The New Evangelization of Catholics
In a New Language

Seán MacGabhann

Order this book online at www.trafford.com/07-1756
or email orders@trafford.com

Most Trafford titles are also available at major online book retailers.

© Copyright 2008 Seán MacGabhann.

All rights reserved. No part of this publication may be reproduced, stored in a retrieval system, or transmitted, in any form or by any means, electronic, mechanical, photocopying, recording, or otherwise, without the written prior permission of the author.

Note for Librarians: A cataloguing record for this book is available from Library and Archives Canada at www.collectionscanada.ca/amicus/index-e.html

Printed in Victoria, BC, Canada.

ISBN: 978-1-4251-4228-5

We at Trafford believe that it is the responsibility of us all, as both individuals and corporations, to make choices that are environmentally and socially sound. You, in turn, are supporting this responsible conduct each time you purchase a Trafford book, or make use of our publishing services. To find out how you are helping, please visit www.trafford.com/responsiblepublishing.html

Our mission is to efficiently provide the world's finest, most comprehensive book publishing service, enabling every author to experience success. To find out how to publish your book, your way, and have it available worldwide, visit us online at www.trafford.com/10510

www.trafford.com

North America & international
toll-free: 1 888 232 4444 (USA & Canada)
phone: 250 383 6864 ♦ fax: 250 383 6804
email: info@trafford.com

The United Kingdom & Europe
phone: +44 (0)1865 722 113 ♦ local rate: 0845 230 9601
facsimile: +44 (0)1865 722 868 ♦ email: info.uk@trafford.com

10 9 8 7 6 5 4 3

ORDER OF CONTENTS

Do Catholics Need To Be Re-Evangelized? 17
Jesus: Source And Summit Of The New Evangelization 20
We Are Never Fully Catholic 23
Encountered By Jesus 26
Meeting Jesus In Scripture 29
Baptism: John's or Jesus'? 32
Bishops Too Are Catholic! (i) 36
Bishops Too Are Catholic! (ii) 39
We Still Bid God 42
Church: Chicken With Its Head Chopped Off! (i) 46
Church: Chicken With Its Head Chopped Off! (ii) 49
Church: Chicken With Its Head Chopped Off! (iii) 52
Sit Down Beside Me 55
Slow Down Frank! 58
Formation For Matrimony 61
A New Language For Mass Goers (i) 65
A New Language For Mass Goers (ii) 68
A New Language For Mass Goers (iii) 71
A New Language For Mass Goers (iv) 74
A New Language For Mass Goers (v) 77
A New Language For Mass Goers (vi) 80
A New Language For Mass Goers (vii) 83
A New Language For Mass Goers (viii) 86
A New Language For Mass Goers (ix) 89
A New Language For Mass Goers (x) 92
Year Of Eucharist Resolution 95

New Language For First Communion (i) 99
New Language For First Communion (ii) 102
What Is Your Religion? (i) 106
What Is Your Religion? (ii) 109
What Is Your Religion? (iii) 112
What Is Your Religion? (iv) 115
"Let My People Go" (i) 119
"Let My People Go" (ii) 123
Whose To Blame? 126
Distorted Thinking Retards 129
Preferential Option For The Poor 132
Preached And Directed Retreats 135
Give Up Your Addictions 138
A Confessional Awakening 141
Sin Bravely! 144
Cross And Crib 147
To Know We Don't Know (i) 151
To Know We Don't Know (ii) 154
To Know We Don't Know (iii) 157
To Know We Don't Know (iv) 160
Wanted: Reformers 163
Catholics Worship Images 166
Where Was God? 169
God: Elusive As A Pot Of Gold 172
Give Up Your Projections Of God 175
Dropping Your Projections Of God 178
Throw Your Images Into The Fire 181
Free Of Your Images Of God 184

"Late Have I Loved You"	187
Mysticism Is 'catholic'	190
"We Need....A New Saintliness"	193
Peel Your Onion	196
Attention! Attention! Attention!	199
You Can Experience God (i)	203
You Can Experience God (ii)	206
You Can Experience God (iii)	209
You Can Experience God (iv)	212
You Can Experience God (v)	215
We Too Are Lepers	218
We Don't Create We Irrigate	221
Vatican State Is Real Estate	224
The Coffin And Diana	227
Pope Too A Disciple	230
Evangelize The Curia	233
Cardinal Sins	236
Relationship Grace (i)	240
A Common Language Of Grace (ii)	244
Grace Is Always Already (iii)	248
Theologians Too Are Learners	251
Theologians Must Kiss!	254
Benedict Benedict Benedict	257
Sacraments Are Secondary	260
Power Of Sacramentors	263
Fiddling While Rome Burns	266
People Strength	269
The Salmon And The Triduum	272

We Have Colonized God	275
Slow Learners!	278
Watch Your Language	281
The Dark Side Of Jesus	284
Institution As An Obstacle	287
Shut Out By The Institution	290
Patron Saint For The Institution	293
Patron Saint For Bishops	296
Patron Saint For Excluded Women	299
Patron Saint For Excluded Laity	302
Patron Saint Of Sex Scandals	305
But What Do You Think?	308
Duc In Altum	311
No Shortage Of Priests	314
Involve The Children	317
Ways To Involve The Children	320
Dualism Shuts Us Out	323
No Expectations No Disappointments	326
Same-Sex Marriage And Our Response	329
More Dreams - Fewer Meetings	332
A Matter of Justice?	335
The Rabbi and Evangelization	338
A Miraculous Marriage!	341
Little Shockers!	344

REMBRANDT'S PORTRAIT OF CHRIST'S FACE
painted about 1650

He was born Rembrandt Harmenszoon van Rijn on the 15th of July, 1606, in the Weddesteeg at Leyden, Holland; the son of the village miller, Harmen Gerritzoon van Rijn, and Neeltgen Willems-dochter van Zuytbrouck, the daughter of a local baker.

More than any other artist of the period, Rembrandt strove to give *earthly reality to the face of Christ;* and, at the same time, no other artist endowed that face with more *radiant kindness* - particularly in his later paintings. Such works, *though radically different* from most of so-called Christian art, reveal a true depth of spiritual understanding and sentiment.

Rembrandt was also a painter of the *common people* of history and of his time. Because of his profound experience of humanity, he was able to portray his subjects *not only as sinful yet repentant,* but also as being *created in the likeness of God their Creator.*

Rembrandt's portrait of Christ's Head was endowed with *indescribable goodness and purity,* the essence of one who would make the *ultimate sacrifice.*

As a painter, Rembrandt's works *reveal a new kind of beauty, far removed from the classical kind - a vision and an interpretation of the human person which transfigures the least beautiful face, or the ugliest body.* Rembrandt was a painter of the *insignificant or little people.*

REMBRANDT AND THE NEW EVANGELIZATION OF CATHOLICS

The Jubilee of the Year 2000, ended on January the 6th, 2001 with an exhortation of Pope John Paul II titled: *"At the Beginning of the New Millenium."* I wonder if he had Rembrandt in mind because, no less than seventeen times in this short reflection, he exhorts us to "Contemplate the face of Christ." In asking what is the core of the great legacy the Jubilee leaves us, he says: "I would not hesitate to describe it as the contemplation of the face of Christ: Christ considered in his historical features....the experience we have had should inspire in us new energy and impel us to invest in concrete initiatives the enthusiasm we have felt."

Because the Pope holds up before us the historical face of Christ to be contemplated, I offer Rembrandt's Face of Christ as our best historical icon. For this reason, I italicized some key phrases in my brief description of *Rembrandt's Portrait of Christ's Face.* For example, more than any other artist of the period, Rembrandt strove to give *earthly reality to the face of Christ.* It is the human and historical Jesus that we are called to contemplate in the Gospels. We can rest assured that we will not remain at this level. But we have to begin here. The historical and human Jesus will lead us to experience the God who lives in us; in whom we live and move and have our being. Rembrandt's face of Christ attract us because no other artist endowed that face with *more radiant kindness.*

The late John Paul II issued a wake-up call to the whole Church, to be infused with new energy and enthusiasm in implementing the *New Evangelization* of Catholics. Playing it safe and sitting on the fence is apathy. Like Rembrandt, we have to dare to risk and dare to dream as he did. He stood out on a limb because his Face of Christ is *radically different from most of the so-called Christian art* of his period.

Commentators on Rembrandt's paintings tell us that he was a painter of the *common people, the insignificant or little people.* Like Jesus, he had a preferential option for the poor. The poor come in many shapes and sizes and in the light of the *New Evangelization* they are the laity. They are poor in the sense that they are at the bottom of the totem pole in terms of having any significant voice in the Church. Their dignity as a chosen race, a royal priesthood, a holy nation and God's own people is largely ignored. They are seen more as a threat than as a complement to the overall functioning of the Body of Christ.

Rembrandt had deep insight into both the enormous potential and dignity of people. He portrayed his subjects *not only as sinful yet repentant, but also as being created in the likeness of God their Creator.* His moving painting of the father and prodigal son is a sound testament to our openness to and capability of conversion. The call of the *New Evangelization* could be summed up in one word: *conversion.* The more we contemplate the face of Christ the more we are moved to change our lives. Repentance then is less about turning away from sin but more about a fresh encounter with the person of Jesus. Created in the likeness of God means that we are God-bearers because God lives in us. It follows then that we are capable of having a direct experience of God. The little people, the laity, have not been taught this and suffer from an inferiority complex.

As we contemplate Rembrandt's Face of Christ, we see a Christ endowed with *indescribable goodness and purity, the essence of one who would make the ultimate sacrifice in order to secure the redemption of humankind.* The *New Evangelization* calls for great sacrifice. Change and risk are painful. Like Peter, to have Jesus throw a rope around us and lead us where we prefer not to go, is scaring. We fear the unknown. But we have been on the outer journey long enough and now it is time to set out on the inner journey - the longest and without any road signs!

Like Jesus, Rembrandt dared to be different, to be counter-cultural. His works reveal *a new kind of beauty, far removed from the classical kind - a vision and an interpretation of man which transfigures the least beautiful face, or the ugliest body.* Vision and newness describe well the *New Evangelization.* It is not just another program, of which we have enough, but evangelization with a difference: it is *new*. We are to embrace it with new energy and with a vision that is new in *ardour, method and expression*. Perhaps we could take Rembrandt as our patron saint for this new endeavour which, John Paul II believed, will result in a new Springtime for the Church.

INTRODUCTION

These pages are the result of several years of reflection on the urgency of an Evangelization with a difference. Right after ordination I left for the mission fields of South America to Evangelize non-Christians because only they were the recipients of Evangelization - I thought! But not any more! The late Pope John Paul II, opened my eyes when he included *Catholics* and challenged the *whole* Church, not just to be re-Evangelized, but *Newly Evangelized.* This indeed is a new language that will take a lot of getting used to! In the following reflections I attempt to flesh out what this would look like in practice and everyday life.

They are aimed primarily at the average Catholic in the street, in the home and in the workplace. I can't say in the pew because, in the West at least, our buildings are empty and only a *New Evangelization* will fill them again. It is my experience that most Catholics do not engage in much reading that could be classified as spiritual, church, biblical or theological. For this reason each reflection is short, devoid of theological jargon, down to earth, chatty with a spice of humour! It's a very healthy sign when we can laugh at ourselves while being serious at the same time!

Only a friend will tell you that your breath smells! Johann Baptist Metz was a friend, former student and critic of the great Karl Rahner and he respected Metz for this. Rahner too was a critic of the institutional Church and he was often not tolerated much less respected. It failed to see where he was coming from as Metz tells us: "He has the Church in his guts, and he feels its failures like indigestion." It was out of his love for his Church that Rahner criticised the leadership. It is in this light that I am critical of the institutional Church in these reflections which, like the rest of us, needs to be Newly Evangelized.

While in theory and belief we the Church are one, in actual practice we are two: the institutional/structural/hierarchical/leadership aspect and the laity. The latter suffer from a debilitating inferiority complex and do not believe *they,* along with the institution, are the

Church. The institution on the other hand, suffers from a destructive superiority complex that keeps the laity in their subordinate place. The *New Evangelization* calls for a double conversion, metanoia and repentance here: the laity become who they are and the institution surrender control. It must return to a John the Baptist style of leadership and point to Jesus instead of to itself. Conversion demands that it return to its roots where Jesus was the focus. It has ousted him, taken centre-stage and turned in on itself.

I present the *New Evangelization* as uncomplicated, uncluttered and very simple - but not easy! It's new in that it calls us away from more knowledge, more meetings and more programs to a fresh encounter with Jesus. He is our point of reference. He is our North Star. Obviously, a personal encounter with Jesus involves a relationship with him. This too is new because our main focus and teaching is knowledge *about* Jesus instead of simply *knowing* him.

Our Pelagian, doer, and control attitudes must go because they are obstacles to a fresh encounter with Jesus. We cannot forge a relationship with him and do not need to because we are *already* in relationship. All we need do is just become *aware* of what already is and pay *attention* to it. This too is simple but not easy. Because we *are,* we do not need to strive *for.* We are already graced, saved, in relationship, children of God and loved sinners. But we Catholics, particularly the institution, are set in our ways and resist change. As Simone Weil puts it, "It is easier for a non-Christian to become a Christian than for a 'Christian' to become one!" Our sin is not that we are bad but that we have settled for the good. However, the *New Evangelization* calls us to embrace what is *best* and the best is a relationship with a person; not knowledge of dogma, belief in a creed or following a religion.

The call to a fresh encounter with Jesus and an intimate relationship flowing from it, form the basis for each of my reflections. Put simply: The *New Evangelization* is Jesus-centred and relationship-focused. Because of this it transcends religion, all programs and is holistic in that it is a way of life impacting every aspect of it.

If programs could change and convert us we would all be saints by now and not need to be *Newly Evangelized!* Whatever little there is going on at the moment in an effort to evangelize, is program-oriented and going nowhere. Programs will not and cannot stir up in us a *New Evangelization* that is new in *ardour, method and expression.* But a personal relationship with the great Evangelizer will set us on fire. I stress over and over again in these reflections that we must get out of our heads and live from our hearts. Dan Brown in his book, "Angels and Demons," makes an interesting point in this regard: "Sometimes divine revelation simply means adjusting your brain to hear what your heart already knows." The *New Evangelization* gets right to the heart of the matter!

Along with Pope Benedict, I make the same comments and request the same of my readers that he does in his new book, *Jesus of Nazareth.* At the outset, he makes it clear that it reflects his own opinions, which are not necessarily those of the Church's official teaching office. His book, he writes, is solely "an expression of my personal search 'for the face of the Lord' (Psalm 27:8). Everyone is free, then, to contradict me. I would only ask my readers for that initial good will without which there can be no understanding."

Seán MacGabhann

DO CATHOLICS NEED TO BE RE-EVANGELIZED?

"**N**o," says the Pope!

In 1997 Pope John Paul II met with a Special Assembly of the Synod of Bishops for America: North, Central and South. This was in preparation for the Great Jubilee of the Year 2000. Two years later in 1999, the Pope summarized the discussions in what is now known as *The Church in America.* It is his Apostolic Exhortation to the Catholics in America. He calls us "not to a re-Evangelization but a *New Evangelization*—new in *ardour*, *method* and *expression*."[1] Throughout his exhortation he stresses that the starting point for this new initiative is "encounter with the Lord." This relationship with Jesus is so central that he mentions it sixty-six times!

On night four of the parish mission, the missioner preached about hell. He had the people squirming in the pews. This parish was going straight to hell! Right in the front pew a man sat with arms folded and a grin on his face that really irked the missioner. He couldn't take it any more. Looking him straight in the eye, he demanded "And what have you to smile about?" "Oh, I don't belong to this parish," was his smug reply.

When we Catholics hear the word "Evangelization" we tend to think that's for the people in the other parish! Evangelization is what missionaries do in Africa, Asia and Latin America. We're

---

1 **Pope John Paul II:** *The Church in America: #6*

Catholic. We don't need to be evangelized. Correct! We need a *New Evangelization*! How does that make us feel? It's a bit like the surgeon telling me that I don't need by-pass surgery, I need a new heart! Basically that was the message of the prophets throughout the Old Testament. True and genuine conversion could be expressed only in a change of heart.

In this series of reflections I will try to flesh out in a practical way this *New Evangelization* we Catholics are called to. Because discipleship and the Gospel are essentially simple—not easy—I will keep it simple. What would a fresh encounter with Jesus look like in my personal life and lived out in my parish? I look back to my seminary days with regret. I spent five years studying about Jesus and never met him! What a tragedy! No wonder I need a *New Evangelization*! Scripture would have come alive for me had I been taught to pray with the Word. This is something I stumbled upon many years after ordination. Now I have a personal relationship with Jesus and what a difference it makes in my life! For sure my reflections will include ways of praying with scripture that's certain to lead to a fresh encounter with Jesus.

On one occasion I met with representatives of the United and Pentecostal Churches to plan a service at sun-rise on Easter Sunday. The Pentecostals had been without a minister for a long time. Jim, their lay-leader, was happy that they were getting a new minister. Just out of seminary, 23 and his first assignment! But Jim's response to that was, "He has a passion for the Lord." That's what a fresh encounter with Jesus is meant to stir up in us. Passion! Fire!

A *New Evangelization* that is new in *ardour, method* and *expression*. Now that's a tall order! In fact, it is radical! What would that look like in my parish? It calls for an enthusiasm and excitement that comes only from a fresh encounter with Jesus. Risk and great courage are called for. Change is painful. But a relationship that is alive is always changing and risking. New methods, not gimmicks, demand risk, courage and change. If we are alive in Jesus they will automatically happen. And new in expression! Central to this is a new language. When the British occupied Ireland they found that the natives "Speak a language that the stranger does not know!" Frustrating! Try reading a lawyer's letter! Impossible! I believe the institutional Church speaks a language that most of us find hard to comprehend. A kind of a lawyer's language! It is heavily intellectual lacking personal flavour. Cognitive rather than affective. More head than heart. Simplicity too is dangerous! How do we express in a simple way, not simplistic, our fresh encounter with Jesus? I will attempt to answer that in the rest of my reflections.

JESUS
Source and Summit of The New Evangelization

We also call Him, "The Lord," "Jesus Christ" and "Christ the Lord." The most personal title for me is "Jesus." One that Catholics tend not to use a lot. We associate the usage with Evangelicals, Charismatics and Pentecostals. The title Jesus is relational. It has feeling and intimacy. Whereas The Lord is more formal, cerebral and distant. Many times I have heard a husband refer to his spouse as "the wife." Not very flattering! Ask the average husband to describe himself as a husband. "I work hard, mow the grass, do the maintenance etc." A non-relationship description! No mention of his wife. Ask the average Catholic to describe him or herself as a Catholic! "I go to Mass. I pray at home. I went to a Catholic school." A non-relationship description. Where is Jesus? Where are we? A fresh encounter with Jesus is primarily relational.

Jesus calls us to intimacy. So why not speak the language of friendship and intimacy! Take the liturgy for example. The presider addresses the congregation with, "The Lord be with you," and, "Go in peace to love and serve the Lord." What would it sound like if he said, "Jesus be with you," and,"Go in peace to love and serve Jesus?" Relationships are dangerous! When we get close to Jesus and others heavy demands are made on us.

Like his first disciples, Jesus invites us to, "Come and see." And the Gospel writer John, says they spent the day with him. Notice the first thing Jesus did. He invited them to a relationship with him.

Then he taught them. We tend to do the opposite. Someone inquires about joining the Church and we send them to the RCIA. Or a man inquires about the priesthood. We send him to the seminary. We teach them. What if we first introduce them to Jesus and then teach them? Or rather, let Jesus teach them. It's good to inquire about the Church, and go to the seminary. It would be better if their first desire was like some Greeks who said to Philip, "We wish to see Jesus." Matthew has Jesus tell his disciples to go, "Make disciples, baptize….and teach…" Notice the order! Relationship is first. Teaching is last.

Speaking to the director, St. Ignatius of Loyola, sternly warns him or her not to get in the way. He says, "It is more appropriate and far better that the Creator and Lord himself should communicate himself to the devout soul….allow the Creator to deal immediately with the creature and the creature with its Creator and Lord." It is a fact that most of the newly initiated into the Church at Easter drop off fairly soon. The same with our students in our schools. It's not that we haven't "educated them in the faith." Maybe that's the problem. Have they met Jesus? Who do they say Jesus is for them? I couldn't answer that question till many years on in the priesthood. And I spent five years studying scripture and theology! I was educated! But I was not formed. I was catechized but not Evangelized. I knew about Jesus yet didn't meet him. It was a case of the good becoming the enemy of the best. Of course it is good to be educated. But it's best to have a relationship with Jesus.

Ignatius of Loyola saw how a director can be an obstacle to a relationship between Jesus and the directee. It is not outlandish to say that the institutional Church too can be an obstacle to a person's relationship with Jesus. Look at the Crusades, the Inquisition and, nearer home, the bishops' and priests' scandals. Peter, the first Pope, was an obstacle! He tried to get between Jesus and his mission. I have a feeling that most Catholics see the Church as their main conduit to Jesus. An unhealthy dependence develops. We do speak of the Church being a dispenser of grace. The fact is that, as children of God, we already have a relationship with Jesus and so are graced.

The Church doesn't grant it. It nourishes the graced relationship. The servant is not above the master. The Body is not above the Head. The dog wags the tail! Not the other way round! Like Peter, the church must keep behind Jesus. So when the Pope calls for a fresh encounter with Jesus, he is speaking to the whole body, including himself.

WE ARE NEVER FULLY CATHOLIC

A major obstacle to the *New Evangelization* of Catholics is the illusion that one day we are fully Catholic. We see this all the time in sacramental celebration. The sacraments of initiation; Baptism, Confirmation and First Eucharist are seen by many parents as graduation sacraments. They believe the children are now fully Catholic! The above order or sequence of the sacraments of initiation is correct. Eucharist, not Confirmation, is the completion of initiation. Bishops have to stop delaying Confirmation and using it as a means to keep our young people in the church—which it does not.

In his Post-Synodal Apostolic Exhortation, *The Eucharist as the Source and Summit of the Church's Live and Mission, (#17, 18),* Pope Benedict XVI calls for a restoration of the correct order of the sacraments of initiation for children. He says: "It must never be forgotten that our reception of Baptism and Confirmation is ordered to the Eucharist. Accordingly, our pastoral practice should reflect a more unitary understanding of the process of Christian initiation...in this regard, attention needs to be paid to the order of the sacraments of initiation."

Presently there is an imbalance between Jesus and the Church which needs to be corrected. I believe we put too much emphasis on joining, entering, confirming and marrying in the Church. The danger is that the institution can take precedence over a person. That person is Jesus. When the institution comes first, we unconsciously, or consciously, convey the notion that the Church is all powerful. In which case it makes sense to experience the sacraments as rites of entry into the club. And like membership of any club, when we are initiated we are full members.

Switch the focus. Sacraments are celebrations of what already is. Long before baptism or any other sacrament, we have a relationship with Jesus. The Church does not initiate that relationship. The Church helps us to respond and at different stages celebrate that intimate relationship. Nobody ever initiates a relationship with Jesus. We always respond. We need to focus more on this relationship with Jesus that already exists. If you doubt me listen to the profound and sometimes, embarrassing questions that a four-year old child has! Or observe their art. It's natural for children to talk to and about Jesus. We need to build on that. Little three-year old Andrea, on Good Friday, cried when she saw the crucifix covered. She asked her mom why Jesus had gone!

Talking about art! The teacher asked the children to draw some of the beautiful things God created. Little Johnny drew God painting the sky and clouds with his left hand. When she asked Johnny why God draws with his left hand, he replied, "Well last week you taught us in the Creed that Jesus sits on the right hand of God!"

With the primary focus on Jesus we will be relationship-oriented. When the Church is the primary focus the sacraments are things to be done, hoops to be jumped through, devoid of a relationship. Relationship is not our forte as an institution. This shouldn't surprise us. We are an all-male leadership! Men tend to be more head than heart. More thinkers than feelers. More abstract than concrete. More cognitive than affective. More in touch with our animus than our anima. We men are not comfortable with our feelings. The New Evangelization calls for a correction of this imbalance. Is this ever a hard nut to crack!

Relationships are never complete. There is always what Ignatius of Loyola calls the "more." Our relationship with Jesus is the same. I never have a full relationship with him. Nothing is ever complete this side of the grave. It's like the seminarian asking his confessor when he would be rid of sexual temptations. "About ten minutes after you are dead," was the response. Because all sacraments are primarily a relationship, I am never fully a priest. A couple is never fully matrimonied. You are never fully Catholic. Maybe ten minutes after we are dead! So when asked if you are fully Catholic, matrimonied or a priest, the correct response is: "I am a little bit more (or less!) Catholic, matrimonied, a priest today than I was yesterday!" Karl Rahner said somewhere that all symphonies remain unfinished. A relationship with Jesus is definitely an unfinished symphony.

ENCOUNTERED BY JESUS

The basic premise of the *New Evangelization* is that only a fresh encounter with Jesus will get this process rolling. In using the words, "new" and "fresh," Pope John Paul II is saying in effect that Catholics need to start all over again! This is not good news for Catholics but it is true. It's like failing your driving test and you must repeat it!

I will touch briefly on five ways we resist being encountered by Jesus. We need to be absolutely clear that it is not a question of our encountering Jesus. The idea that we take the initiative is a heresy condemned by the Church. Jesus has already extended the invitation. He invites us to respond. We cannot take the initiative in this encounter.

The first obstacle stems from the above and is called Pelagianism. A monk named Pelagius, around 400 A.D. taught that we can take the first step in our salvation. He was condemned because salvation is grace, a free gift we cannot earn. There is still a streak of Pelagianism in Catholics today. This is not surprising. We are products of a Western culture that boasts of independence, individualism, power, superiority and control. We are taught and encouraged to be "go-getters" and take control of our lives. Even if you are not old enough to remember Frank Sinatra, you sing his Pelagian song, "I did it my way!"

The second form of resistance is intimacy. Right away of course sex comes to mind. We are brain-washed by our amoral and sick culture. It tells us that you need to be sexually active to be intimate.

And we believe it! But I am intimate with you when I stand before you naked—not physically. When I risk being vulnerable and tell you who I am, I am being intimate. Knowing you might reject me, I take the risk anyway. This is the kind of intimacy Jesus has with us and he would like it to be reciprocal but we back off.

The third is knowledge. We cannot think our way into relationships but we still try. Instead, we feel our way into them. Knowledge gives us a sense of superiority which keeps us in control. It keeps us at a distance. So stay in your head and you will stay out of relationship. Many Catholics know *about* Jesus but do not know him personally. They resist being known by him because then they would not be in control of the relationship.

A fourth obstacle is ignorance. Particularly ignorance of Scripture. Here the Protestants have the edge on us. Saint Jerome translated the Hebrew and Greek books of the Bible into Latin, the language of his day. He taught that to be ignorant of scripture is not to know Jesus. The Gospels in particular are unique for facilitating Jesus' encounter with us. Later I will explain how we can dispose ourselves by contemplating the Gospels.

The illusion that we are at the center of life is the fifth way we resist. We honestly believe that the world revolves around us. This erroneous thinking sets us at odds with life. This attitude develops a dualistic relationship with the world; a subject and object attitude. Instead of living with and being one with creation we set out to control it. This is both selfish and destructive. The damage we are doing to the ozone layer, forests and oceans are evidence of our illusions. We think that we can have a relationship with Jesus on the same dualistic terms.

All five are summed up in one word, "Control." We are taught from an early age to be independent and stand on our own two feet. When we get out of our head and show our emotions we are told to control ourselves. All this leads us to believe that we are in control of life and are planners of our own destiny. This too is an illusion. We could make our own the first of the Twelve Steps of AA: "We admitted we were powerless over alcohol [life!]—that our lives had become unmanageable."

A fresh encounter with Jesus will shatter our illusion and lead us to the truth. Then our life will not only be manageable, but harmonious, fulfilled, peaceful and joyful too.

MEETING JESUS IN SCRIPTURE

Scripture is proclaimed at the Sunday Eucharist, our celebration of thanksgiving. At the end of the readings the Lector concludes, "The word of the Lord." And we respond, "Thanks be to God." The priest proclaims at the end of the Gospel, "The Gospel of the Lord." Our response is, "Praise to you Lord Jesus Christ." The movement here is that Jesus speaks to us and we are thank*ful*. I will now describe how this encounter can continue throughout the week in what I call *Gospel Contemplation*. However, there are two fundamental requirements. You must have the desire and fifteen minutes. Without these you are not ready to meet Jesus.

Remember, you don't initiate the encounter. Jesus does. Your job is to show up and shut up! Just listen! Find a quiet place. Get out of your head. Do some deep breathing. Sit straight and ask Jesus to reveal himself to you.

Let's take the Gospel scene of Bartimaeus (Mk. 10:46-52). Instead of analyzing, use you imagination and senses. Hear, see, smell, touch and feel what's going on. Get right into the event. Keep your head out of the way. See the blind beggar on the side of the road. Hear him shouting for Jesus to heal him. Feel his isolation. See and hear how the crowd react. See Jesus stop. Hear him say to the crowd, "Call him here." See Bartimaeus spring to his feet. Hear Jesus ask him, "What do you want me to do for you?" See, hear and feel with him as he replies, "Let me see again."

Unless you are a block of ice, you have lots of affective experiences. Simply pay attention to what you are experiencing. Remember, you experience at the feeling level. So what are you feeling as you move around this scene? Pay attention to and notice what's being stirred up in you by Jesus. Your response? Talk to Jesus about how you are *feeling*. He is not interested in what you think!

You may see yourself either in Bartimaeus or the crowd or both. Like him you are feeling your pain and need healing. Jesus sheds light on your blindness and you feel overwhelmed, embarrassed, fearful, guilty etc. Jesus says to you, "Come, what do you want me to do for you?" Tell him. Now you feel loved and accepted as you are by Jesus. You feel grate*ful* and hopeful. You see yourself in a new light and feel closer to Jesus. Like Bartimaeus, you too want to be a disciple, a follower of Jesus. Now you know him more *clearly*, you love him more *dearly* and you will follow him more *nearly*, day by day!

Bring your contemplation to a close by thanking Jesus and slowly say a prayer of your choice, maybe the Our Father. You can now use your head! Then take a few minutes to reflect on what happened. What did you experience? Name it, savour it and ponder on it during the day or the rest of the evening. You will be amazed how much this will influence your day. It will be like a mantra or an echo at the back of your mind. Without planning it, you will pay attention to and notice little things in your day. This is because Jesus continues to encounter you and your are listening. He is no more a distant historical figure but a personal friend.

Finally, do like the bee or hummingbird! Return to that flower where you were nourished. Look at the same people returning to Tim Horton's or Starbucks for their coffee every day! Go back to where you were fed in that Gospel scene. You experience feeding in peace, harmony, confidence, forgiven and loved by Jesus. In Gospel contemplation, less is more! It may be just one word, a phrase, a particular scene that has fed you. I know one person who spent five years, daily, praying with the same Gospel passage!

Jesus is shedding light on your life. You see more clearly what you need to grow. At the beginning of your next encounter ask Jesus for that particular grace. Maybe it is generosity, compassion, patience or forgiving yourself.

BAPTISM
John's or Jesus'?

Since the *New Evangelization* of Catholics calls for a newness in *ardour, method and expression*, this means we cannot stay with the status quo. It challenges us to be courageous, creative and to "launch out into the deep." All of which is in keeping with orthodoxy. We should be confident enough to ask questions. The mystics tell us that the sign of a mature disciple of Jesus is one who has more questions than answers. It's scaring to risk being secure in my insecurity! An orthodox disciple is one who is at home with paradox! And a truly wise person is one who knows that he or she does not know!

So whose baptism? Do we prepare parents and Catechumens for John's or Jesus' baptism? Baptism, like all the sacraments, is primarily relationship-oriented. John's is anything but this. His clarion call to repentance is mainly a movement *from* sin. John is big time on sin! So were the old parish missions when I was growing up in Ireland! Clearly, turning from sin is absolutely essential to being a disciple of Jesus. But it's not the whole story. There's much more to baptism. We could compare John's baptism to that of the weaning of a nursing child. Weaning must take place and that's painful! I still hear the "maas" and "baas" of the mothers and lambs when it came time for weaning. It went on for several days and nights. We need to be weaned from John's baptism to the baptism of Jesus. Not, like the lambs, to stand on our own two feet. Rather, moved into total dependence on Jesus.

Relationship and intimacy characterize Jesus' baptism. It's less *from* and more *into*. God, at Jesus' baptism, claimed him as his beloved Son. Jesus lays claim on us as his beloved sisters and brothers. He calls us his friends. The *New Evangelization* calls for a *fresh* encounter with Jesus. The challenge is how to celebrate this in baptism. Sadly, for most of our Catholic parents presenting their children for baptism, it will be their first encounter with Jesus!

The first step is to drop any programs we have for baptism. Programs have little or no relationship content. In his Apostolic Letter, *"Novo Millennio Inuente" (Moving Into The New Millennium),* John Paul has this to say about programs: "We shall not be saved by a formula but by a person....it is not therefore a matter of implementing a 'new program.'"[2] Of course that person is Jesus. We need to slow down the preparation and develop a process that's akin to the Rite of Christian Initiation of Adults. A program ends. A process continues. Jesus took thirty years preparing for his baptism! His was a surrender, a total commitment to God's work. We could say it was a baptism of blood, sweat and tears. That's all Winston Churchill, the English Prime Minister, promised his soldiers going to war. And Jesus asks *us:* "Can you drink the cup that I am going to drink?" Drinking the cup in scripture is always associated with suffering and blood. It's scaring when we link our baptism with Jesus'. And he makes no apology for it!

Baptism for Jesus meant being out of control. The Spirit that seized him was no gentle dove! The Gospel of Mark says that the Spirit "immediately *drove* him out into the wilderness." We go for a coffee, cake and pop after baptism! Jesus was chased into the desert after his! Who wants to celebrate being out of control? Jesus' baptism, and ours, is like Peter's. When in control he fastened his own belt and went where he liked. Not any more. Jesus warned him that someone else would throw a belt around him and take him where

---

2 **Pope John Paul II:** *Moving into the New Millennium: #29*

he would rather not go. Ron Rolheiser describes our baptism as the Church putting a rope around us, taking away our freedom, and taking us where we would rather not, but should go! How do we incorporate this meaning of Jesus' baptism into our preparation and celebration? If parents had even a glimmer of what this involves, they would be less casual answering the question: "Do you still want to have your child baptized?"

BISHOPS TOO ARE CATHOLIC!

part one

※

A long time ago, around 400 A.D., St. Augustine reminded his fellow bishops that they are also Catholic! In a letter to his people he writes: "Secondly, we have already told you that two things are to be borne in mind, first that we are Christians, and secondly, that we have been put in charge of you. Because we are leaders, we are ranked among the shepherds—if we are good. As Christians, on the other hand, we too are sheep like you. So whether the Lord is speaking to the shepherds or to the sheep, we must listen with trembling to everything he says, nor must our hearts be free from anxiety." It's easy to forget that bishops, like the rest of us, are human and also called to daily conversion. Past and recent scandals among bishops are stark reminders.

It was Confirmation in Ballyboreen, a little farming village in Ireland. Among other things, the bishop explained that he was like a shepherd. That's why he carried a crook or crozier. That was blunder number one because in Ballyboreen farmers chased their sheep with a blackthorn stick! Maybe it was a Freudian slip! In those days candidates were questioned. "Seamus," asked the bishop, "on your way to school you see a flock of sheep out in Mr. Murphy's field. Who do you expect to see with them?" Blunder number two! Seamus, without any hesitation, "Paddy Murphy's big black-faced ram, me lord!"

The point here is that Seamus did not make the connection the bishop expected him to. The fault lay with the bishop, not Seamus. In other words, the bishop was not relevant. Obviously shepherd and crook did not mean the same for him and Seamus. The question I will attempt to answer in this and the next reflection: "How in touch are bishops?"

I will answer this in the light of the *New Evangelization.* Here Catholics are called, not to a re-Evangelization, but a *New-Evangelization.* Since the bishops are Catholic, they too are included. Conversion lies at the heart of the *New Evangelization.* This side of the grave, conversion is never complete so we are meant to be in a process of conversion.

The bishops at the Second Vatican Council, (1962-1965), set the ball rolling for a universal conversion of the institution with Jesus as its model: "Just as Christ carried out the work of redemption in poverty and under oppression, so the Church is called to follow the same path....thus, although the Church needs human resources to carry out her mission, she is not set up to seek earthly glory, but to proclaim humility and self-sacrifice, even by her own example" (*Dogmatic Constitution on the Church*).

Around thirty years later, the bishops, gathered for the Synod, "The Church in America," echoed that need for reform: "This conversion demands especially of us bishops a genuine identification with the personal style of Jesus Christ, who leads us to simplicity, poverty, responsibility for others and the renunciation of our own advantage, so that, like him and not trusting in human means, we may draw from the strength of the Holy Spirit and of the Word all the power of the Gospel."

"A genuine identification with the personal style of Jesus Christ" is the key. It is Jesus who converts us. The starting point of a *New-Evangelization* is this personal encounter with Jesus. He began his ministry calling people to an intimate relationship with him. "Come and see" was his invitation when they inquired about him. The same holds true two thousand years later. Jesus, not programs, religion or theology is our point of reference.

Bishops can find excuses for not spending quality time daily, sitting like Mary, at the master's feet. The big deception that they, like the rest of us, can be guilty of is called, "The heresy of good works!" We live in the fast lane of a hectic, materialistic and restless society. We "do for the sake of doing." The Martha syndrome is deeply entrenched in each of us! Saint Francis de Sales used to say that everyone should spend a half hour in prayer each day. And if they are really busy, spend an hour!

Workaholism is an addiction, a sickness, to which bishops are prone. We boast about how much we "do!" To be a fly on the wall of the meetings of Conferences of Bishops! The more appointments we cram into our daily planner, the better we feel. Not, "Who are you?," but "What do you do?" is usually the first question we ask on introduction. We are defined by our workaholism! A bishop working in Africa once said, "If I had a choice between ten active priests and ten contemplative nuns, I would choose the latter." Maybe he had it right!

part two

❊

The *New Evangelization,* conversion and metanoia to which bishops are called, starts with being encountered by Jesus. For it to be genuine, it must be expressed in everyday life. Authentic conversion is tangible and practical. It is this lived conversion that helps bishops to keep their feet on the ground and in touch with real life.

Saint Thomas Aquinas died in 1274. He had a brilliant mind and a humble heart. He refused any ecclesiastical dignity including the Archbishopric of Naples. Clearly Jesus transformed him and freed him from dependence on honour, power and prestige. He taught others what he himself lived for one cannot give what one does not have.

In presenting Jesus as a model, he has this to say: "He was naked on the cross, derided and spat upon, struck and crowned with thorns, and finally given vinegar to drink. Do not then, be attached to fine clothes or riches, for 'they divided my garments among them.' Do not seek for honours, for he knew mockery and beating. Do not seek honourable rank, because they 'plaited a crown of thorns and placed it on my head.' Do not seek after fine foods, because 'for my thirst, they gave me vinegar to drink.'" Here's how a comparison might look:

Jesus	Bishops
Crown of thorns	Mitre
Nails in hands	Rings on fingers
Reed; beaten on the head with it	Crozier
Scarlet cloak; one worn by soldiers	Regalia; expensive, ostentatious
"Crucify him"	Applause, fanfare, honour, prestige
Vinegar to drink	Fine wines and foods
Thought crazy by his family	Cardinals: "Princes of the Church"
Servant, labourer	C.E.Os, Administrators
Crucifix in churches, rectories, offices	Photo in churches, rectories, offices
Considered a failure	Success lauded and sought after

Jesus is always our point of reference. How well does dress and lifestyle reflect the poor man of Nazareth? For example, the crozier and ring are a throwback to Feudalism. The local lord appointed bishops who in turn became his vassals or servants. He gave them a crozier and ring as symbols of their office which had more of a secular than Gospel meaning. Most young people today have never seen a flock of sheep so how relevant is the shepherd's crook? The Pope carries a crucifix. Now that's very symbolic! The servant is not above the master!

And what about that gaudy regalia of the Cardinals who allow themselves to be called "Princes of the Church!" This is both dress and language of the royalty, kings and queens and the palace. How can *they* square this with the poor man of Nazareth? After his election in 1522, the Dutch pope, Adrian VI met with the Sacred College. The historian, Philip Hughes, tells us that "....it had to be explained to him that they were the cardinals, for in dress and manners they were simply Renaissance princes."

During the funeral of John Paul II a nurse at the hospital asked me: "Wouldn't you like to be one of them?" Meaning bishops and cardinals. "Just look at the beautiful and expensive robes you would wear!" People do notice! When a priest is made head of a department in the Curia, he is automatically "raised to the office and dignity of Archbishop." Again, power, prestige and honour as well as an abuse of ordination. One is ordained a bishop to pastor a diocese, not be a C.E.O, Bureaucrat or Administrator. I guess without the title and power they would not be able to control bishops around the world.

Only a ruthless and radical conversion coming from a personal encounter with Jesus will dispose of this baggage. Bishops must represent *Him* if they expect to be relevant, not popular. Other practical steps would be to cut out all the fanfare and paraphernalia at ordinations of bishops. No dignitaries. Invite the marginalized, the poor, mentally challenged and addicts. One bishop is enough to ordain so let the rest stay in their dioceses instead of wasting time and money. The money saved will help with the excessively high budgets of Conferences of Bishops. Instead, send a card or email of congratulations.

A recent Vatican document to bishops tells them that they should reflect Jesus: "Be poor and appear to be poor," living a modest lifestyle equivalent to that of their people. It just needs one or two bishops to kick the traces and get the ball rolling!

WE STILL BID GOD

Because a cow gives birth in a stable her calf is not a foal! At our Sunday Eucharist, we pray what we now call the "Prayers of the Faithful." They were previously known as the "Bidding Prayers." But a different title has not changed our mentality. We still bid God under a new name! In a sense they are our prayers but in another sense they are not. This is what I want to explore. It's all part of the call of the *New Evangelization* to daily conversion. If you think we Catholics do not need converting, we only need to look around us, right in our very homes! Scripture reminds us that even the good person sins seven times a day!

Pay close attention to the title: "Prayers of the *Faithful*." That's us. So in theory they are our prayers. But in actual fact they are not. We are stuck in the mindset of the "Bidding" Prayers. These are announcements we make to God and we bid God to answer them. They are our prayers but we are not involved. For example, we tell God to stop wars, make Mary well, send us more vocations and put fire in our parish. And we feel good about it. All we have done is inform God.

Also, notice how we pray for others to take care of our concerns. We pray that these lazy parishioners get off their behinds and volunteer for the Parish Pastoral Council. That more come forward to bring Holy Communion to the sick and housebound. That the government stop abortion, same-sex marriages, root out corruption and put people before profit. There we are on a Sunday morning all passing the buck! Count me out Lord! Like when there was something messy to deal with on the School Council a unanimous voice spoke, "Father will deal with that!"

If the Prayers of the Faithful are to be truly *our* prayers there will have to be radical conversion on our part. The Prayers *of* the Faithful must also be the prayers *done by* the faithful. A basic principle comes to mind: Don't pray for something if you are not prepared to be involved in what you are praying for. That's dangerous! You don't need to inform God. But you do need God to reform you! Pray for wisdom and courage to implement what you are praying for. God answers our prayers by throwing them back at us saying "You take care of this!" But that's not fair. Now I have to do something about it. This is where the rubber hits the road!

A few examples: When you pray for the Church, remember that *you* are the Church. So how, not where, are you as Church? Are you already involved? Or are you a cafeteria Catholic, picking choosing what you like about being Catholic? Or, as Saint Monica, described her husband Patricius, a "sometime husband." Do you have a catholic, a universal outlook?

When you pray for the world, governments, injustice, wars, corruption, are you part of the problem and will you be part of the solution? How involved are you in politics, social justice, the environment, starvation, unemployment, corruption in the workplace, pro-life, AIDS, multinational take-overs and so on? If you are an employer, do you put your workers before profit? I think it was George Bernard Shaw who said: "All that is needed for evil to triumph is for good people to do nothing." And G.K. Chesterton proclaimed: "It's not that Christianity has been tried and found wanting. It just hasn't been tried."

At the parish level: What is my involvement? Usually it's the same few who carry the load. If I want this parish to come alive it has to start with me. And about the big problem of fewer priests and religious. We inform God, "Send us more vocations." God replies, "I have, lots of them." Like the parishioner who said there is no shortage of money in this parish. "That's right," said the priest, "but it is still in their wallets." When you pray for more priests and religious, are you positively encouraging your son or daughter? If not, is it fair to pray for others to do what you are not doing?

CHURCH: CHICKEN WITH ITS HEAD CHOPPED OFF!

part one

———✤———

Recently I butchered some of my chickens. Two are needed to complete the execution. One holds the body while the other beheads. If not, the headless chicken will run around for a while in all directions. The experience got me thinking about us, the Church, particularly the institutional dimension. We are the body of Jesus and he is the head. This is the theory. But in fact and every day life the two are severed. I will develop this practice in the following reflections.

Scripture is full of intimate descriptions of Jesus the head and the Church his body. One is the vine. Jesus is the vine and we are the branches. To keep us connected and bearing fruit, we need to be regularly pruned. That's what conversion means. Cut off from him we run aimlessly all over the place. It's that simple. The call to the *New Evanglization* is patently clear about this. As many as sixty-six times it hammers home the message that this conversion begins with and is sustained by a *fresh* encounter with Jesus. It calls for a new relationship with the head, Jesus; not the body, the pope, bishops and priests. Again, it is that simple. But simplicity is often an obstacle. We live in a high-powered, technological and sophisticated society. People believe that the more complex something is the better it must be. So we are suspicious of simplicity. Did not Jesus remind us that we must become like little children but not be childish?

Just as children learn to speak a language, we too need to speak a *new* language. New in *ardour, method and expression* as outlined by the *New Evangelization*. Let's now look at the language we Catholics commonly use. Right away we see it is primarily the language of the body, the Church. The head, Jesus, is little mentioned. For example, ask the average Catholic who the Church is and inevitably you get, "The Pope, Bishops and Priests." And who is the head of the Church? "The Pope." Not really! Jesus is the head. And to add insult to injury, we speak of Cardinals as "Princes of the Church!" Push it further. We say that bishops have the fullness of the priesthood. Only Jesus has the fullness of priesthood! It's amazing how we usurp what rightfully belongs to him and appropriate it for ourselves. This is holy plagiarizing!

Perhaps you will object that we don't actually mean all of the above. Well say what you mean and mean what you say! Use a language that is clear, specific, unambiguous and speaks the truth. Children are good at this. If we don't, we just keep adding more confusion. Dare we say, heresy? Other examples of language that favours the body are: A person enters the RCIA to be initiated into the Church. On Sunday, we go to Church. We baptize into the Church and marry in the Church. A man is ordained a priest to serve the Church.

In controversial issues like same-sex marriage and politicians not receiving Holy Communion, we ask what the Church has to say. We teach that the Church is known by its four marks: It is One, Holy, Catholic and Apostolic. The question to ask in all this is: "Where is the head, Jesus?" Doesn't he have anything to say? It is like a husband describing matrimony with no mention of his wife. Is it any wonder that the Church in the West is running around like one of my chickens with its head chopped off?

I am not demeaning the role of the body, the Church. But it is always a subservient role. The servant, the body, is not above the master, the head. The new encounter with Jesus will have to be expressed in the body knowing its place and keeping it. The body, as it were, must keep it's head screwed on! Severed from the vine it bears no fruit. Like the Israelites, our ancestors in the faith, we continue to avoid a close relationship with God preferring knowledge *of* God to intimacy *with* God. But God is a God of the heart, not the head.

part two

❁

Ignorance of scripture equals ignorance of Jesus. This is applies to all Catholics but particularly to the institutional and hierarchical dimension of the Church. It does not follow that because one has studied scripture for years one knows Jesus in the biblical sense of knowing. We can have a lot of knowledge about Jesus yet not have a personal relationship with him. This is the goal of the *fresh* encounter with Jesus called for by the *New Evangelization*. No one more than Paul was on fire for Jesus because Jesus was real for him. Paul is our man to sharpen our focus and return us to a Jesus-centered Church.

So intimate was his relationship with Jesus, that he speaks about being "Captured by Christ." Paul continues on this note of being possessed when he says, "The love of Christ overwhelms us." Jesus was the driving force of his apostolate. His mission was very simple: tell people about Jesus. Clearly Paul first lived what he preached.

Jesus was the source and summit of Paul's life. "Life to me, of course, is Christ," he tells us. While he was not stupid, he says the only knowledge he claimed to have was, "About Jesus, and only about him as the crucified Christ." Just as Jesus was at his strongest when he was weak between two thieves, likewise Paul. So much so that he exclaims, "I shall be very happy to boast about my weaknesses so that the power of Christ may stay over me."

Paul didn't have an identity crisis. He was an ambassador for Christ: "For it is not ourselves that we are preaching, but Christ

Jesus as Lord." Like a genuine ambassador, he played second fiddle. He knew his place and kept it. When people wanted to put he and Barnabas on a pedestal and lavish praise on them, he got angry. He tore his clothes and shouted, "Friends, what do you think you are doing? We are only human beings like you?" He resisted any semblance of power, prestige and honour. Only a person rooted and grounded in Christ has the inner freedom to walk away from these illusions.

Unlike the institutional Church today, Paul was free of trimmings, trappings and distractions. The early Church was not entangled in the government of its day. This would come around three hundred years later. From then on the Church aligned itself with Emperors, Kings, Queens, Lords and Nobles. Wearing the two hats of secularism and the Gospel, it compromised its primary mission of preaching Jesus. Quickly the body became severed from the head. The institution then absorbed the secular model of governing. This mix of oil and water dominated the institutional Church down the centuries and is with us today to a lesser degree. It still operates out of that hand-in-glove, bedfellow mindset.

Only a radical and ruthless conversion of heart will break this unholy marriage. We need to return to the purity and simplicity of Paul, free of our trimmings, trappings and distractions. A daunting challenge! As an institution, we are like Martha, distracted with many things while only one is necessary: Tell people about Jesus! The Pentecostals and Evangelicals have converted twenty-five percent of Catholic Latin America because they preach Jesus first.

We tell them about the Church first! Like the security personnel at our airports, we do a check before putting them on board with Jesus! This is power and control, a vestige of bygone days. The truth is that Catholics in the Western world have lost hope in the institutional Church. History shows that when this happens people turn to Jesus. They are making the same request today as the Greeks did of Philip: "We want to see Jesus." Notice they didn't ask to see any of the apostles. Philip went and told Jesus.

Paul and Philip set the challenge for the institutional Church. Put people in touch with Jesus, drop them off and get out of the way. For this to happen the institution must experience the inner freedom, detachment and trust that results from a *fresh* encounter with Jesus.

part three

Spring follows Winter. Life follows death. John Paul II, optimistically, predicts a New Spring-time for the Church. For this to happen the institutional Church must first experience the death of winter. Like the rest of us, it must undergo profound conversion. Since it is only Jesus who can convert us, a *fresh* encounter with him is an absolute requirement.

In the *Decree on Ecumenism,* the bishops at the Second Vatican Council preceded the Pope in their call for conversion: "Christ summons the Church, as she goes her pilgrim way, to that continual reformation of which she always has need in so far as she is an institution of men [people] here on earth. Therefore, if the influence of events or the times has led to deficiencies in conduct....these should be appropriately rectified at the proper moment."

If we were to name the root sin of the institutional church, it would be *power.* This is expressed in myriads of ways but most evident in control and paternalism. A child developmental psychologist, Erik Erikson, sums it up like this: "Religions often thwart confidence by keeping the adherents infantile. Enforcing dependency is a distorted form of care."

Severed from the head, Jesus, the body resorts to this. For example, we speak an impersonal language to describe ourselves like, "The Catholic religion, the Catholic Church, the Catholic faith." While they are not bad, they do lack the warm language of a personal relationship with Jesus. The stilted, ecclesiastical language we use reflects this divorce. We write in a lawyer-like, cold and formal language that the average Catholic cannot comprehend. Compare this to the language of friends and lovers! Compare it to the language of the Song of Songs in scripture and the mystics!

Clearly, the institution has many obstacles to overcome if it is to stop controlling and be more relational. An all-male leadership is a major hurdle. It's like a twin-engined plane flying with one engine shut down! We men in general are not comfortable with intimate relationships. Yet, this is what Jesus calls us to. Not an intimacy of heads but of hearts. But men find it safer to stay in their heads. The institution sets the tone so it is inevitable that the rest of us stay clear of relationships too. Most of our parish communities would not set you on fire on a Sunday morning!

An obvious consequence of this is the institutional leadership's escape into intellectualism. It's bizarre that we have no dearth of theologians telling us about God. Yet few who write from their experience of being known by God in the biblical sense. I believe Karl Rahner said that all theologians are liars! So he was one of the greatest liars! But he was right. Theologians have a speech impediment when talking about God. A good definition of a theologian would be, "A 'stammerer' in the face of the reality of God."

Knowledge is power. It gives a false sense of certainty and security. It fools us into believing that we have all the answers. We also confuse knowledge with wisdom. A wise Jesuit seminary professor knew the difference. Entering the classroom he announced, "Gentlemen, I am here to speak to you about that which I know nothing: The Trinity." My chickens have more wisdom than many intellectuals! A *fresh* encounter with Jesus will enlighten and awaken us to ask more questions and have fewer answers. Meister Eckhart tells us, "Seek God so as never to find him." It is in this relationship that we find liberation and freedom. Free to live in mystery where we possess all the answers! As John of the Cross put it, "It is in unknowing God that we know God."

Enlightenment, being truly catholic, knows no borders and is not the monopoly of Catholics. A laywoman, Simone Weil, was never baptized. But she was enlightened and died at the age of thirty-four. Her words of wisdom should challenge the institutional Church to reflect. "Intelligence," she says, "can never penetrate the mystery."[3] And, "The mysteries of faith are degraded if they are made into an object of affirmation and negation, when in reality they should be an object of contemplation."[4] The Pope presents Jesus as the object and calls us to, "Contemplate the face of Christ."

The intellectual genius, Thomas Aquinas came to the same conclusion as Simone Weil. No theologian has had such an impact on Catholic thought as he. Yet, when he became enlightened he quit writing. Like Paul, he considered it all rubbish in comparison to his new experience. Conversion does that—it shatters our illusions!

---

3   **Simone Weil:** *Gravity and Grace: 185*
4   Ibid., 183

SIT DOWN BESIDE ME

John Main grew up in London. He became a lawyer and worked for the British colonial government in Malaya. A desire to deepen his prayer life led him to seek direction from Catholic priests. Dissatisfied, he turned to a Hindu guru for help. The Guru's simple response was, "Sit down beside me and say your mantra." That wasn't the answer he expected. A typical Westerner, he wanted to be "taught" how to pray. However, he trusted his teacher and sat down.

Several years later, he became a Benedictine monk in England. Soon he was sharing his experience of Eastern spirituality. His quiet prayer led him to see a very close connection between the spirituality of the East and Western monasticism up to the first millenium. This simplified prayer attracted many. Like his Hindu guru, he simply invited people to "Sit down and say your mantra." When I applied to make a directed retreat with him in Montreal, his reply was: "I don't direct anyone. You are welcome to come and sit with us for four periods of silent meditation each day." I did!

Jesus is the source and summit of the *New Evangelization* to which Catholics are called. John Paul II is emphatic on this. In *The Church in America,* he mentions the urgent need "To encounter Jesus" sixty-sixty times. And in his *Moving Into the New Millenium,* seventeen times he stresses the need "To contemplate the face of Christ." Jesus is the master guru and spiritual director. We just need to sit at his feet and be quiet.

This is an almost impossible task for us in the West. Our busyness, intellectual orientation, analytical mindset, our preference for complexity, workaholism, the need to prove ourselves by "doing," our fear of silence and simplicity, are some of the obstacles. To "waste time" and "to be" do not sit well with us. As a species, we are named *human beings*. We are born *to be*. We are not named *human doings* but we sure behave as if we are! Is it any wonder we are all messed up? Miguel Elizondo is a Jesuit priest and spiritual director in Latin America. In his article, "Jesus and Prayer," he says, "The problem of prayer has been made far too complicated in comparison with the simplicity that we see in Jesus." This is because we are so hung up on *doing*.

On my departure from sitting for eight days, I expressed to John my fears returning to the missions in South America. It was easy to sit, to be and "waste time" in a monastery! What would happen when I got back to my busy active missionary life? Being a man of few words, he looked at me and asked, "And what alternative have you?" He turned and walked away! That was a typical Irish response! The Irish rarely answer your question. They respond by asking another! Jesus must have been Irish for he too rarely gave a straight answer. He just asked another question! Frustrating! Just tell me what to do. Don't ask me to reflect!

Jesus taught the Beatitudes on a mountain, sitting down. This depicts the Eastern tradition of the student sitting at the feet of the master or guru on a mountaintop. Teaching from the sitting posture reflects authority. The authority of lived experience. The authority of Jesus having first climbed his mountain! He spent thirty years "being" and only two and a half "doing." Jesus first lived what he taught. "He had to take his seat." Buddhism teaches that the student must sit at the Buddha's feet. Catholics must learn to sit at the feet of Jesus. But who will teach them?

The Beatitudes, more than any other body of teaching, highlight the consistent paradox of Jesus' teaching. His teaching and lifestyle defy our Western logic. Sitting at his feet seems such a useless waste of time. That's how Martha interpreted her sister's stance before Jesus. A core experience of the *New Evangelization* is to start getting used to living with paradox. That doesn't make sense to us. It's not meant to! In my day, the bishop questioned candidates at Confirmation. He asked Johnny what he knew about the Trinity. Shaking and wetting his pants, Johnny mumbled something. The bishop asked him to repeat. The same mumble. After several more attempts and same reply, the bishop became frustrated and blurted out, "I don't understand."

Johnny, loud and articulate, shot back, "You are not meant to!" That too would be the typical response of the Eastern tradition. We need to return to our roots. John Main drew on the affinity of East and West to teach people how to sit. In this regard, we in the West are breathing with only one lung. We need to breath with both lungs: East and West.

"SLOW DOWN FRANK!"

Francis Xavier was a great Jesuit missionary. He worked in Goa, South East Asia and Japan. He died on his way to China. In his zeal, Francis baptized anything that moved! His boss, Ignatius, had to tell him to slow down on the baptisms. Some basic cathechesis was necessary.

The challenge to the *New Evangelization* calls us to slow down on baptism today: not only the preparation but the actual ceremony. The rite is so rich that we cannot do justice to it in the celebration of the liturgy. This doesn't give us permission to celebrate it outside the Eucharist! It is mind-boggling when you think of what we try to accomplish in one hour, or less, at a Sunday Mass! In this reflection I give a thumbnail sketch of how I am slowing down the preparation and celebration. It is my small response to the *New Evangelization* that calls for a newness in *ardour, method and expression.* This skeleton outline follows the RCIA process. It consists of four short meetings and four short celebrations. Less is more!

Meetings:
At The Door
Name, Role of Parents/Godparents,

Sign of cross
At The Book
Listen to God's Word, Speak God's Word, Oil

Celebrations:
At the Eucharist
Welcome into community, Litany of Saints, Present a cross
At the Eucharist
Blessing of ears/mouth
First anointing

	(catechumens) Prayers of the Faithful (from the rite) Present bible
At the Font Conversion to Jesus What we believe Water	**At the Eucharist** Renunciation of sin Profess faith in Creed Bless water, baptize, clothe with garment Give holy water bottle
At the Altar The Eucharist: where baptism leads to Sunday: Day of the Lord	**At the Eucharist** Anointing with oil of Chrism Baptism candle/certificate given

These four sessions and celebrations can be longer than a month. Parents are comfortable with this when it is well explained. Plus, something happens every time so they feel they are progressing. Using this model, it would be best to have baptisms four times a year. Fall: *Feast of the Holy Cross.* We sign them with the cross. They are baptized into the death and resurrection of Jesus. Winter: *Holy Family.* Spring: *Easter Season.* Summer: *Corpus Christi:* Baptism leads to Eucharist. And Eucharist, not Confirmation, is full initiation. With short celebrations spread over a long period, I am more relaxed in the liturgy. So is everyone else! It's no longer a hundred meter dash as happened when I incorporated the full rite. I hesitate to say "celebrate" because I just breezed through it as parishioners sat there looking at their watches!

Most of our parents today are uncatechized and definitely not evangelized! Many are not even fully initiated, just baptized. How can we expect them to bring their children to a "fresh encounter with Jesus" called for in the *New Evangelization*? Basically we have children forming children in the faith. We need to shift the focus from the child to the parent. When addressing the Godparents, the priest asks, "Are you ready to help the parents of these children?" Notice who needs the help! The parents! So do the Godparents! I should stress that it is for the uncatechized, who are the majority, that I use this model.

For many parents baptism is a private event. They often resist celebrating it in the liturgy but this is the norm. To stress the place of the community into which the child is baptized, I involve parishioners. Before we process, I link up parents with a family who will process in with them and sit with them. Not up in the front pew but scattered throughout the congregation. Sitting in front isolates them from the community. That family brings them to the front for the different celebrations, stays and brings them back. I find a different family the next Sunday and so on. This gets them rubbing shoulders with many parishioners.

My Latin teacher's wise advice was, "Divide et impera." Divide and conquer. So when faced with a sentence a mile long, he taught us how to tear it apart. Look for the object, the subject, the verb, the dative and so on and it would all come together. This is the principle I am using for baptism preparation and celebration. It's the same principle the RCIA uses. Throughout, the rite tells us to adapt, adapt. Similarly, the *New Evangelization* calls us to adapt to: a newness in *ardour,* a newness in *method,* and a newness in *expression.*

FORMATION FOR MATRIMONY

The following outline is based on the call to the *New Evangelization* and the Rite of Christian Initiation for Adults process.

Period of Enlightenment and Precatechumenate:
- **FOCCUS**
  (Facilitating Open Couple Communication, Understanding and Study) Couple inventory deals with key aspects of matrimony.

Rite of Enrollment-during the Eucharist

Period of the Catechumenate:
- Faith formation—6 sessions
  Catholics: The family into which we marry
  The Church: The Bride of Christ
  From Covenant to Sacrament (marriage to matrimony)
  The Eucharist: This is my body given for you. Couples say this on wedding day.
  Sacrament of Reconciliation: Couples need to heal regularly.
  Natural Family Planning: 1% divorce rate for couples who live this lifestyle.

Rite of Engaged-during the Eucharist
- Immediate formation stage:
  Engaged Encounter Weekend or Evenings for Engaged

Rite of Scrutiny-during the Eucharist

Period of Purification and Enlightenment:

- Day of reflection on their vows and rehearsal for wedding

Period of Mystagogia:
- Reflection on wedding
- Reflection on honeymoon
- Meal

I am convinced that an integral component of the *New Evangelization,* is the need for a new language. The title reflects this. "Preparation" is academic. It focuses on knowledge. It deals more with the head than the heart. "Formation" looks at the whole person. A key element in this approach is less teaching and more dialogue. And this can be laborious! Often it is more efficient to teach! But then the couples sit there with blank faces and fall asleep! To get them to interact can be like drawing blood from a stone! Catholics for the most part are very reticent to talk about their faith. Sadly, I think this is because of their ignorance. They are just embarrassed. Young couples are appallingly ignorant of the basics. That's why we have to slow down and do a little formation in the short time we have with them. On the bright side, I find that as we move along a sense of bonding takes place, around the third session, and they become more open.

"Marriage" and "Matrimony." Most couples presenting themselves for a sacramental relationship do not see any great difference. Anyone can get "married" but to be "matrimonied" is a horse of a different colour. The other reason for dropping the title "marriage" is because it no longer means a man and woman only. Now this could be a blessing in disguise. Many countries still celebrate the sacrament of matrimony along with a civil marriage in one ceremony while most do not. The sooner we separate the two the better. It clarifies for the couple the difference between sacramental matrimony and civil marriage. Have your sacramental celebration and then go elsewhere for your civil. It used to be the case in England that the Registrar would do the civil bit in the sacristy afterwards. So when a couple calls up wanting to "get married in the Church," as they put it, what would be a good response? Something like, "The State performs marriages. The Church celebrates the sacrament of matrimony. Which route do you wish to take?" Formation has already begun!

A NEW LANGUAGE FOR MASS GOERS
The New Evangelization Approach

part one

I desperately needed fresh air. All weekend I was the victim of second-hand smoking in the days when you smoked where you liked. Just about everyone lit up in the crowded parish hall in Scotland where I facilitated a workshop. Returning from my bike ride I passed Protestants heading for church with their bible under their arm. Catholics strolled down the street to Mass with the Sunday newspaper under their arm!

Had I asked the Protestants where they were going, they would have responded, "We're going to worship." And the Catholics! "We're going to Mass." Protestants advertise times of "worship" on their signs. Catholics advertise times of "Mass." "Going to Mass" can sound as flippant as going to work or the grocery store. Apart from obligation, many Catholics, particularly our young, do not understand the deeper meaning of the Eucharist.

In response to the call of the *New Evangelization*, I propose a new language for what should be the high-point of the week for Catholics. The Eucharist is the source and summit of the life of a Catholic. Yet, few appreciate this. In exhorting us to eagerly and urgently implement the *New Evangelization*, the Pope is quite radical. And no where should this be expressed more in *ardour, method and expression*, than in the Sunday celebration of the Eucharist or liturgy.

"I am going to celebrate thanksgiving this morning." That's the kind of language I would love to hear Catholics use on any given

Sunday or weekday. It's so simple! After all, the very name of the celebration is called "Thanksgiving." That's what Eucharist means in Greek. A great reformer of the liturgy was St. Basil the Great. Commenting on his wisdom, one writer says about him: "Perhaps the simplest and most direct way to characterize the teaching of Basil, and a way that recalls that he was the author (reviser) of the liturgy that bears his name, is to say that it is essentially **eucharistic:** that is, humanity's relationship to God is to be one of thanksgiving." The Second Vatican Council calls for a renewal of the liturgy that would be characterized as a "noble simplicity." Could anything be more noble and simple than celebrating thanksgiving every Sunday! Easier said than done! We in the Western world have lost the sense of gratitude. The poor know how to be grateful because they know what it is like to depend on God. We in the West feel we no longer need to depend on God, or anyone else for that matter.

Because we are immersed in a me-centered culture, our narcissism is the very antithesis of gratitude. Often I hear people say "I don't go to Mass anymore because I don't get anything out of it." Notice where the focus is and that Mass is an "it." That's our narcissistic, neurotic self-preoccupation response. Switching the focus will not be easy. But using the language of "thanksgiving" is a start. Thanksgiving for what? Put simply, thanking God for Jesus who died for me, who points me in a whole new direction and gives me hope in death. Thanking him because all is pure gift. I own nothing. All is on loan. I came with nothing and I will leave with nothing. Thanks to him, I can die healed. There's a lot more but that's plenty for starters. Would that we Catholics appreciate more this great magnanimity of Jesus! You would have to be quite a heartless Catholic to know this and not take one hour out of one hundred and sixty-eight to celebrate thanksgiving on a Sunday.

The Eucharist is for Catholics what the Passover was for the Israelites: a celebration of gratitude for passing over from slavery to freedom. Jesus, the new Moses, is leading us to our promised land. We haven't arrived yet. He continues to pass over our sins. He continues to save us for we are never fully saved this side of the grave.

Because he passed over death, we can look death in the face with dignity. The focus of our Sunday thanksgiving then is Jesus, not what we get out of it. Leaving our ego at the door and watch at home would be a start in this direction.

part two

T he communist, Karl Marx, described religion as the opium of the people. We look at our parishes today and wonder if he had a point. Expressions like "going to Mass" can sound empty and have the same effect as opium. It's an intellectual statement that lacks feeling, commitment and depth. The need for a new language to wake us up is urgent. Her husband's head was buried in his chest during the homily and the priest could not take it any longer when he began to snore! "Wake him up madam," he shouted. "You wake him up," she retorted. "You put him to sleep!"

The new language I suggest is, "I am going to celebrate thanksgiving." Keep in mind that Eucharist means "Thanksgiving" and so it makes sense to speak the language of celebrating thanksgiving on Sunday. This has feeling, is joyful and spontaneous. The focus shifts from head to heart, from what I get out of "going to Mass" to thanking and praising God for Jesus.

For Catholics, "Jesus" language is new and threatening. It can be too personal and emotional. Yet in the *New Evangelization* the Pope, sixty-six times mentions the need for a fresh encounter with Jesus. We prefer to keep our distance with the more formal language like "The Lord" or "The Christ." It's like the story of the woman who jumped up during Mass raising her hands and singing, "Thank you Jesus, praise you Jesus." Immediately, the Knights of Columbus rushed in with drawn swords. She resisted being dragged out saying she only met Jesus. "Not in this church madam," replied one of the Knights! It's sad, but true, we can "go to Mass" and not meet Jesus! But we cannot celebrate thanksgiving without Jesus.

Gratitude should be the hallmark of a Catholic in everyday life but in particular when we gather on Sunday. How much easier it would be for parents to get their children out if more gratitude was lived at home. It's sad that many parents pay their children to do chores which should be done gratefully and gracefully. A simple exercise like grace before and after meals is a constant expression of gratitude. We have lost the sense of gratitude because we have lost the sense that all is gift. When Catholics are possessed by an attitude of gratitude they will move beyond just "going to Mass!" And that would be great! Once they recognize their need for gratitude, they will gladly express it in celebrating thanksgiving on a Sunday morning. This is far more positive than simply fulfilling an obligation.

A brief look at the liturgy of the Eucharist confirms that it is a thanksgiving prayer. It opens with the Preface with the presider appealing to the people: "Let us give thanks to the Lord our God." And the people respond: "It is right to give God thanks and praise." Both invitation and response should raise the roof instead of a murmur! Most times it is a whisper and often just silence! "We come to you Father, with praise and thanksgiving....," begins the first Eucharistic Prayer. Recalling the Last Supper at the Consecration, we are reminded of Jesus' attitude of gratitude: "He took bread....he gave you thanks and praise." "He took the cup; again he gave you thanks and praise." And we go forth from our celebration of thanksgiving with gratitude: "Go in peace to love and serve the Lord." "Thanks be to God."

I begin Mass on this note of gratitude. It is good to call to mind our sins but it's better to call to mind why we are gathered in the first place. A brief reminder that we are here to celebrate thanksgiving followed by silence, sets the tone. This should change the focus from me to Jesus, from beggar to receiver, from obligation to privilege, from duty to worship. We mistakenly believe that "Full, Conscious and Active participation" in the Mass is primarily physical and intellectual. It is more important to be fully conscious of why I am there. This inner awareness will spill over into genuine active participation expressed in praise, thanksgiving and silence.

The poet, T.S. Eliot says that, "The last temptation that is the greatest treason, is to do the right thing for the wrong reason." Celebrating thanksgiving is the right thing and done for the *right* reason.

part three

Sacrifice is not politically correct in our affluent culture riddled with "me-ism." This poses a major obstacle to experiencing our celebration of thanksgiving as sacrifice. Added to this is how we were taught that the sacrifice of Jesus was primarily to placate an angry God whom we had sinned against. So the celebration of the Eucharist was mainly about making reparation and appeasing God. I am sure glad that I do not subscribe to this kind of God anymore! There has to be, and there is, a better way of understanding Jesus' sacrifice. Jesus sacrificed himself for you and me right from the day he was born and all through his life, not just on the cross. The cross was the appalling and brutal culmination of a sacrificial life. His sacrifice is the kind we see in parents who, day in and day out, make heroic sacrifices for their children, particularly if they have a mentally or physically challenged child.

A recent saint, wife and mother, doctor and surgeon, Giolla Molla, canonized in 2004 mirrors spectacularly Jesus' sacrifice. Giolla gave up her life that her unborn daughter, Gianna, would have life. Late in her pregnancy in 1962 she was diagnosed with a uterine tumour. A hysterectomy would have meant the abortion of her baby so she refused. "If you have to choose between me and the baby, save it, I insist," she told her husband. In April of that year doctors delivered a healthy baby but a week later Gionna died from septic peritonitis. Forty-two years later, Gianna and Giolla's husband, Pietro were at her canonization!

We need to celebrate with profound gratitude the sacrifice Jesus made for us. We do this by celebrating thanksgiving on a Sunday. I am sure that Saint Giolla's daughter, Gianna, is continually grateful that her mom died for her. Can you hear the appeal of Jesus to us to remember to be grateful when he said: "Do this in memory of me?" Celebrating the horrendous sacrifice Jesus made for us is meant to stir up gratitude in us which is our only meaningful response to such sacrificial love. When we are in pain we ask the obvious question: "Why me?" When I see how much Jesus suffered for me I should ask the same question: "Why me?"

This sacrificial aspect of the Eucharist is little appreciated or understood by most Catholics. "Stripped of its sacrificial meaning, it is celebrated as if it were simply a fraternal banquet," says John Paul II in "The Church of the Eucharist." He goes on to say that when this happens it is reduced to a mere proclamation. Our celebration of thanksgiving is not a reminder of what happened two thousand years ago. It is a re-presentation. It is a real presence of the death and resurrection of Jesus. "To remember," for the Israelites, was more than recalling the event of the Passover. To remember was to make happen again. They relived their liberation from Egypt and exodus to the promised land.

Gathered at Ground Zero in New York City a year after September 11, 2001, people were asked to observe a moment of silence. Commenting on this in his book, *Coming to our Senses,* Jon Kabat-Zinn points out that this exercise is not just about memory, a kind of mental recalling: "It is a confluence of memory and now. It is honoring the dead and the harmed and the heroic in the present moment, which is always now, for now is the only actuality that endures." On a Sunday, we relive in the now, in the very present moment, the sacrifice Jesus made for us two thousand years ago. When a person recalls a nightmare, a serious accident or childhood abuse, they actually relive it. It is so vivid that they experience the fear and pain again. This is how we are meant to celebrate thanksgiving. For the Israelites, the abused and Ground Zero, pain is central. Pain too is at the heart of the sacrifice of Jesus and the Eucharist. I read recently that worship without sacrifice is a sin!

Another great obstacle to our experiencing the connection between Eucharist and sacrifice, is our head. Being the independent, me-centered people we are, we try to figure it out. But we have to get out of our heads. The fresh encounter with Jesus that we are called to in the *New Evangelization* is one of heart to heart! It is not in knowledge but in relationship that we will appreciate the sacrificial meaning of the Eucharist.

Note well that at the Last Supper Jesus did not give his apostles a lecture, knowledge, as his farewell gift. He gave himself: "This is my body given for you. This is my blood poured out for you." This is what stirs us to make a sacrifice on a Sunday morning and gladly celebrate thanksgiving for the excruciating sacrifice made for you and me.

part four

※

We're stuck! We get nothing out of "going to Mass" because we are getting nothing out of life. The Eucharist is experienced as static because we are stagnant! So we project our lethargy and inertia onto the Eucharist. In order to experience the Eucharist as a "celebration of thanksgiving," we need first to begin living as opposed to merely existing. The Eucharist is what life is at its most fundamental level: rhythm, movement, dynamic and pulsating life. The Indian Jesuit, Tony deMelo's mantra was "Wake up! Awareness! Awareness!" Maybe this is why he is not popular with some of the leadership of the Church! We are sleepwalking! Get with the dance of life!

A meeting of scholars of the history of religions was held in Tokyo in the 1950's. The participants were shown the major Shinto shrines and witnessed Shinto religious ceremonies and celebrations. A distinguished western sociologist chatted with an equally distinguished Shinto priest named Hirari. He thanked Hirari saying how impressed he was by the beauty and solemnity of the Shinto ceremonies. But, (typical westerner!), he said, he didn't quite understand what the participants thought they were doing in the ceremonies. Would Hirari mind explaining the meaning of the actions. "What," he asked, "is the theology behind these celebrations?" Hirari listened respectfully, thought a moment, and replied, "We have no theology. We dance."

The Eucharist is a dance. Before your blood pressure sky-rockets, let me quickly qualify this! It is the celebration of the rhythm of life. Don't ask philosophers or theologians to enlighten you on this! Ask matrimonied couples who are awake, aware and living a vocation as opposed to being just married. We have to be awake, aware and alive to experience the rhythm of life. None are more awake than these couples because they strive to deepen their relationship. Nothing other than relationship will plunge you into and teach you the rhythm which is romance and disillusionment! It is yang and ying. Relationships are not static. We either experience romance or disillusionment. There's no neutrality, no sitting on the fence here. The rhythm is also experienced in consolation and desolation; in the flow and ebb tide; in light and darkness; in good and evil. We can't think our way into relationship no more than we can learn to dance with our head! We feel our way. Our head is also an obstacle to the rhythm of life!

The Eucharist is rhythm and dance because it celebrates all of the above in terms of resurrection—death—resurrection. This may look cyclic but it's not. It is a spiral movement going deeper into life. The romance, consolation, flow-tide and resurrection are experienced through spiraling down to yet another layer. Notice that we grow down to live! We grow up to exist! A tree has to grow down before it can grow up! The disillusionment, desolation, ebb-tide and death are the other side of the rhythm coin. As we spiral down we inevitably rub up against sharp rocks that cut and tear off pieces of flesh. But no pain no gain! We can experience another layer only through spilling some blood.

Eucharist then is the celebration of the very pattern, rhythm and dance of life. Jesus, as it were, puts flesh and blood on the Eucharist. It is the celebration of his embracing the rhythm of life; of his spiraling down and leaving his torn, bloody flesh on the jagged rocks. His resurrection is the guarantee and hope that each layer issues forth new life. This is why we show up every Sunday to celebrate resurrection—death—resurrection, because this is the reality of life.

I prefer to put resurrection experience before death because without it we do not have the energy to die!

Like it or not, every day is experienced as romance-disillusionment, consolation-desolation, flow tide-ebb tide, resurrection-death. The problem is that we are not aware of it and so pay no attention to it. We can choose to fight against it but the rhythm carries on because we have no control over the flow of life. So why not dance! Why not strike a match instead of cursing the dark! In "celebrating thanksgiving" each Sunday, we celebrate life, hope, joy and gratitude, among other things. Then we are energized to enter daily life again to continue spiraling down. And we return the next Sunday to "celebrate thanksgiving" for the many ways we experienced spiraling down as resurrection—death—resurrection. It's o.k. to die daily when you know for sure you will rise the same day! The Eucharist is indeed a dance, a "celebration of thanksgiving!"

part five

The death and resurrection of Jesus, which we celebrate on Sunday as thanksgiving, is less about the next life and more about this life. Jesus assures us that eternal life is *now,* in the Gospel of Saint John. Jesus wants us to experience life *now.* Resurrection is the experience of Jesus redeeming and saving us *now.* This is no pious platitude but an absolute fact and dead practical too! You mean I am not fully saved! Correct! As the saying goes, "May you be in heaven half an hour before the devil knows you're dead!"

The parish priest dropped into the local pub late one night, part of his pastoral visit of course! After berating the guys about all the sins committed through alcohol, he yelled over the blaring television, "Stand up all who want to go to heaven." All staggered to their feet except Murphy in the corner with a pint of Guinness in either hand—his idea of a balanced diet! "You mean you don't want to go to heaven Murphy," demanded the priest. "Of course I do Father but I thought you were going right away!" Murphy had found new life right where he was!

The rhythm of life is a spiraling down to new layers of new life. Unfortunately we can't avoid the jagged rocks on the way down. Notice how after his resurrection Jesus appears in his risen body with the marks of the nails and wound in his side! There's new life in those wounds. That's why Jesus is our wounded healer, but more, he is our hope. There is life in death—right here. Jesus is also our saviour. He saves us from despair and hopelessness in our daily deaths.

Death and resurrection is the universal experience of the rhythm of life. We experience it in practical ways like disillusionment-romance; desolation-consolation; darkness-light; ebb tide-flow tide; despair-harmony; anxiety-peace. This is the cross of every human being and not just Catholics. Thanks to Jesus, we, like him can choose to embrace the rhythm. It's always a choice. We can also choose to just "go to Mass" or celebrate thanksgiving!

When Jesus invites us to take up our cross *daily,* he calls us to dance with the rhythm of life. That's what he did. Mistakenly, many think that Jesus means that we take up his cross. But he doesn't say, "Take up my cross." Or, "Give me your cross." He says, "Take up *your* cross daily". Take up life daily. We don't have to go looking for our cross. We just need to become aware of it. You are either fighting and cursing it or living and embracing it right *now,* as you read this! There's no middle ground here. No sitting on the fence1 You are either in desolation or consolation, experiencing death or resurrection.

Jesus, in the Eucharist, celebrates the truth of life and ask us to join him. That is, take up our cross. But to accept the cross we first have to accept Jesus. Here's where we in leadership need to refocus our catechesis or religious education. We place too much emphasis on putting people in touch with the Church first instead of Jesus. Only he makes sense of the cross of life. That's why the *New Evangelization,* sixty-six times, calls us to a fresh encounter with Jesus. Not more knowledge but a relationship with him. Again, we in leadership tend to be fixated with knowledge. Only in a relationship with Jesus do we have the key to peace and harmony: Jesus and the truth of life. So when we accept the truth we accept Jesus. And when we accept Jesus we accept the truth. They are one. The truth is that the cross of life is essential to human growth. Jesus made it quite clear that, "I am the truth and the truth will set you free?"

Now we can see why and how the Eucharist is the "source and summit" of the life of a Catholic. You could say it's the "be" all and "end" all of who we are. Not only does it give meaning to the cross of life, but we can actually celebrate it. The cross is not an imposition but part and parcel of being human in a broken world. When we take up our cross, take up life as it is, we experience resurrection. Not without pain of course! But pain need not be suffering. Suffering is despair and hopelessness. This we cannot celebrate. Pain is suffering injected or infused with hope. It's the assurance that we will experience resurrection in this life. And this we can celebrate as thanksgiving, in the Eucharist. It's not the pain itself we celebrate but the conversion of suffering into pain and hope—just as the bread and wine are changed into the Body and Blood of Jesus.

part six

When I'm in pain, even a headache, I want a quick-fix! So I reach for Tylenol, extra strong! Many Catholics "go to Mass" for a quick-fix! They go as beggars rather than worshippers. Like me, they want their Tylenol! And they pester Jesus to deliver it. In a sense they are at loggerheads with Jesus. Their focus is primarily on themselves. They beg Jesus to remove the pain of the cross of daily life. They believe the cross is to be circumvented, not taken up. "Why me?" is their mantra. Even Jesus can't answer that! The right question is, "What does it mean?" Jesus has all the answers to that question! Bonhoffer, the German Lutheran pastor, reminds us that there is only costly grace. He knew. He died in the gas chambers of Auschwitz.

I developed a kind of website which I turn to in my pain and suffering. It goes like this: WWW.H! They are four questions I ask Jesus: What does it mean? Where are we, Jesus and I, going? When will I know? How am I to respond? You notice I omitted the useless question Why? From painful experience I know Jesus does not reply so I have given up banging my head against a brick wall!

All this I do in prolonged prayer of at least half-hour periods and I persevere till I get an answer. I always do! That's why I have the hope to go down this road. I experience the answer in the form of resurrection, peace, harmony, consolation and joy returning. So I have spiraled down to another layer of life experienced first in my suffering as death, anxiety, fear and desolation.

Though it does hurt, we can be alive in our pain because we experience it as growing pain! It is the inevitable pain of human growth. Our peace and harmony are compatible with pain. It's like the ocean. There can be great turbulence on the surface while deep down all is calm. Now if we are to bring all this to our celebration on a Sunday, it has to take longer than the sacred hour, or forty-five minutes, or, God forbid, thirty-five! It needs to be open-ended. We have no problem with open-ended events like soccer, hockey, baseball or football! Even when the game goes into overtime we hang in there!

Begin our celebration of thanksgiving at eleven and end.....! Close is a better word. Like the Triduum of Holy Week. Holy Thursday Eucharist doesn't close till the great Alleluia at the end of the Easter Vigil! If our Sunday liturgy were truly a celebration of thanksgiving, it would be a weekly Triduum celebration and flow into our daily life. Celebrating thanksgiving on Sunday and the rest of the week is difficult but absolutely essential if we are to stop just "going to Mass!"

Meanwhile, there are several things we need to work on. One, don't restrict the word "Mass" to describe the Eucharist. It has become so commonplace and trivialized that it no longer represents the "source and summit" of Catholic life. Language evolves over the centuries. Words today don't mean what they did even a few years ago. Take "gay" for example. And closer still, "marriage." It no longer means a man and a woman. So we adapt. Use "matrimony" instead.

Two, we priests and bishops have to stop "saying Mass" at the drop of a hat. We have Mass for just about everything. We ask couples, "Will you be having Mass for your wedding?" It's like asking if they will be having two or six bridesmaids! Doing his rounds of the hospital, the chaplain asked the patient if he would like Communion in the morning. "No, thank you," he replied, "I prefer cereal for breakfast." Just before the Eucharistic celebration for the death of her mother, an Italian lady asked if I would, "Put some of that bread (Communion) in the casket with my mother!" She was quite offended when I emphatically said I would not. The Eucharist has been reduced to the props, the dessert, the frills. We have too many "Masses" and too few celebrations of the death and resurrection of Jesus.

In this regard, Pope Benedict calls us to examine the situation and question if we should have Mass at all for some weddings and funerals. Other circumstances are where Catholics have long ceased to participate at Mass along with others, because of their lifestyle, cannot receive the sacraments. He says: "Wherever circumstances make it impossible to ensure that the meaning of the Eucharist is duly appreciated, the appropriateness of replacing the celebration of the Mass with a celebration of the word of God, should be considered."

The urgency to raise the bar is blatantly evident.

part seven

Awareness! Awareness! Awareness! Only this will help you make the connection between celebrating thanksgiving on Sunday and the rest of your week. One is meant to flow into the other. We are called to live holistic, not compartmental lives. So, you need to pay attention, notice and smell the roses!

There are a few other preliminaries though to work on. One, is desire. Without a deep desire and longing for a rounded and fulfilled life (with the cross!), you can't proceed. Two, is a change of lifestyle. No connection will happen so long as you are living a frenzied and crazy life. You can't smell the roses on the run! So get off the tread-mill of the fast lane! Three, is faithfulness. Simple! So, how can each day be a celebration of thanksgiving that leads to Sunday Eucharist and flows back into your daily life? Remember, while this looks cyclic, it is not. It always spirals down.

The daily prayer exercise, "Awareness Examen," which I use is second to none. Let me be absolutely clear, this is not "examination of conscience!" We do the latter before celebrating the Sacrament of Penance. The former is best done at the end of the day. This is such a fitting way to bring closure to your day and live the rhythm of life. We're so busy that day and night are the same for us! Ten minutes at the most is all it takes. Desire, lifestyle change and faithfulness is all that is needed. It's not as daunting as it looks!

Begin with talking to Jesus. Ask *him* to show you your day. He's better at it than you! And he is more gentle too! Begin with resurrection and ask him to first show you what was life-giving, positive, uplifting, what brought you peace, harmony and consolation, (with the cross of course!). Go for a stroll with him beginning from when you got up. Jesus will communicate with you, not through your head, but through your feelings. So you need to be in touch with your emotional side. Feelings, not thoughts, are the best indicator of who you are. Feelings have no morality. They are neither right or wrong. It is what we do with them that is right or wrong. Your feelings are unique and original just like your fingerprint! But there is no original thought!

Pay attention then to how you are feeling. Any major or little event in your day that stirs up peace, harmony, new life and joy is suffering changed to pain, to consolation, to resurrection! You have spiraled to a new layer of life. Linger, stay with it and savour it. Tell Jesus how you *feel,* not what you think, about these moments. Above all, thank him.

Then ask Jesus to show you the times when you felt fear, anxiety, guilt, shame, sadness, suffering and desolation. Feel the feelings. Don't try to analyze them. Talk to Jesus about how you *feel,* not the event. Where you brought these on yourself (called sin!), say sorry. There is healthy guilt! You will notice a pattern in one or more areas like anger, gossip, judging others and so on. Focus on just one for tomorrow and ask Jesus to help you. Then say goodnight to him and sleep in peace! You have paid attention to, been aware of, and noticed your rhythm of death and resurrection in your day!

On Sunday you show up to celebrate thanksgiving. Now you do have something to celebrate! Not only Jesus' death and resurrection, but your own death and resurrection! Maybe you are weighed down by the cross of the rhythm of life. Really suffering. You can still celebrate because you have *hope.* From your awareness and paying attention during the week you *know* you will come back to pain, consolation and resurrection. You died and rose every day! The important point is that you noticed it.

Rejoice! You have made your connection between the Eucharist and your daily life. Now the celebration of Jesus' death and resurrection, and yours, does not end with the dismissal, "Go in peace!" There is no end! You leave to continue dying and rising during the week—if you pay attention, be aware, notice and smell the roses! Next Sunday, you return to a deeper celebration because you will have spiraled to yet another layer. And you have blood on you to prove it! You can even say with Jesus: "This is *my* blood poured out for *you*."

part eight

※

Recently, I hitched a ride with a group of loggers. That every word was not a swear word was my first observation during the forty-minute ride. The second was the dedication of these tough guys. It was five-fifteen in the morning. At the end of the drive they would catch a ferry. This would take an hour to their logging site. They repeated this day in and day out. Talk about commitment! What caught my attention the most though was their 'bitching!' One had been short-changed half an hour's overtime. The poor accountant was in for a rough day! Then their Union representative! And, of course, their company. I was left in no doubt of their love-hate relationship with Weyerhauser!

Does this in any way describe "Mass-Goers?" I believe it does. First: the focus. Like my good friends, Catholics are often centred on number one. We go primarily for our own benefit: to put bread on the table as it were, maybe to tank up for the rest of the week. We can do the right thing for the wrong reason. Whatever the intention, "I" am the focus. Then: the relationship. A love-indifference attitude might better describe our relationship with Jesus and the community. And indifference is worse than rejection.

When I left my comfort zone in Catholic Ireland for Protestant England, it was the indifference that got to me. Unlike during the sixteenth and seventeenth centuries, Catholics were not persecuted. Nobody cared what you did. It was this indifference, no support or encouragement, which caused many Irish to fall away. The same indifference in North America has a similar impact on Catholics today. It's subtle but extremely effective.

Finally, we Catholics do our share of 'bitching!' "That homily! He's so liberal! He is too conservative! It was over my head! There was no meat in it! And he's so long-winded! He went on for a full eight and a half minutes!" A parishioner once timed me and told me exactly how long I was! As for the singing! "And he kept us for a full forty-five minutes!" Like the music and the homily, all of us can be way off-key at Mass. Even when some pay compliments like, "That was a good homily; the singing was great!" I have yet to hear a parishioner say something like, "That was an enriching Eucharist." We can "go to Mass" and not celebrate Jesus', and our own death and resurrection. For many Catholics, the high points of a Sunday celebration are the homily, singing and Communion. In reality, it has been for them a Liturgy of the Word with Communion, although the priest presides. I have often been tempted to omit the Eucharistic prayer and see how many would notice!

We have two major problems here. First, most Catholics are not fully aware of the difference between a Liturgy of the Word with Communion and the Eucharist. Comments like, "Mary said a lovely Mass last Sunday" are common. Second, a lot do not distinguish between "going to Mass" and "celebrating thanksgiving." We have a lot of formation to do. I say formation in contrast to education. Formation deals with the whole person, both at the affective as well as the cognitive level. Education is primarily cognitive—knowledge. Because the Eucharist is a celebration of thanksgiving, it is relationship focused. The very centre of this celebration is a person, the host, Jesus. So the emphasis has to be on formation—an attitude of gratitude.

We would then leave our celebration making the words of the poet, Rainer Maria Rilke, our own: *"Oh, tell us, poet, what do you do? I praise. But the deadly and the violent days, how do you undergo, take them in? I praise."* Rilke experienced death and resurrection. As a child he suffered greatly, locked up in the attic by his mother for long periods of time. We are meant to return to daily life hope-filled to continue the dying and rising rhythm because we have just celebrated it. We experienced what Julian of Norwich calls, "A great *oneing* between Jesus and us because when he was in pain we were in pain." And we can add: When he rose, we rose and continue to rise. So I praise!

part nine

※

"If the only prayer you say in your whole life is *'thank you,'* that would suffice." That is the advice of the German mystic, Meister Eckhart. To arrive at this profound awareness would surely simplify not only our prayer and our spirituality, but our entire life. Imagine a world alive with gratitude! No more ecological crisis because we would treat it as a pure gift and give it the reverence it demands. We would learn to live *with* our environment, not demand that it accommodate itself to our greed and irresponsibility. There would be an end to AIDS, STD and abortion because we would handle our bodies as gifts, not our own. Our own and others' would be revered and respected as the temples of the Holy Spirit that they are. No more hunger because grateful people don't take more than they need of the gift. A thankful person instinctively shares.

'Thanks' comes from the Latin word *gratis,* meaning *grace.* We refer to a gift being "free gratis." It is something we have not earned, is not ours, but we are given it anyway. That knocks the wind out of "this is mine and I do with it as I like" attitude. It's just a short-term loan. In the English language there is no half-full of thanks! We are grate*ful* and thank*ful.*

The public schools are calling for extra money to help stem bullying. How absurd! Fifteen thousand professionals met in Bangkok recently to discuss the AIDS disaster. The solution? More money! Billions! Crazy! Dealing with the soaring Health Care cost, Janice

McKinnon, hit the nail on the head. "Canadians," she said, "must be responsible. Don't abuse the system or your body. Take responsibility for a healthy lifestyle that will prevent illness." It is attitude, not money, which will solve our problems. And gratitude is the key.

Teachers would do well to study the following advice of the writer, Pablo Casals: "When will we teach our children in school who they are? We should say to each of them, 'Do you know who you are? You are a marvel. You are unique. In the entire world there is no other child exactly like you. In the millions of years that have passed there has never been another child like you. And look at your body—what a wonder it is! Your legs, your arms, your cunning fingers, and the way you move. You may become a Shakespeare, a Michelangelo, or a Beethoven. You have the capacity for anything. Yes, you are a marvel. And when you grow up, can you then harm another who is, like you, a marvel?'" Throw in Psalm 139 and Matthew 25:31-46 for good measure and what a rich recipe we have! It's so simple and doesn't cost a cent! Teach children, and parents, to be thank*ful* and live grate*ful* lives.

There we have the model of formation for a child's full participation in the Eucharist for the first time. As things stand, preparation for "First Communion" is just another hoop to jump through. It is impossible to celebrate thanksgiving without living gratitude. This goes for adults as well as children. No miracle happens on a couple's wedding day. They don't suddenly change from being "I" focused to "us" centred or from a single mentality to oneness. That's the work of matrimony. Nor do miracles happen when Catholics gather on Sunday. We are not microwaves! We do not suddenly switch on to our grate*ful* and thank*ful* channel! Yet, we are there to celebrate thanksgiving. There to celebrate Jesus' and our death and resurrection instead of just going to Mass.

It may be simplistic, but we have to get back to basics, and begin by teaching our children good manners. That may seem primitive but it is real. Remember how only one leper had the good manners to return and thank Jesus. We do not need more books, more programs, curricula or crash courses for First Eucharist children.

Neither do we need these for their parents and Catholics in general. It cuts much deeper. Not even a re-evangelization will shake us out of our stupor. Only a *New Evangelization* will melt our hearts and awaken an attitude of gratitude.

part ten

※

Principles and foundations! We cannot function properly without them. Math: 1+1 = 2, for example. The law of gravity: Respect it! Reading and writing are essential for a decent job. On what do you build your house? Prevention is better than cure! Take your compass when hiking! And keep to the trail! Don't drink and drive! Basically, principles and foundations are common sense. Not so for a lot of people.

Just as for life in general, there are principles and foundations for Catholics. Indeed for all Christians. There is no one better than St. Ignatius of Loyola to lay these out for people making a thirty-day retreat. He calls them the "Principle and Foundation." To even begin the long haul, a retreatant must be firmly grounded in these. Then the long retreat will be an overwhelming conversion experience. It begins with a personal encounter with Jesus and feeling loved by him as a sinner. This leads to a renewed commitment to be his disciple, to generosity in taking up the cross of daily life and to the profound experience of joy because right *now* the person shares in the resurrection of Jesus. The thirty-day marathon concludes on a note of gratitude. Ignatius says, "Stirred to profound *gratitude,* I may be able to love and serve God in all things."

His "Principle and Foundation" applies to all. We are pilgrims on retreat and passing-over. The latter can happen anytime. He helps clarify for us the difference between "Going to Mass" and

"Celebrating Thanksgiving." Here is the "Principle and Foundation" in his own words:

"Human beings are created to praise, reverence, and serve God our Lord, and by means of doing this save their souls. The other things on the face of the earth are created for human beings, to help them in the pursuit of the end for which they are created. From this it follows that we ought to use these things to the extent that they help us toward our end, and free ourselves from them to the extent that they hinder us from it. To attain this it is necessary to make ourselves indifferent to all created things, in regard to everything which is left to our free will and is not forbidden. Consequently, on our part we ought not to seek health rather than sickness, wealth rather than poverty, honour rather than dishonour, a long life rather than a short one, and so on in all other matters. Rather, we ought to desire and choose only that which is more conducive to the end for which we are created."

There we have it in a nutshell! Our priority is to *praise, reverence* and *serve* God. This is the end and purpose for which we are created. Creation is a *gift*, so not ours. It is not an end in itself to be used as we like, but a means to our end. Detachment (indifference) is the proper attitude to life. "Attachment," says Simone Weil, "is a manufacturer of illusions and whoever wants reality ought to be detached. We only possess what we renounce."[5] We hold dear only that which helps us attain the end for which we are created.

Any other principles and foundations of life we have are sheer illusions. If we want to measure the depth of our illusions, just feel the power of our attachments. To be real we must get rid of them.

All this gives new perspective to the Eucharist as a celebration of thanksgiving. Our only purpose for showing up on Sunday is to *praise* and *reverence* God with Jesus. The cross of the daily rhythm of life is woven into this but doesn't deter us from celebrating. We bring with us our experience of death-resurrection each day of the past week. We know that roses without thorns are an illusion!

---

5   **Simone Weil:** *Gravity and Grace:* 59

Sunday is the highpoint, the *summit* of our week because we celebrate Jesus' death-resurrection and he is our *source*. The Eucharist is both *source* and *summit* because it is a person, Jesus. He is our principle and foundation!

We build on Jesus then. Without a personal relationship with him you cannot celebrate thanksgiving on Sunday. It's that simple.

YEAR OF EUCHARIST RESOLUTION

I wrote this reflection for the end of the Year of the Eucharist in 2005. I figured there would be all kinds of resolutions and most would be theological and academic. So I took a more practical approach and summarized it in one word: *Accountability.* We presiders need to be held accountable for the way we preside at the Eucharist or liturgy. We owe it to our people.

Even cleaning up the very introduction to the Eucharist would be a giant step forward. Showing up with his hair not combed and vestments thrown at him instead of on him, made him look more like a scare-crow! The perfunctory and sloppy sign of the cross was more the action of a robot than a human. If I hear that empty invitation again, "Let us call to mind our sins," I will scream, I said to myself as I concelebrated for the fifth time. Not to mention as we paused, my brother was flicking through the pages of the sacramentary to find his bearings. Unfortunately this kind of automatic and non-engaging attitude is all too common and enough to put people to sleep from the very start.

A team of high-powered therapists I know who work in an institution, once a week video-tape a session and then critique each other. In this way they are holding one other accountable because they owe it to their clients. How about installing a camera in each parish? The parish pastoral council or the liturgy committee could periodically gather with the presider for critique. It is too easy for us to slip into bad habits that we would not get away with in any other respectable profession. Imagine the president of Microsoft Works showing up shabbily dressed and unprepared for the company's Annual General Meeting!

Since the liturgy is described as the work of the people, it is also the work of the presider. Sadly, many of us have settled for "saying Mass" which requires no work at all. Working at presiding is draining. That's why some priests feel they can do justice to presiding only at two Sunday liturgies at the most. We can "say" many Masses and not work up a sweat.

As presider of the Eucharist I am called to be fully engaged with my people and doing the work *with* them. I have the privilege and awesome responsibility of reliving the death and resurrection of Jesus. To make this event come alive for and with my people means that, as best I can, I am integrating it into my own life. We priests boast about being called an *Alter Christus,* another Christ. This is much more than a nice title, at least it should be. With privilege comes responsibility and accountability.

My people have to experience me *living* what I celebrate. Meaning, the death and resurrection of Jesus is real in my life but more alive in this celebration of his death and resurrection. The pain is real because being a companion of Jesus in daily life is costly. I also feel the joy when I spiral down to a new level of living and enlightenment. It is this spirit that my people must catch and experience me as the *Alter Christus,* another Christ. In this sense I preside as one living and being drawn deeper into Christ's death and resurrection and drawing them with me. Presiding at this level demands energy, feeling and communication.

On the other hand, when I simply "say Mass" I reduce the death and resurrection of Jesus to an exercise of devotion instead of a living, challenging and joyful event. The focus is mainly on me doing something *for* my people that does not require much personal involvement. From this mentality it follows that receiving Communion is the highlight for them. The truth is that if I am not trying to live and celebrate the death and resurrection of Jesus in the here and now, should we receive Communion at all? Why should we if we have not done the work! Johnny was just five and used to put his own money in the children's collection. But he felt he too should be receiving Communion so one Sunday, in protest, he kept his money. When his dad inquired why, Johnny replied: "If I don't eat, I don't pay!" If, as priest, I am not accountable and preside well neither should I "say Mass."

NEW LANGUAGE FOR FIRST COMMUNION

part one

※

"Johnny got his First Communion last week." "Mary is preparing to get First Communion in the summer." Till recently I used that language without batting an eyelid! Now I see how inaccurate and superficial this is. So I need to watch my language!

With this erroneous thinking, Johnny does not need the celebration of the Eucharist. He could get First Communion at a Liturgy of the Word with Communion. It would be no problem so long as Johnny gets his Communion. It's like when Johnny got "done" at Baptism! Look at the focus. It's all about getting. This is typical of our "me-centered" society. It is impersonal too. Communion is reduced to an object, a thing.

We are lacking the very basics here. It's like a computer monitor but no hardware; the car with no engine. Where is the Eucharist, the core and heart of Communion? By Eucharist I mean the celebration of the death and resurrection of Jesus. Eucharist is a person. Sadly, Johnny and Mary can get Communion but not encounter the person—Jesus!

The cart is before the horse. Communion and the celebration of the death and resurrection of Jesus is one event. It is a re-presentation of the Last Supper and Calvary. That's why Communion apart from the celebration of the death and resurrection is wrong and leads to confusion. For many Catholics, Communion is the Eucharist. The death and resurrection of Jesus don't figure. For this reason, I am convinced that when a priest is not available on a Sunday we should have a celebration of the Word alone without Communion.

There is order in our Sunday celebration. We first celebrate the death and resurrection of Jesus, and our own. Then we share in Communion, all in the one celebration, of course. To put it rather crudely, to clarify, Communion is the finished product. Communion is a consequence of the re-presentation of the death and resurrection of Jesus. It is one event.

We call the Eucharistic celebration the "liturgy." This is a Greek word and means *the work of the people.* So if you haven't done the work, don't expect to get paid! This work consists of being in communion with Jesus prior to celebrating his death and resurrection, and our own. This is much more than being free of serious sin. It's all about lifestyle. To the best of my ability, I need to be working at living the death and resurrection on a daily basis. This is communion with Jesus' death and resurrection. Now I am ready to celebrate fully the Eucharist and receive Communion. This is full, active and conscious participation at its best. To receive Communion without that prior communion is hypocrisy. What does it express? Receiving Communion is meant to be an expression of and celebration of a communion that already exists.

So where do we begin with First Communion? As always, we should begin in the home. Mary is formed from day one by the example of her parents. This is the remote stage. It's not about teaching Mary. The formation is rooted in one word, "gratitude." Not a quick grace before and after meals, or "please" and "thank you." It's a whole lifestyle of her parents based on the truth that all is gift.

In experiencing gratitude lived everyday in her home, Mary early on celebrates death and resurrection like her parents. Grate*ful* people know how, when, where, what to say "no" and "yes" to. They know how to make life-giving choices. Thank*ful* people are free and detached to live a balanced life. All this is possible only because Mary's parents have a personal relationship with Jesus into which she is drawn. Does this lifestyle involve dying and rising? Try living it!

Because Eucharist is already lived at home, Mary, from an early age, experiences the Eucharist on Sunday as a celebration of thanksgiving. By grade two she is well formed (not educated) and ready to share fully in the Eucharist for the first time. She will not "get First Communion" but celebrate fully Jesus' death and resurrection as well as her own. And as a consequence, she will receive Holy Communion. Because of her prior communion with Jesus, she experiences Holy Communion as an extension and deeper expression of that intimacy.

part two

The Irish have a saying that if you were born into a wealthy family you were born with a silver spoon in your hand! The good news is that we were all born with that silver spoon, wealthy or not! Every child comes into this life already in communion in the sense he/she is in a loving relationship with God. How could it be otherwise? The seed of communion is present but now must be nourished. This is primarily the responsibility of the second communion the child enters at birth, the family. So the child is now experiencing two communions! At baptism, parents are reminded that they are the first and best educators of their children in this respect. The family is the little and domestic church, the first and basic cell of society. Judging by the mass exodus of children after what we wrongly call, "First Communion," we have to conclude that few Catholic families are in and celebrating communion. This is the crisis. The seed of the first communion, a loving relationship with God, is not watered and fertilized and so it dies.

Jesus told the parable of the sower and it highlights this neglect. Seed fell at the edge of the path, some on rocks and in thorns, and all died, of course. He says that the seed in the thorns is the person who is caught up in the worries of this world and the lure of riches. It is fair to say that this describes the life of many Catholic families today. They are so busy that there is little time for family communion. Parents and children are on the run and are exhausted at the end of the day. Not even time to say a quick grace before and after meals. Never mind the family Rosary! Then what should be rest and Sabbath day, Sunday, is instead "catch up" day. So much for this second experience of communion for Johnny and Mary.

Recently I listened to a doctor describe the awful damage the television is doing to children. The major one is attention deficit. Then she gave the following alarming statistics: The average child spends four hours a day before the television; fifty-percent of children have one in their bedroom; twenty-five percent of two-year olds also have a television in their bedroom. Imagine children being brainwashed for twenty-eight hours a week! Then, only a few days later on the radio, I listened to a mother being interviewed about a raccoon that got into the house. It was the last bit that really caught my attention. She was so grateful that it didn't make its way into the basement because that's where her two-year old goes alone to watch television!

Add the Internet to all this and is it any wonder that we have a generation who cannot communicate? Germany is the first country to have opened a rehabilitation centre for teenage Internet addicts. They spend up to twelve hours a day on it. Some are obese from eating just junk food and some are underweight from not eating at all!

In my last parish I regularly watched a father drop off his little child before eight in the morning at my neighbour's across the street. The child was then picked up around five in the afternoon by its mom. I once spent a few days close to a day-care centre in a large city. Children were dropped off as early as seven-thirty and collected at five-thirty. Add to this the time spent in busy traffic and the children must have gone from bed to bed. I mention this not by way of criticism of parents but simply to point out how little time is left to nourish communion. Often busy couples say to me that they are like ships passing in the night.

We have a major problem on our hands when it comes to preparing children for what should be their third experience of communion. Because the first was not nourished by the second, the communion in the family, they are incapable of celebrating, for the first time, the death and resurrection of Jesus and receive Holy Communion.

What's the solution? As part of the *New Evangelization*, cease linking this third experience to an age or grade. This would also get away from the fashion parade that goes with group "First Communions" day! It does not follow that because Johnny and Mary are seven years of age they are ready to celebrate the Eucharist fully for the first time. We need to retrace our steps back to the home and focus primarily on the parents. What's the alternative?

WHAT IS YOUR RELIGION?

part one

Since these reflections are written for Catholics, it may seem ludicrous then to ask a Catholic: "What is your religion?" I hope to show that it is not as crazy as it seems! The call to the *New Evangelization* challenges Catholics to stop, look and listen. And the call is much more than mere window-dressing, a kind of band-aid or papering over the cracks. It is nothing less than a radical conversion.

In my part of the world, the bears hibernate for six months of the year. They sleep so soundly that their cubs are born and their moms are not aware of it! Like the bears, have Catholics gone underground into hibernation? Well it's springtime and time to wake up! The bears wake up in the spring basically because they are hungry. Catholics will wake up when they experience a hunger for more than religion. Bridie shouted up to Paddy that it was seven o'clock and time to get up. There was no movement twenty minutes later so she yelled again. Finally, at seven-thirty she ran up the stairs right into the bedroom roaring at him to get up or he would be late for work. But Paddy was dead in the bed. "It serves you right," said Bridie. "If you answered the first time I called you, you would still be alive." Could it be that religion has put us to sleep and it is from this that we need to wake up?

The Scottish philosopher John MacMurray makes a powerful distinction between false and true religion. Illusory religion runs like this: "Fear not; trust in God and He will see that none of the things you fear will happen to you." That of true religion is the opposite: "Fear not; the things that you are afraid of are quite likely to happen to you, but they are nothing to be afraid of." In light of this and as a Catholic, how would you answer the question, "What is your religion?"

Back in my seminary days, we had a philosophy professor who should have been at Oxford or Harvard! His patient endurance with us must surely have guaranteed him direct passage to heaven! Karl Kruger was a German refugee and a brilliant academic. His pastime was spent translating Karl Rahner's "Theological Investigations" into English! I am sure he found this much more exciting than a seminary classroom! What I remember about his classes I could write on the back of a postage stamp! I judged him to be a stubborn old German because he never gave a direct answer to our questions. Wasn't Jesus like that too? Frustrating! Karl responded to every question with another question, "What do you mean?" Now I realize he was a very wise teacher. He forced us to think for ourselves and keep asking questions.

A hibernating Catholic is one who has no questions. An awake Catholic is one who asks questions. And a wide awake Catholic is one who has more questions than answers! The first step then, in this new conversion process that we are called to, is to begin asking questions. The exciting point about this is that it becomes addictive! It's like gambling. You win a little, you gamble more, and then you are hooked. Asking questions is like that. The question is like a key. It unlocks unknown depths and opens up new horizons. Because of the new life, new insights, new wisdom and new potential you experience, you feel driven to experience what Ignatius of Loyola calls the "more." It's like being on a roller coaster! You just cannot and you don't want to get off because you have found the treasure of which Jesus speaks. It's impossible to hibernate when you ask questions!

Children are fully awake! Look how inquisitive they are. They never stop asking questions. Simple, stupid and sometimes so profound that we are shocked and stumped! The child in us never dies.

It's just that it has gone into hibernation, so wake up your inner child. "Unless you become like little children you will never enter the kingdom of heaven," Jesus warns us. The best are the "what?" questions. They are objective and will always evoke more. Steer clear of the question we most ask, the "why?" This is subjective and will turn us in on ourselves.

part two

Most Catholics today, like me, were educated in and grew up on what I call a "creedal" religion. I remember staying up late at night learning by heart the penny catechism. My mother would pound me with repetitive questions like, "What is a sacrament and how many are there? What is grace? Name the ten commandments, the six commandments of the Church, the seven spiritual and corporal works of mercy." By age eight I was a budding theologian and ready for ordination!

I am not knocking this. Unlike most Catholic children today, I had a fair bit of knowledge as a country youngster! While this was very good it was inadequate to sustain me later in life right into priesthood. It is this that I want to pursue in these reflections: How a "creedal" religion is not only insufficient but is actually an obstacle to Catholic Christian growth. It is fair to say that this is where the majority of Catholics are at today—stuck in a "creedal" religion that sends them into hibernation! Someone said that Catholics today are not just lapsed but have collapsed!

Just think for a moment how we rattle off the Creed at the Sunday Eucharist as if there was a fire in the building! And then how casual and flippant we are with the renewal of our baptismal promises at Easter: "Do you reject Satan, and all his works and empty promises?" Instead of raising the roof, we get a barely audible murmur, "I do!" This is religion in the bad sense of the word from which we need to be rescued.

How can "creedal" religion be an obstacle to our spiritual growth? To begin with, it leads us to believe that knowledge is everything. This fools us into thinking that religion is mainly about facts to be accepted and believed. This leads to settling for religion as blind faith. Finally, it draws us into an unhealthy relationship with and dependence on the institutional Church in the form of the hierarchy. This stifles independent thinking and slows us from taking initiatives. We can make lofty statements of belief but if they are not integrated into our everyday life, they are empty. This is a kind of spiritual divorce that is all too evident in our Catholic people. Sad to say, but what they profess on Sunday has little or nothing to do with how they live on Monday!

This "creedal" religion is like spouses who have no real relationship with each other but are staunch believers in matrimony. You would never invite them to give a presentation on matrimony and certainly not to run the preparation classes! But it does happen! The sacrament of matrimony is first of all a lived relationship and only couples who are working on this have the authority to share. True and authentic religion is exactly the same: it is first and foremost a relationship. The knowledge I had as an eight-year old should have blossomed into a personal relationship with Jesus. I am sad to say that it took more than thirty years! The major obstacle to this was "creedal" religion. Seminary life and post-ordination formation were mainly about acquiring more knowledge. This was good in itself but not good enough to connect me to Jesus.

For years I was faithful to my annual preached retreat. More knowledge! No wonder I was bored and distracted for the whole retreat! It was not until I made guided or directed retreats that I finally met up with Jesus on the road to Emmaus! Like the two disciples, I invited him into my life. From then on I can say with them, "Did not our hearts burn within us as he talked to us on the road and explained the scriptures to us?"

A guided retreat lasts at least six, but preferably eight days and always begins with how you are experiencing Jesus, or 'where you are at' as they say! True religion is like that: it's primarily about how we are experiencing our relationship with Jesus. A non-Christian, Simone Weil, says that religion should begin with a personal encounter with Jesus and not doctrine and creeds. She holds that religion ought not to be a matter of what we make ourselves believe but of what we know. ("Know" in the biblical sense of a relationship and intimacy). She insists that the test of religious truth is always a practical one: "Truth is bread," she says, "you know it by its taste!"[6]

---

6   **CBC Ideas:** *Enlightened by Love: The Thought of Simone Weil:* 21

part three

❧✺❧

Instead of calling on Catholic theologians to support my point in these reflections, I look to a non-Christian and a Protestant! God transcends individuals and institutions! Peter was showing a group of Protestants around heaven. A continuous twenty-foot wall caught their attention so they asked Peter about it. "Oh, the Catholics are behind there. They think they are the only ones in heaven," explained Peter! Catholics are called to transcend, to go beyond a merely "creedal" religion.

Simone Weil was born in 1909 in France to middle-class Jews. She was never baptized and is considered a mystic. Though she was an academic—she taught philosophy—her heart was with the poor, the farmers, the factory workers and the soldiers of World War One. At age eight, to identify with the soldiers, she stopped using sugar in her tea and wearing socks. She was frail and suffered daily from migraine headaches. Yet she worked on the farms and in the factories. At age 34 she died in exile in England from exhaustion and self-imposed malnutrition. What she has to teach us about religion is frighteningly challenging!

She whips the rug out from under the feet of Catholics who consider themselves safe with just a "creedal" (belief only) religion. Simone maintains that the unbelief of atheists is closer to a true love of God and a true sense of his nature, than the kind of easy faith which, "Never having *experienced* God, hangs a label bearing his name on some childish fantasy or projection of the ego."[7] There's the difference between false and true religion: knowledge about God versus *experiencing* God. Elsewhere she claims that "It is easier for a non-Christian to become a Christian, than for a Christian [Catholic!] to become one [a Christian]."[8]

The point is that we Catholics can become very smug and complacent. We settle down, we feel we have arrived. We don't need to be converted! Faith and belief lull us into a false notion of security. We want the consolations of God rather than the God of consolations. In this sense, "In so far as religion is a source of consolation, it is a hindrance to true faith."[9] Weil does not let us off the hook! The consolation syndrome fools us into believing that religion means comfort and peace of mind. She brings us the terrible reminder that Jesus promised not peace but the sword. Her writing as a whole is marked by extreme statement, paradox, contradiction, and the importance of myth.

Myth for her is the opposite of intelligence. She insists that we know God only in mystery. Not through intelligence, creeds or religion. Take the iceberg as an example. Only ten-percent is above the water while ninety is below. The ten-percent represents our intelligence, our ego. The ninety-percent below represents mystery, the unknown and the unconscious. Yet, paradoxically, it is here that we meet God. Like all the great mystics, she teaches that it is in unknowing that we know! Myth, mysticism, and mystery are the same for her. We live mystery through silence, passivity, and paying attention. This is because God is always present to us trying to get our attention, always communicating with us. God alone takes the initiative. We respond. Religion turns this the other way around.

It is "looking," says Simone, which saves us. "It should also be

---

7   **Simone Weil:** *Waiting for God: IX*

8   Ibid.,

9   **Simone Weil:** *Gravity and Grace: 168*

publicly and officially recognized that religion is nothing else but a looking."[10] Looking, the mere turning of the head toward God, is equated by Simone Weil with desire and that passive effort of "waiting for God." Every day after work a simple labourer would drop into the local Church. The priest was curious to know what he "did" during that half hour so he asked him. "I just look at Him and He looks at me," was his humble reply. He was a true contemplative.

In writing about belief as a relationship, Kathleen Norris says, "....faith does not conform to ideology but to experience....for the Christian, this means the person of Jesus Christ....it is this faith in Christ as a living person that is most inexplicable outside of the experience of faith, and also most fragile, in that the Church as an institution has often seemed bent on preserving a dead idol." Faith outside the context of a relationship with Jesus is hollow, and faith as a relationship does not conform to religion!

---

10 Simone Weil: Waiting for God XXXI

part four

"Look! You can *experience* what you believe—your religion can live!"[11] What powerful words of hope and encouragement from a Swiss Protestant and pioneer in psychology, Carl Gustav Jung, (1875-1961)! Please copy that precious sentence in bold and stick it on your bathroom mirror where you will see it many times in the day. Later on in these reflections I will develop this revolutionary idea that your faith and religion can be *experienced* as opposed to just known! Imagine a Protestant saying clearly and simply the goal of the *New Evangelization!* He grew up in a religious environment. His father was a pastor as were several relatives. Through his psychology he challenged people to go beyond their traditional rational "blind-faith" religion which is the one-tenth of the iceberg. To truly experience God we need to go below to the nine-tenths, the mystical, mystery and the very depth of our being.

Above his door, Jung had the following motto in Latin: "Vocatus atque non vocatus Deus erit!" Translated, 'Summoned or not, God will be there.' The numinous, the divine, the higher power transcends all and is in all. God is already at the very core of our being; the only place where we find life in abundance. It is there religion becomes alive, fulfilling, experiential and exciting.

---

11 **Kenneth L. Becker:** *Unlikely Companions: 311*

"Make friends with your shadow" is a well quoted saying of his. Our shadow is that part of us, the nine-tenths below the water, we don't want to know! It's the dark side of us that we keep the lid on but now and then explodes. Sadly, and to our own detriment, we forget that Jesus dared to embrace it for all of us. We actually find Jesus right there! That part of us is also saved and redeemed so it's alright to take the plunge, painful though it is initially. But it is more painful repressing it! So make friends with it! "Who looks outside, dreams. Who looks inside, awakens" claims Jung.

Jesus loves this part of us as much as our light side. Most Catholics do not know this, and those who do, need to experience it. Jung encourages us to transcend knowledge and experience the *experience!* It is what Ignatius of Loyola calls "The *experience* that I am a loved sinner." Like Jung, he taught that without this there is no conversion and we remain stuck in a "creedal" religion which keeps us on the outside, dreaming!

To live on the outside only is to remain a child. Jung says of this childishness "....the faithful try to *remain* children instead of becoming *as* children. They cling to the world of childhood....Faith.... tries to retain a primitive mental condition on merely sentimental grounds....one must give up remaining a child in order to become a child....and they do not gain their life because they have not lost it."[12] We must plunge below the surface of the iceberg and it is there we will encounter the child Jesus, born in a cold and drafty stable.

To become *as* a child is to have the Incarnation happen in us. Jesus must be born in us. This is the repentance, conversion and rebirth Jesus preached. While it is symbolized in baptism it has to be personalized, embraced and actualized. I have to take ownership of and responsibility for my baptism because it is not magic. This is the difference between childishness and childlikeness. The former is the one-tenth of the iceberg. The latter is the nine-tenths! To be childlike is to be Jesus-like. His life in us is dynamic, unpredictable, uncontrollable, and creative as witnessed in the mystics.

---

12 Ibid., 182

"Only the mystics bring creativity into religion....the creative mystic was ever a cross for the church, but it is to him [her] that we owe what is best in humanity,"[13] boasts Jung. They wake us up and shock us just like Jesus did! It is the mystics who teach us the difference between religion and spirituality: Religion teaches us the answers while spirituality questions the answers! Religion teaches us to live with certainty while spirituality teaches us to live with a healthy doubt—like Thomas in the Gospel.

We can only live this paradox with a personal encounter with Jesus. Remember, he takes the initiative. He can encounter us only in empty space. Doubt creates this void and vacuum in us. Then we question the illusion of certainty. "What is my religion?" is a must question!

---

13 Ibid., 175

"LET MY PEOPLE GO"

part one

❦

This is the warning that God addressed to Pharaoh through Moses. After his personal encounter with God in the burning bush, Moses was sent by God to lead the enslaved Hebrew people from Egypt to freedom. Catholic leaders are called to a similar encounter and to be *newly*-evangelized.

I was present at the ordination of a bishop when the homilist, looked the future bishop in the eye and warned him, "Remember, the people of your diocese are not yours. They are God's people first." Yes, he must lead them but not possess them. My observation tells me that theologians, the hierarchy, and the Roman Curia, are holding God's people captive. For the most part, this is unconscious. I will focus only on one reason for this possessive style of leadership.

Strange though it may seem, but God is the problem! Not God in God's self but how they interpret God. I was going to say "understand" God but that would compound the problem even more for we cannot understand God! But all too often leadership leads us to believe that we can. The fundamental flaw is that they present God as an object. It is this that leads to possession of people. An object is something outside us that we can know, define, control and relate to. Today we are discovering all sorts of objects in space that we can now relate to. But God is not an object in this sense. God is not someone out there that we can define, know and relate to like we can with a friend in another part of the world. God is unknowable in God's self. Saint Augustine, the great intellectual though he was, used to say, "If you understand, it is not God!"

The Old Testament people knew this so they described their relationship with God through the medium of myth, which was the only way they could. Myth is the opposite of our logic, reasoning, speculating, intellectualizing and discursive thinking. It's like the difference between the Western thinking of democracy that we are trying to impose on Iraq and Afghanistan, and their understanding of it. We presume they think like us but they do not. The cultures of the Old Testament were similar. They dealt with mystery and the unknowable through symbolism and intuition. Unlike us, they did not attempt to solve the problem of God but tell us what our attitude should be in the presence of mystery and the unknowable. Myth *describes* God. Leadership tries to *define* God. To describe and define something is not the same.

When leadership intellectualizes myth they make God an object to be defined. They replace myth with their cognitive, intellectual and rational powers. Myth *described* God as male, powerful, almighty, a punisher with absolute authority. Leadership *defines* God with these same attributes. But God is beyond all definition. Unconsciously, or consciously, they project onto God and create God in their own image. Leadership then appropriates for itself these roles or attributes of power, might, maleness, punisher and authority. God becomes an object of study, known and defined only by an elite group.

The result for the masses is spiritual bondage. The "uneducated" are held captive in childish dependence, benevolent paternalism, obedience and even guilt. Because leadership, wrongly, believe they have all the answers, it is to them the people must turn. Leadership possesses them. They are stripped of their innate ability to *experience* the unknowable and unpredictable God.

Moses says to leadership today, "Let my people go." A few people like the mystics, happen to break free. But mysticism is the vocation of all God's people. Sadly, however, what should be the norm is the exception. Mystics are a thorn in the side of leadership because they challenge the latter to return to myth. Mystics, like myth, speak a language of paradox and contradiction, and have more questions than answers. This makes leadership feel very uncomfortable and insecure. Conversion involves dropping the apparent certainty of knowledge, taking up the uncertainty of myth and live mysticism. Myth, the mystical, and mysticism, are compatible. Myth and intellectualism are opposites.

Karl Rahner's prediction years ago is now a stark reality: "The time is fast approaching when one will either be a mystic or an unbeliever."[14] Mysticism was central to his theology because, as Fischer says, "He has himself originally had it."[15] Vorgrimler endorses this: "Rahner's theology has grown out of prayer, is accompanied by prayer, and leads into prayer."[16] The fourth-century desert monk, Evagrius Ponticus, defines a theologian like this: "A theologian is one who prays and one who prays is a theologian." My mother was a theologian!

---

14 **Karl Rahner:** *Spiritual Writings:* 24

15 **Philip Endean:** *Karl Rahner and Ignatian Spirituality:* 248

16 Ibid., 141

"LET MY PEOPLE GO"

part two

Saint John Leonardi was born in 1541 in the middle of the Reformation begun by Luther. John too became a reformer, for he witnessed great scandals and laxity among the priests, bishops and religious. He was courageous and took risks for which he paid a price. Here is part of his letter to Pope Paul V: "...reformation must be undertaken among high and low alike, among its leaders as well as its children; we should therefore direct our attention first towards those who have charge of the rest, so that reform begins among those from which it should be communicated to others. Every effort must be made to ensure that cardinals, patriarchs, archbishops, bishops and parish priests who have the immediate care of souls, are such that the direction of the Lord's flock can be safely entrusted to them."

The call of the whole Church to the *New Evangelization*, nearly five hundred years later, proves that there is nothing new under the sun! Naturally there was a strong reaction by the hierarchy to the Protestant Reformation. They became extremely defensive and protective to the point where Catholics were discouraged, even forbidden, from reading the Bible. This led to a childish and submissive laity who depended on the hierarchy as a baby depends on its mother.

An area where this continues today revolves around the *experience* of God as opposed to knowledge of God. The hierarchy is still reluctant to admit that every Catholic can experience God. They tend to view this as dangerous post-Reformation thinking. Worse still, because they cannot control experience, they view an individual's experience of God as a threat to their authority. By and large, they and theologians would argue that God's presence among us is beyond our experience. The conclusion then is that we can only *believe* it is true and we depend on them to teach us that it is true. This is a subtle but real form of bondage and captivity.

Most evenings I walk on the beach across the road from me. I think of the frustrated young Coho salmon who spent his first two years looking for the ocean! Then one day he met up with grandmother Coho who sat him down. She gave him a brief lesson in awareness and said, "Look around you!" The penny dropped! In becoming aware he realized he was in the ocean! Prior to that, he saw himself apart from the ocean. That's pretty much our image of God, a false one of course, which leaves us frustrated and unenlightened. We cannot be anything else but *in* God, not apart from God. Theologian and writer, Catherine M LaCugna says it well: "One finds God because one is already found by God." Like the young Coho salmon, we don't need to go looking for the ocean because we are already in it! We just need to wake up and become aware.

God is Immanuel, God with us. Each Christmas we celebrate that God, in Jesus, has become human, one of us, part of creation and is with us. While we celebrate it, do we actually believe it and live the consequences? Or are we like that young Coho frantically searching for God while God has already found us? Speaking of God Immanuel, God with us, Karl Rahner put it graphically in one of his prayers, that God "Has *become human experience.*" It follows then that each person can and must experience God *in*, not despite of, our everyday human experience. In no way is this in opposition to the teaching role of the Church. But it does mean that if our leaders and theologians are not doing the job of grandmother Coho, they are not just failing us, they are controlling.

The great Jesuit poet, Gerard Manley Hopkins, as only poets can, shares his experience of God as God among us. He writes: "The world is charged with the grandeur of God." To be *charged* is to be electrified and on fire. Maybe we need fewer theologians and more poets! An experience of God is the privilege of every person, and to speak about it is to speak with authority. In fact, to *know* God through experience is more authoritative than knowing about God through knowledge. The role of leadership is to lead their people to this and not just be teachers of an objective theology. While God's self-gift of presence is incomprehensible and cannot be explained, it can be *experienced.*

WHOSE TO BLAME?

In a very short time Ireland has experienced a rapid decline in vocations and church attendance. Secularism and moral relativism are now the order of the day in what was once the land of 'saints and scholars.' Gone are the days when Ireland was shipping out missionary nuns, brothers and priests all over the world.

Since Ireland entered the European Union the economy took off, giving the Irish a standard of living that could be previously had only abroad. Apart from Norway, it has the most thriving economy in Europe. This prosperity has allowed them to achieve many great things but the greatest by far is higher education. Now the kids from County Council houses can rub shoulders at high school and university with the farmers' children! All now can have a bull in the field and a son or daughter at university!

But what is experienced as a blessing for most is seen by others to be a curse and the cause of Ireland's 'loss of faith.' Ecclesiastical circles blames higher education and prosperity for the "secularization" of the country. The subtle implication here is that if the religious institution could keep the Irish poor and uneducated, Ireland would still be a Catholic country. But those days are gone—thank God. As in bygone days the people will no longer ask, "how high?" when the institution commands them to jump. The laity are now telling their leaders that for too long they have been Catholic on their terms. Now they say we will be Catholic on our terms and it's your turn to listen to us.

Religious leaders must undergo a massive conversion: from commanding to invitation, from driving to leading and from denial to transparency. This is the kind of radical conversion demanded by the *New Evangelization* which the institution needs to experience if it is to reclaim any credibility. However humiliating it is, leadership has to ask itself: "How much are we responsible for the alienation of our people? How much are we part of the problem?" One doesn't read a lot about this kind of frank and open honesty. It's much safer to blame the economy, and in doing so blame the laity, for the empty seminaries, convents and churches.

They say there is a silver lining behind the darkest cloud and in fact we find this in Archbishop Diarmuid Martin of Dublin. He takes a different line to those in leadership who see the standard of living enjoyed by the average person today as the root cause of the problems in the Irish church. He says:

> *"Others will say to me that it is precisely the style of prosperity created within the European Union that has brought a climate of materialism and rejection of Christian values. For me, taking huge sectors of the European population out of poverty and precariousness is an achievement about which the Christian must rejoice."*

Here's a case where one sees the glass half-full and the other half-empty. We should be grateful that at least one person in leadership is prepared to stick out his neck in support of the laity. And he goes a step further when he challenges leadership of the Irish church to do some self-scrutiny:

> *"If such prosperity has been accompanied by a change in belief patterns within the E.U., then this may be due to a lack of dynamism in the churches' own pastoral structures for evangelization in a cultural climate that is changing, just as much as a result of the economic prosperity fostered by the E.U."*

He's hit the nail right on the head! Irish leadership faces an enormous challenge to even say the word 'evangelization,' never mind to undergo it. Just like the lawyer in the Gospel of the good Samaritan could not bring himself to say 'Samaritan.' For fourteen-hundred years they have been the evangelizers so how can they admit that they now have to be evangelized! The New Evangelization is going to be a bitter pill to swallow for the Irish institution! Add to this a hostile anti-clericalism throughout the country and leadership might be tempted either to dig in their heels or throw up their hands in despair.

But while the Irish fight at the drop of a hat, they are also capable of forgiving and moving on with life. Time and time again throughout the centuries they made allowances for their leaders' short-comings. "Sure Father has bit of drink problem" they would say and love their alcoholic priest all the same. I have no doubt they can rise to the occasion again. They will accept leaderships' sinfulness, only if they admit it, but will despise any semblance of self-righteous arrogance. In this regard leaders could take hope from the advice the psychologist, C.G. Jung, has to give: "Power that is constantly asserted works against itself, and it is asserted when one is afraid of losing it. One should not be afraid of losing it. One gains more peace through losing power."

Maybe Murphy's blunt advice, after a few pints of Guinness and in the vernacular, might bring leadership to its senses: "For God's sake lads, would yis go and take a shaggin good gander at yerselves in the lookin-glass!"

DISTORTED THINKING RETARDS

Jane Doe asked me to be her spiritual director. Her written interview revealed some major distortions which severely retarded her desire for a personal relationship with Jesus. Most of us can relate to Jane in our distorted thinking. For example, we feel frustrated because life falls short of our expectations. We honestly believe that we are in control of the future. Expectations will nearly always lead to frustration and desolation because they are unreal. The most you can have about the future is hope. Another example of our distorted thinking is that we see one single negative event as a never-ending pattern of failure. So we say things like, "I am always a failure and I never do anything right." which, of course, is a lie. Sometimes you fail and don't get things right. But not always. Change your distorted thinking and you change your whole attitude towards yourself.

"I don't have the same kind of relationship with the Lord that I once had," wrote Jane. You are not meant to Jane! Distorted thinking keeps Jane a prisoner in the past. She wants to go back to slavery in Egypt instead of journeying to the Promised Land! Jane is the product of our Catholic education which by and large is heady and therefore static. Relationships are dynamic, alive, and meant to develop. Because of this they have a certain insecurity about them which can scare us.

"I want to make some serious strides in controlling my weaknesses." Notice the control freak Jane is! Just like you and me! She doesn't need Jesus as Saviour! She wants to do it all alone. To be in control means to have my act together which, of course, is an illusion. The most she can do is manage her weaknesses. We will have our act together and be free of our weaknesses about ten minutes after we are dead! She is uncomfortable with her weaknesses. Like Jesus and Paul she will have to learn to embrace them and trust that her very weakness is her strength.

"I am tired of taking so long to defeat my weaknesses and struggles; I want to be holy today." Well, Jane, you are not going to defeat them and you don't have to. Again, like Jesus, accept your humanness and let him help you manage them in a joyful and peaceful way. What do you mean that you want to be holy? Wake up! You *are* holy; part of a holy nation, a royal priesthood, a people consecrated to sing the praises of God. You are graced and saved, so rejoice! Quit navel-gazing and look at Jesus. And don't praise God because you believe in God but praise God because God believes in you!

"I feel like my life is out of control and I get anxious and overwhelmed about where I am." Of course you do. Who told you that you could ever control your life? You are addicted to control and now your addictive distortion has thrown you in the gutter. Now this is a good place to be because, instead of you raising yourself out of it, you have to turn to your Higher Power.

"I really don't know who I am." Do any of us really know who we are? Another illusion and distortion. In this respect we are victims of two major negative influences. The first is what society tells us about ourselves: We are valued by what we do, what people think about us, how much we earn and the likes. The second is our ego. Our ego is the level of life we are conscious of and out of which we live. But it is only one-tenth of who we are. We commit the unforgivable sin of believing we are our ego. So what claim do we have to knowing ourselves when we live a lie, and at such a shallow level? This is the root cause of all our distorted thinking. When we begin living the other nine-tenths then we might have some idea of who we are.

As Jane prays with scripture and keeps the focus on Jesus, he will lead her below the one-tenth into the "Kingdom within." Only he can reveal to her the unique and beautiful person she is. Once she *experiences,* not knows, that Jesus loves her *as she is,* Jane will become free. This will be for her a conversion experience, her *new-evangelization.* Jane can now live in peace and freedom with her dark side, free of distortions, precisely because she encounters Jesus deep below the surface of her ego.

PREFERENTIAL OPTION FOR THE POOR

This often-quoted challenge of John Paul II sounds like we have a choice and that it is indeed a noble one. The truth is that we have no choice in the matter—not if we claim to be orthodox disciples of Jesus. He was born poor, lived poor, began his mission to the poor, preferred to be with the poor, demanded poverty of his followers both in fact and in the beatitudes, and died poor. Nobody, whether pope or bishop, is excluded from being physically poor and consciously choosing the poor. We have no other option.

Thanks to the media, we witnessed the powerful effect the Pope's simple coffin had on the world. The point is that public image does matter, whether as a source of good or scandal. A picture is worth a thousand words! Heeding the demand of Jesus to be poor is of the essence of the *New Evangelization*. The picture the Vatican presents suggests that it has not taken seriously this command of Jesus. I am not suggesting, as many are, that it sell off its paintings and art but that it reflect more the poor man of Nazareth and his Gospel.

Statistics prove that Catholics don't do well when it comes to stewardship. Other denominations far outstrip us in generosity to the point of tithing. The reason? Ask any priest in parish ministry and he will tell you the same old story he gets from Catholics: "The Church has lots of money." Of course they mean Rome. The Vatican, as an independent State, is not a third-world country so they are convinced they are right. And since a picture is worth a thousand words, it is useless arguing with them. Images do matter!

Two receptionists worked at the front desk of the hospital where I collected my list of Catholic patients. Olga was her usual bubbly self and was excited as she related how she had just been explaining to Maria the blessings of tithing. Olga is a Baptist. Maria, a collapsed Catholic, looked bored and lost. It's Catholics like Maria, not the Pope, who force us into celibacy! Until she starts tithing we may forget about married clergy for we all would be on social welfare and a burden on the tax-payer!

Recently I discussed this with my congregation in the Anglican church I use on Sunday and presented concrete facts. The married Anglican priest's budget is eighty-thousand dollars with fewer parishioners than us. My budget is thirty-two thousand and my annual collection seven! So I will not be rushing to get married!

Read the signs of the times and you notice that something is at work in this whole question of Gospel poverty. It would seem that the institution either embraces it voluntarily or it will be imposed on us. Just look at how dioceses are being stripped of Real Estate to pay victims of abuse and some are bankrupt. Maybe Jesus did have a point: "You cannot serve God and mammon." Immediately after selecting the twelve apostles, he dispatched them to evangelize without even the bare essentials: "Provide yourselves with no gold or silver, not even with a few coppers for your purses, with no haversack for the journey or spare tunic or footwear or a staff."

King David would make a good patron saint for the Vatican—in the wrong sense of the word! His conscience began to disturb him as he relaxed in his lavish house of cedar while the ark of God dwelt in a tent. So he decided to modernize God and build him a similar house and then all would be hunky-dory! Strange that he didn't accommodate himself to God; sell his house and live in a tent!

Well God refuses to be domesticated and he soon put David straight: "Are you the man to build me a house to dwell in? I have never stayed in a house from the day I brought the Israelites out of Egypt until today, but have always led a wanderer's life in a tent. In all my journeyings did I say: 'Why have you not built me a house of cedar?'" God was quite contented to live in a tent while Jesus didn't have such luxury! Only a fresh encounter with Jesus will move the Vatican staff to have a preferential option for the poor and be poor.

PREACHED AND DIRECTED RETREATS

"I could never go back to preached retreats," state people who have experienced a directed retreat and I fully agree. My own experience of directed retreats tells me that women by far outnumber the men attending. This suggests several things. Men tend to be more head oriented. Since preached retreats are primarily knowledge oriented, here is where they feel comfortable. We men prefer to stay here rather than to touch on the affective, feeling level. Feelings threaten us so we shy away. Women, on the other hand, handle feelings much better. They prefer the affective approach and so opt for directed retreats. Women too have a greater capacity to deal with the pain that comes with conversion. I find it refreshing to see how many laypeople; women in particular, are making directed retreats.

A priest friend made his first directed retreat, a thirty-day Ignatian retreat. It was a powerful experience which really churned him up. Back in the parish he felt like a fish out of water, not in control as before and very scared. Feeling very insecure he called me up one day. He felt relieved and was surprised when I told him that he was in good space. All it meant was that he had a personal encounter with Jesus. And as Jesus tends to do, he disturbs the comfortable! He could easily have asked the same question as the poet Rilke, "Who is this Christ, who interferes in everything?" My friend had a conversion experience, and an integral part of that is to encounter one's shadow side. A good retreat is meant to shake us up and leave some scars! If it doesn't you should ask for your money back!

The churning up comes from a movement that is experienced only in a directed retreat. This is experienced primarily in our affective and emotional life. We experience God more at this level rather than in our heads and that is why there is no movement in preached retreats. The movement in a directed retreat is mainly that of consolation and desolation. This is the reality of daily life which means we are in one or the other at any given time. It's just that we are not used to noticing and paying attention to them. In a directed retreat however, we give them our full attention and they become the very basis of our prayer. The secret of discernment is that at any moment I can stop, notice and know where I am by how I am feeling. Since there is no middle ground, no fence-sitting, it has to be either desolation or consolation. What to do in this will be material for another reflection on "Discernment of Spirits."

Ignatius of Loyola, the founder of the Jesuits as well as the Spiritual Exercises, tells the director to pay particular attention to this movement. If the directee is not experiencing, in the sense of not being in touch with desolation and consolation, then the director must facilitate this. Most directors will agree that this is the greatest challenge in guiding directees! If they continue to resist they might as well go home for it will be a wasted retreat. The other warning Ignatius gives the director is that he/she must know his/her place and keep it. The Spirit is the director of a directed retreat. Therefore, the director must stand back, and allow the Spirit to deal directly with the directee. None of this happens in a preached retreat. That's why a directed retreat is personal and custom made while a preached retreat is like buying a suit off the peg!

Since a preached retreat keeps us in our heads, I believe it is an obstacle to spiritual growth. It does not stir up conversion as called for by the *New Evangelization*. Here is where the good becomes the enemy of the best. Change occurs where we feel, not where we think.

In a directed retreat we are alone with Jesus, and the demons, in the desert. Total solitude is absolutely essential. We are stripped naked of all our props and become very vulnerable. We retain the props and invulnerability in a preached retreat. Over the days a personal relationship with Jesus develops primarily through contemplating Scripture. This evokes the movement of consolation and desolation. It takes time to settle down and prepare for this so an eight-day retreat is preferable while six is the minimum.

In the early days of missionary activity we were mainly providers. Then someone came up with the saying: "Give people a fish and you keep them dependent. Teach them to fish and you free them to feed themselves." The same principle applies to retreats. Preached keep people dependent. Directed leads them into the freedom of the children of God.

GIVE UP YOUR ADDICTIONS

This is another item to be addressed on the road to conversion! We sin by doing what is positively evil and by abusing what is good. Alcohol for example is good but can be abused. Food is good but we can eat too much. I heard recently that there are more obese people in the world than there are starving. Since we are all addicts to a greater or lesser degree, we are all called to be converted, every day!

Just the thought of converting turns us off because we have such a negative view of it. This is definitely true of older Catholics because of how we were raised at home, taught at school and the sermons we heard on a Sunday morning. We see our glass as half empty instead of half full. No wonder we feel helpless and discouraged. And of course we know the pain of the withdrawl symptoms and feel scared. Worst of all though we make the terrible mistake of believing we alone can convert and change ourselves. Well, ask any recovering alcoholic and he or she will put you right on this. First you need the help of your Higher Power. Second, it is worth it because you receive the gift of sobriety which brings peace, harmony and joy. Then you see your glass as half full!

Look at "giving up" our addictions in another positive light. Take the simple example of someone trying to lose weight. The more support they get the easier it becomes. Most likely they will join a group for this purpose. In this way they are giving *themselves* up or handing themselves over to others to help them. Conversion then is more about giving up, handing over *myself* than focusing on the particular sin or addiction.

We Catholics don't talk about giving up and handing over our lives to Jesus. That's for the Pentecostals and Evangelicals! Maybe it is time we not only talked about it but did it! How else can we have a personal encounter with him? Now wouldn't that be some conversion! He is not only our Higher Power. More important, he is our Saviour. But then again, we see salvation in a negative light too, as being saved primarily *from*. In this case it is being saved from sin. There is nothing much personal about this. Rather, Jesus saves us *into* a personal relationship with him. So surrender, give up, and hand over yourself and your addictions to him!

Our addictions are deeply grafted on a three-pronged taproot bearing the titles Riches, Honour, and Pride. We can trace them all back to these three capital sins of addiction. Riches, in themselves, are good. It is the abuse of Riches that becomes an addiction. Is not the love of money the root of all evil? We act out this abuse in many ways. For example, time is money, and with it we can buy anyone's time. Money fosters privilege and the privileged will get money by fair or foul means. Money also means power, and the rich are getting more powerful. It is this that leads them to be dictators and authoritarians.

The rich automatically believe that they have a right to be noticed and honoured, simply because of what they have. They are not only addicted to but possessed by their riches. What is meant to be a means to an end has now become an end in itself. During the Athens Olympics I heard a good antidote to this addiction to fame and honour. The commentator remarked how the athletes were under great psychological stress because of the pressure of having to be the best. His advice was, "You don't have to be the best. You simply do your best."

Riches and honour bolster your pride to the point that you demand: "Look at ME!" Because you feel totally in control of everything you believe it is your right to control others. You are totally blinded to the truth that all is gift and that you are not the source of who you are and what you have. The evil one has tricked you and now you are trapped. From the unholy trinity of Riches, Honour, and Pride flow all the other vices. Conversion begins with counteracting each one with the values and attitude of Jesus: Simplicity and detachment work against riches. Desire for non-recognition works against honour. And cultivate humility in opposition to pride.

A CONFESSIONAL AWAKENING

Being the only priest on the island I manage to get to Confession only a couple of times in the year. The ferry takes six and half hours one way to the mainland, on a good day! It can be several days in the winter as I know from experience having spent twenty-three hours once in the stormy Pacific! So my visits to the noisy and busy mainland are few.

Recently I was in Vancouver working on a Retrouvaille formation weekend. This was for couples who had made a regular weekend and now want to be involved in helping hurting couples heal. It was an opportunity to get some needed items so I stayed over for a few days. On Monday afternoon I went early to the five o'clock Mass at the Cathedral. What a surprise to see a line for Confession on a weekday! I joined them.

Even on a remote island I find a lot to gossip about! This reminds me of the priest, rabbi and minister who were good friends. One day they decided to be totally open with each other. "I steal from the collection," confessed the minister. "And I cheat on my wife," confessed the rabbi." "I am a compulsive gossiper," admitted the priest, "and I can't wait to get out of here!"

When I confessed my sins of gossiping, I was taken aback by the confessor's question, even felt some resentment. "What's at the root of your gossiping, where's it coming from?" he inquired. I was put on the spot. It was the kind of question that called me to walk my talk. On the formation weekend I had been challenging the couples to search for the source of their marital struggles. That source is our family of origin. Inevitably we will find a connection between our present negative behaviour and family of origin. After all, we are formed for life by the age five.

The negative experiences I have from my family will always show up later in life, particularly in relationships. So if I was not loved and affirmed I will find it difficult to love and be loved as well as to affirm others. If I grew up in a home where feelings were taboo I am in deep water. I am scared of my feelings, avoid them, deny and repress them and can't be affectionate. This plays havoc in relationships, particularly matrimony but also with me and my parishioners. The bottom line here is that my present behaviour is heavily influenced by my past experiences as a child. I am always pleasantly amazed to see how couples grow on a Retrouvaille weekend when they get hold of this and look at their family of origin, painful though it is.

Since all families are dysfunctional to some degree, I too have negative experiences. This is where my gossip is rooted. In asking me to reflect, the priest directed my focus to within. In reflecting and pondering on my family of origin, I would begin making connections like the couples. He asked the right question and I have the answer. My gossip is both projection and compensation for my negative experiences.

When I gossip I drag people down. It's a mean way of getting attention at the expense of others' reputations. I focus on their negative side because that's how I see myself. In pulling them down I build up my own ego. My gossip can also be related to my floating anger towards my parents and teachers.

My reflection was an awakening to new insight which put my gossiping in context. I now experience a new-found freedom. The question challenged me to bring to my consciousness what I had been unconsciously denying and repressing. This kind of surfacing the root cause brings healing. It gives me a kind of power over gossiping and a confidence to manage it. In his Rules for the Discernment of Spirits, St. Ignatius reminds us that keeping sins a secret is dangerous and plays into the hands of the evil one: "But when the person reveals them to his or her good confessor or some other spiritual person who understands the enemy's deceit and malice, he is grievously disappointed."

This awakening experience reaffirms for me the value and importance of Confession. It also taught me that it is more important to ask the right question than to presume I have the correct answers. Giving advice is less important than helping people reflect.

SIN BRAVELY!

This is the advice of the Augustinian monk and reformer, Martin Luther! But he is not encouraging us to sin. However, he does demand honesty with our sins. Don't play the denial game. I have spent a lot of time in group dynamics. Group facilitators, counsellors and psychotherapists abhor, with a passion, liars. There is no place in the group for dishonesty, for people who will not spit out the truth. Sin itself is not the problem. It's our rationalizing, covering up and blatant dishonesty in not admitting it that is totally unacceptable. We can slip into a self-deceptive pattern where we truly believe we don't sin. "But I don't do anything wrong!" We no longer realize that we are actually sick, spiritually and emotionally.

God, too, has no time for lies. This is what John warns a church community in Laodicea, in the book of Revelation, as he calls them to conversion. God admonishes them, "I know all about you; how you are neither cold nor hot. I wish you were one or the other, but since you are neither, but only lukewarm, I will spit you out of my mouth." God can't stomach dishonesty and denial. Elsewhere John is brutally blunt with us. He says that we are liars if we say we don't sin. We must call a spade a spade and quit lying.

"You are as sick as your sickest secret." This is a phrase used by groups like Alcoholic Anonymous. They challenge people to be up front and speak the truth. If not, there is no place for them in the group. "I'm Jo Blo and I am an alcoholic," is how one introduces oneself to an AA group. That frankness and honesty is the first step to recovery. The sick secret that has been tightly kept for years is finally out in the open. Healing begins when the lying stops.

There is a movie called *Sex, Lies and Videotape*. It's about a dysfunctional young man. Maybe himself, the maker who was twenty-six when he made the movie. His addiction to sex makes him severely neurotic, from which he desperately wants to be liberated. So he vows that he will never again lie, no matter what other addictions he may be enslaved to. Then he invites others like him to join him in his endeavour to be free.

Next he sets up a video camera around which he gathers his friends. He encourages them, like him, to be as truthful as they can and tell the camera about their sexual aberrations. The result? All who were honest about their perversions experienced healing and liberation. They felt peaceful and were gentler with themselves and others. On the other hand, those who rationalized could not speak the truth but lied, became even more enslaved to their addictions. Unlike the others, they could not spit out their sickest secret and so became more ill.

Isn't this what we do in the sacrament of Penance? Yet few Catholics go to Confession today. Whatever happened to sin! Would that we didn't sin any more! The scriptures tell us that the good person sins seven times a day! Original sin is alive and well! Self-deception, rationalization and dishonesty seem to account for our absence from Confession. Along with honesty and truthfulness, what else might help us to celebrate the Sacrament of Penance?

One, experience it as a celebration of being loved by God as a sinner. This is unconditional love. Confession is less about asking for forgiveness and more about receiving it and celebrating it. This view is crucial. We tend to focus only on the sin and grovel. Remember, we are forgiven long before we go to confession. Once we acknowledge our sin and repent, we are immediately forgiven. This is how God's unconditional love works. Then why go to Confession? To celebrate what has already happened. Go to spit out the sin so that it doesn't cling to us and become our sickest secret. We go to Confession primarily to experience healing.

Two, we priests must facilitate this celebration and healing process. People should leave absolutely convinced that they are loved sinners. Exposing the secret is a start. They need help to see where it comes from, how it is enslaving them and robbing them of inner peace. Asking the right question will often be enough. But here is where we need converting because we were taught from day one in the seminary that we have all the answers! More lies!

CROSS AND CRIB

Today is Christmas-Eve and I feel sad. Not depressed. It's just a heaviness and a feeling of loss that mingles death with life, and end with beginning. This may sound terribly morbid but deep down I feel peaceful and grounded in inner harmony. How can you be sad and joyful at the same time, particularly at Christmas?

A few days ago I heard from a religious Brother and long-time friend. I spent six years in his nursing Order before studying for the priesthood. He brought me up-to-date on who died and now there are only a few left and all well on in years. With no vocations and the closure of houses, it is the end of an era. I have fond memories of those committed, generous, happy and dedicated Brothers going back forty-six years. They, more than the seminary, shaped and formed me into the person I am today. Not by their teaching but their example: love in action.

With the compassion of Jesus they cared for the mentally challenged and nursed the physically ill in their hospitals. Brother Bernard was the last to die in October and had just celebrated seventy years of vowed heroic service. I shed a tear because he was the very first Brother I met when I inquired about entering the Order of Saint John of God. What a welcome home it must have been for them to hear Jesus say, "When I was sick you cared for me. When I was hungry you fed me....."

The truth is that their death experiences fit in very well with the birth of Jesus our Saviour. Notice the title of this reflection. The order is deliberate and theologically correct as well. You see, the disciples did not begin their preaching with the birth of Jesus. They started with the end of his life preaching and teaching that Jesus died, rose and ascended. This does not make sense to us Westerners. It means that we must read the bible as it was written and not impose our logical mindset.

For years there was no mention of the birth of Jesus. Then only two Gospel writers, Matthew and Luke, wrote about his birth. But they didn't start there. Like the rest, they began with his death, resurrection and ascension and worked their way back to his birth. The point is that the birth of Jesus was of secondary importance in their proclamation. Sounds blasphemous! Maybe to us but not to them. Easter was, and still is, the most important proclamation and celebration. But sadly, this is not so for most Catholics. The crib outstrips the cross and this does not pay any compliment to Jesus! We must correct the imbalance.

Seen in this context, my sadness is not out of place on Christmas-Eve! Neither should yours be. We have this crazy notion that everyone should be upbeat at Christmas. The truth is that for many it is the most painful time of year. It's easy to forget that Jesus comes as *Saviour*. His birth was just a start, a means to an end, if you like. But we tend to make it an end in itself. We don't want Jesus to grow up! Isn't this true of most parents, mothers in particular? Jesus is no threat to us as a baby. But does he ever challenge us as an adult!

The crib didn't appear until introduced by St. Francis of Assisi in 1223 as a form of devotion. Obviously it is not essential to the birth of Jesus. In fact, I think it is has become a distraction. It is keeping us childish instead of adult Catholics. It is blurring our overall vision of the life and mission of Jesus, particularly his death and resurrection. The controversial writer, Fr. Andrew Greely, warns us about taming Jesus: "When we have domesticated Jesus, we may have a very interesting person on our hands, even a superstar maybe. Alas, it is not the real Jesus."

The Christmas prayers and carols repeatedly remind us that Jesus comes as our *Saviour*. He didn't save us as a baby, but as a rejected adult at the end of a very turbulent life hanging on a cross. Do I experience Jesus as *my* Saviour? This will happen only if I start at the end of his life and work my way back to his birth. This is a conversion experience that puts things in perspective. Then my sadness, pain and loss are part and parcel of celebrating Christmas just as they were part of his birth. Born in a manger not his own and wrapped in a swaddling cloth foreshadowed his death: wrapped in a shroud and buried in a tomb not his own. Yes, Christmas can be a celebration of peace and joy, a peace, Jesus says, the world cannot give. His peace, unlike the worlds, is all inclusive in which peace and the cross are compatible. Cross and crib are one. That's why I believe the correct place for the crib is right beneath the crucifix!

TO KNOW WE DON'T KNOW

part one

❊

I would put my money on a wise person instead of an intellectual! Jesus chose wisdom against knowledge. Instead of going to high school and then university, scripture tells us that, "Then he went down with them to Nazareth....and Jesus increased in wisdom and in years and in divine and human favour" (Lk1:51-52). We have what we call in the Bible 'wisdom literature.' These are: Job, the Psalms, Proverbs, Ecclesiastes, Song of Songs, Wisdom of Solomon and Sirach (Ecclesiasticus). In these books, 'knowing' and 'wisdom' are practically synonymous. Incidentally, the bible is not one book but a library of books—73 in all. There are 47 in the Old Testament and 26 in the New Testament.

The conversion called for in the *New Evangelization* will come from wisdom, not knowledge. God knows there is no shortage of knowledge but there is a great dearth of saints! This means that we need to be clear about the difference between 'knowing' in the Bible and 'knowing' as defined in the dictionary. "To know," according to the latter, is to apprehend, comprehend, grasp and understand. This is the knowledge we engage in every day and are most familiar with. But now the time has come that we must learn a new language!

On the other hand, "to know" in scripture is not primarily an intellectual exercise. "To know" in the Hebrew language is experiential and relational. It is about intimacy, the kind of intimacy a husband and wife experience in sexual intercourse. It is a holistic intimacy of mind, heart, spirit, and body. Because we are a people brainwashed by the ways of the world, all this is foreign to Catholics. For example, we don't even distinguish between sex and sexuality. When I explain to people that, like every other human being on the planet, I am sexual, they laugh. They hear sexy, not sexual. Moreover, neither do Catholics distinguish between recreational sex and relational sex.

If conversion is to happen at every level of our lives, we desperately need to get a grip on this level of 'knowing.' Unlike our Protestant sisters and brothers, we Catholics are at a great disadvantage right from the start. We just are not familiar with the Bible. It's not all our fault. Our leadership; pope, bishops and priests not only discouraged us from reading the Bible, but actually penalized us. This was their reaction to the Reformation in the sixteenth century which made the Bible available to the people. It's not that 'knowing' as we understand and practice it, is wrong. It's just that it is totally inadequate. Of course the Bible expects us to use our heads in the everyday sense of 'knowing' but the other 'knowing' is superior, more fundamental and essential. The truth is that we cannot know God at all in the sense of understanding and comprehending God. Unfortunately this kind of knowledge prevails today. Many theologians talk and write as if they know God in this sense. Nothing could be further from the truth. God is 'known' only in relationship which is a kind of pre-knowledge. I am waiting for a theologian to write about his or her *not* knowing God!

Let's now look at the difference between biblical 'knowing' and secular 'knowing.' Mary's response to the angel Gabriel was, "I am a virgin." Literally, this means, "I do not *know* man." The best concrete experience of how God loves us is the relationship between a wife and husband. "I will betroth you to myself with faithfulness, and you will come to *know* Yahweh," speaks God to his people (Hosea 3:22). Notice the close connection between marriage and knowing. To 'know' God is to have a close and intimate relationship with God. So when God complains throughout the Bible about his people not 'knowing' him, he is talking about the denial of a relationship. By the way, adultery in scripture is not primarily sexual. When God calls the people adulterers, he berates them for having walked out of a relationship. When they worship idols they commit adultery and live like their pagan neighbours.

"You 'knew' me through and through....when I was being formed in secret, knitted together in the limbo of the womb," says Psalm 139. When God calls Jeremiah, he reminds him, "Before I formed you in the womb I 'knew' you." To be 'known' by God is to be possessed by God who is known as creator in the context of a relationship.

Similarly, when God "makes God's-self known" to his wife, his people, it is through the medium of a covenant, a loving, unconditional relationship. Likewise, we "know God" in our response to this love relationship with every fibre of our being, not just our heads. It is always a heart response. A husband and wife can have a lot of knowledge about marriage but not have a close relationship. Most Catholics have some knowledge *about* God but do not *'know'* God. Conversion calls us to be wise and admit that we do not know God!

part two

They say that practice makes perfect! Because it is absolutely crucial to our conversion, we will keep looking at 'knowing' in the biblical sense. I grew up in rural Ireland and worked in South America where 'who you know' was all that mattered! Obviously this was far more than an intellectual acquaintance. The more intimate the relationship the more certainty that you could get away with murder! It got you a good job and promotion. A little bribery and the police, judges and customs officers turned a blind eye! I always carried a dollar with my driver's license in Guyana! When stopped by a policeman you got out and met him at the back of the car with your dollar bill! It didn't matter a hoot if you had four bald tires and no lights! Things haven't changed even in our so-called 'developed' world where corruption continues on a massive scale. Just look at our politicians!

I know of and about many of these men and women elected by the people, but who soon forget those of us who put them there. However, I do not know any of them intimately enough to be at the receiving end of their favours! On the other hand, I 'know' and am 'known' by my spiritual director to the point that I can be very open and honest. The bottom line in all this is that 'knowing' for Catholics is meant to be primarily about relationship. You will not find God with the help of a dictionary but you will in an intimate relationship.

They also say that it is hard to teach an old dog new tricks! Because we Catholics are stuck in a mindset where the only 'knowing' we are familiar with is the dictionary knowing, it will require a major effort to break free. But there is a greater obstacle to negotiate. Remember when Church leadership taught and believed we were the centre of the universe! And God help you if you didn't subscribe! The Inquisition took care of you! Then came along the great astronomer, Galileo, who proved that the institution was out of its mind and that we are not at the centre! The sun does not revolve around us. We orbit around the sun. Because he knocked us off our pedestal, he was condemned and sentenced to life imprisonment by the Inquisition in 1633!

But we Catholics are slow to learn and we still believe that we are at the centre of life. Just look at our self-preoccupation, our navel-gazing, our narcissism and our illusion that we are in control! On any given day, who do we think and talk about the most? Just listen in on a casual conversation which is really a monologue and competition for attention! I'm telling you all about me. No listening of course! We just have to be the focus and at the centre! This is our major barrier to 'knowing' God. Because we are convinced that we are at the centre, we believe we must take the initiative here as in every other aspect of life. So God is out there and we take the lead in getting in touch. We do this primarily through prayer and study. The latter is more subtle. We fool ourselves into believing that if we have a degree in theology then we not only know a lot about God, but we actually know God! Before God we all stand as morons and illiterates!

When we behave like this, we put the cart before the horse! It's the tail wagging the dog! Our only stance before God is always one of receiver. This cannot be stressed enough. We do not, I repeat, do not take the first step in a relationship with God. Only God takes the initiative. We respond. Since the relationship then has already begun, we need to move from centre-stage and just welcome it! Can you imagine how much pressure this would take from us if we really believed and acted on it! Why search frantically for the ocean or the forest when you are already immersed in them? God does not revolve around us!

Another hurdle is our failure to appreciate the difference between the culture in which the Bible was written and ours. Because we didn't understand and appreciate cultural differences, we made terrible blunders in the mission fields and with the Aboriginal people. And the institution still has a colonial mind! The biblical writers were wise people who wrote for their own, not for us. The Israelite people 'knew' with their hearts. 'Mind,' 'intellect' and 'knowledge' as we understand them, were foreign to them. Their Hebrew language has no words which correspond exactly to our English words "mind" and "intellect."

We must study the scriptures from *their* perspective and not impose our cerebral colonialism. We first read or study the Bible in *their* culture and context. Then we apply it to ours and not vice versa. This is basic respect, good manners, common sense and—an awakening to admit that we don't know!

part three

※

It's amazing how little we actually know! And the bit we do know is not ours because we are all plagiarists! Strictly speaking, none of us has an original idea. As the saying has it, "There is nothing new under the sun." Our thoughts are an accumulation of ideas that we glean from other people. I guess we do toss them around a bit to make them look as if they are ours. But really it is still only mutton dressed as lamb! This whole question of knowing ourselves, or self-knowledge, is a major leap forward in our 'knowing' God in the sense of being in relationship with God. Self-knowledge is the most neglected while 'knowing' God is the least practiced!

Knowing ourselves is not primarily cognitive. It is not mainly an intellectual exercise. Rather, it is affective and we shy away from this. It is a sense-knowledge involving intuition, reflection, insight and an awareness of our creatureliness: a child of God and a loved sinner. When we are truly aware of this, we experience our relationship with God as one of total dependence. Awareness and experience are far deeper than intellectual knowledge. They are feelings, our emotions which rise from the very core of our being.

It is not the academics we look to for guidance in this kind of self-knowledge but the great spiritual masters and mistresses. St. Benedict, in his Rule for his monks, lists some of the qualities needed like: listening, silence, obedience and humility. When practiced, these will help deepen our self-awareness and discover who we really are, not who we think we are.

The great Franciscan, St. Bonaventure stresses the emptying of the false self to discover the true self. This may sound complicated and difficult but it is not. It just calls us to face the truth and quit fooling ourselves! Now this is not easy! All too often we lie when we talk about self because we are not really talking about self at all! What we call self is in fact our ego. That's why we speak about people talking off the top of their heads! Our ego is what we are aware of and conscious of which is only one-tenth of the iceberg! No wonder we are so darn cold when we live at this shallow level! This is the level we are at for most of, if not all our lives.

Our real self, on the other hand, which we are not aware of, and do not want to be, is the nine-tenths of our sub-conscious. It's the nine-tenths of the iceberg submerged in the ocean. The work of self-knowledge and self-awareness is to be more in touch with that deeper level of who we are. To achieve this we need to grow down! Intellectuals grow up! Then our real self will surface to the same awareness as our ego. Of course this does not happen over night! It is much easier, and less painful, to grow up than to grow down! But then only down-to-earth people are in touch with self, with themselves, hence, the importance of humility, which means 'humus' or earth. Self-knowledge and self-awareness are rooted in the soil of our subconscious.

A couple of scientists argued with God that today they can create anything they like. So God replied, "Fire away!" Then one of them took his spade and began to dig. "Hold on," said God. "Create your own soil first."

St. Catherine of Siena was a laywoman, the twenty-fourth of twenty-five children, had no formal education, died at the age of thirty-three, and became a doctor of the Church and patroness of Italy. Speaking of the soul, she says, "She has become accustomed to dwell in the cell of self-knowledge in order to know better God's goodness toward her." Elsewhere she emphasizes that self-knowledge is born when we recognize that our very existence is an unmerited gift from God. Again, humility is stressed. We must humbly admit that everything is pure gift, and this includes the ability to 'know' God in relationship.

St. Teresa of Avila describes our journey towards 'knowing' God as that of an intimate relationship with Jesus, the bridegroom, culminating in marriage. She uses the image of a mansion with many rooms. A Spiritual Betrothal takes place in the sixth and Spiritual Marriage in the seventh mansion. However, she warns that from mansion one to five it is not one long honeymoon! Taming our ego is painful. But the new life of freedom, peace and inner harmony we experience makes it all worthwhile.

part four

"You're going around with your head in the clouds!" How many times people have said that to me! And it certainly was not meant as a compliment! But I hope to show that it can be the richest compliment paid to us. When it comes to 'knowing' God, all of us, popes, bishops, clergy, religious and laity are going around with our heads in the sand! We can take comfort that we are a motley crew in the same boat of ignorance. The truth is, as we shall see, in the clouds is the right place to be. Was it not in a cloud that God was best experienced in the Old Testament?

Nobody has better articulated this with utter conviction than the anonymous fourteenth- century author of *The Cloud of Unknowing*. All we know of him is that he was English, a mystic, a theologian and a superb spiritual director. He is clearly writing from personal experience. From the outset it is crucial that we put the emphasis in the right place. As you read this, your focus is almost certainly on the word *cloud*. But let the author clarify: "When I speak of darkness, I mean the absence of knowledge. I have not said *'cloud'* but the *'cloud of unknowing.'* For it is a darkness of *unknowing* that lies between you and God." There it is in a nutshell! When it comes to 'knowing' God intellectually we are literally in the dark. And that's how it should be, so don't panic! Just hold your head high in the clouds!

The author challenges us to lose our minds, in the right sense of course. So when next someone tells you that you are out of your mind, take it as a nice compliment. You are on the right track. He calls us to "Reject all thoughts [in 'knowing' God], for God can be loved but he cannot be thought." And we thought God could! How disappointing! This all fits in beautifully with Jesus' call to deny ourselves [our false self] for it is only in losing ourselves, our ego, that we find our true self. Perhaps now we are seeing more clearly, that being Catholic and a disciple of Jesus is pure paradox, an apparent contradiction and completely counter-cultural!

Why couldn't Jesus think like us! As only Fr. Andrew Greely can put it: "Jesus would be a less troublesome house guest if he played by our rules. A Jesus who does not disconcert and shake us up is not Jesus at all!" His paradoxical life and teaching sure do disturb us. Moreover, he is no respecter of power, titles, position, garb, dress or education. Not one of us has the edge on Jesus. When we think we have domesticated him, like sand he slips through our fingers! So the sooner we accept him on *his* terms the better.

The author of *The Cloud of Unknowing* is just as paradoxical as Jesus which proves he is on the right path. For example: "There is that most divine knowledge of God which takes place through ignorance. So leave behind the operation of the intellect and strain upwards in *unknowing*." Two hundred years later, the great mystic St. John of the Cross would reiterate this with his unsettling claim, "We know God through unknowing!" For John, relationship and union with God is by way of darkness. On a clear night out in the country, look up at the stars and you will fully appreciate the value of darkness! Or try watching a movie in the light!

By now it should be obvious that the *New Evangelization* of Catholics cuts very deep. This is no mere window-dressing or papering over the cracks. It calls for a newness in *ardour, method and expression*. We Catholics in the West are at a crossroads. So we need to halt, discern well and make the right decision. We can take the road of least resistance and continue in our complacency. Or we can go down the road of short-term band-aiding. But Jesus invites us, hierarchy included, to take the highroad with him. This calls for a fresh and personal encounter *with* Jesus. He's not interested in us knowing *about* him. But he longs for us to *'know'* him.

WANTED: REFORMERS

Calling priest-abusers to Rome, resignations, zero tolerance and kicking them out of ministry, is only a start. A universal reform of bishops and clergy is desperately urgent. Another name for this is conversion, not just *from* the abuse of power but *to* our higher power: Jesus. I believe that the abuse of power is at the root of all abuse in ministry. Leadership can be so preoccupied with lawsuits, bankruptcy and public opinion that they put reform on the back burner if it even gets a thought. But it has to be absolute top priority. They have put a lot of energy into drawing up detailed preventative abuse plans, and this is good, but they must not mistake legislation for reform. I sincerely hope they will put at least the same amount of effort into implementing reform. It is one thing to be a legislator but it's a horse of a different colour to be a reformer! Will the first reforming bishops and priests please stand up!

A quick glance back at Church history reveals few reformers. In one way or other it cost them dearly. The great reformer of the Carmelites, St. John of the Cross, paid a heavy price. His own Friars locked him up in a dungeon for nine months and beat him up! He could blame the other Carmelite reformer, St. Teresa of Avila, for this because she coerced him into her reformation plan for the Carmelite nuns! So were the prophets of the Old Testament dragged kicking and screaming by God into reforming the Israelites! Reformers for the most part do not volunteer for the job! But this is no excuse for leadership because it is part of their job description!

We Catholics are blessed with people who dared to risk reform and so we can draw strength from them in this time of appalling clerical crisis. The priesthood, as it is today, was in poor shape in the sixteenth century. The Council of Trent was called to deal with Catholic Reformation. It lasted for eighteen years and ended in 1563. Among the myriad of issues discussed, the reform of the clergy received much needed attention. Then individuals bravely took the initiative.

Top of the list was the mystic and founder of the French Oratory, Cardinal Pierre de Berulle. He came to see that his special vocation was to work for the education and sanctification of the diocesan clergy. He was convinced that the vocation to holiness needed to be stirred up in the diocesan clergy which he called, "The Order of Jesus Christ." It is Jesus our founder to whom we the clergy must turn, and by whom we must be reshaped. This will happen, as Berulle taught, when we have a deep personal relationship with Jesus. Renewal for him started within.

Berulle had a great influence on others who in turn risked reform. St. John Eudes focused on establishing seminaries and rooting seminarians in the interior life. A similar approach was followed by St. Vincent de Paul with his Congregation, the Vincentians. Two Italian saints from around this period also dedicated themselves to the reform of the clergy: St. Cajetan, founder of the Theatines, and St. Anthony Mary Zaccaria, founder of the Barnabites. They pursued this primarily by the example of a fervent religious life and their love of the priesthood. There has been no major thrust towards the reform of bishops and priests since. Hence the urgency today.

We cannot go on fiddling while Rome burns! Individual reformers among us must set the ball rolling without counting the cost. As Zorba the Greek said to his employer, "It's difficult, boss, very difficult. You need a touch of folly to do it; folly, do you see? You have to risk everything." I believe our Catholic people are calling us priests and bishops to risk everything and get on with reforming—*now*. A touch of folly is an essential ingredient in a reformer! The great reformer, Jesus, was considered out of his mind by his own family!

Reform begins with me and prayer is a good place to start. Karl Rahner's first published reflection was called, "Why We Need to Pray." He was only twenty-two when he wrote it! "You must pray. We must pray. If we don't pray we remain attached to earthly things, we become small like them, narrow like them, we get pressured by them, and we sell ourselves to them—because we give our love and heart to them. We must pray."[17] We in leadership would do well to stick this admonishment on our bathroom mirror.

---

17 **Karl Rahner:** *Spiritual Writings: 32*

CATHOLICS WORSHIP IMAGES

I am not talking about statues of Jesus, Mary, Joseph or the saints. Bridie and Johnny Doogan lived close to the seminary and many of us often retreated there for a cup of tea. Their house, like my own, had statues all over the place with a light burning before the Sacred Heart. Well, one day when Bridie was dusting she knocked it over and, of course, it was damaged. "Thank God it wasn't Mary," exclaimed a relieved Bridie! Here I am talking about our images of God that we Catholics worship and we call this idolatry. The bottom line is that an image of God is not God. It's that simple. Just like a photo—it is only an image of me, not the real me. To help clarify what I mean I will explain in more detail the meaning of images.

Going back to my photo; images are things that stand for something else. Often these are things that we cannot put into words. Don't we all know how our imagination can run crazy? What else are our daydreams but our imagination gone wild! Exactly the same happens with God. All of us; popes, bishops, priests, religious, laity, saints and theologians are guilty of worshiping images of God. There is no *one* false image of God. *All* images of God are false precisely because they are not God. Spectacular though Rembrandt's 'Head of Christ' is, it is only an image.

When images are recognized for what they are, as representing some deeper reality, they function as symbols. Now symbols are helpful and can act as vehicles by which we are brought into touch with reality. But when images are taken *as* the reality that they are supposed to represent, they become idols. However learned or profound theologians' images (ideas, thoughts, or insights) of God might be, they are only images. But look at how these are taken for real and taught as real! When we teach that an image of God *is* God, we lie and teach idolatry too! The truth is that God is beyond all images. This reality that we call God, we can never capture, comprehend and verbalize. It's when we don't recognize and accept this that we become idolaters.

The story is told of a distinguished theologian that, when addressing new students for the first time, he would enter the lecture hall, go to the podium and begin by saying, "God." Then he would pause while the students waited to find out what he had to say about God. He would then tell the students, "Whatever came into your head when I said the word 'God,' is not God."

Our image of God reduces God to an object or a noun but God is better described as a verb! It's our way of trying to control or get a handle on God. We then proceed to presume that we can know and understand this object we call God. But God ain't no object! God *is*. Period! This is the reality that no image can make real. We have to be satisfied to live in a state of incompleteness when it comes to knowing God and we Westerners are not happy with this limitation. Easterners, on the other hand, are very comfortable with it! We view God as a problem to be solved. They see God as Mystery to be lived. It's like the Irish plumber visiting Niagara Falls: "If I had my tools I could fix this thing," he exclaimed! For Paddy it was a problem to fix! For others it was a wonder to savour!

We indulge in images instead of accepting the limitations of reality because it feels safe and comfortable. Also, it gives us a false sense of security because we believe we are in control. We see this in its extreme in mental illnesses like schizophrenia, psychosis and severe neurosis. People withdraw from real life into their own imaginary world. While this can be quite comfortable it is totally destructive. The cure is to help people move from image to real. Therapists will tell you this is difficult. In regard to God, we Catholics stay with our image of God because it is more pleasant than dealing with the reality of God. But this is destructive escapism.

God seemed to foresee the trap we would fall into! So in the very first commandment God warns us: "You shall have no other gods before me, you shall not make for yourself an idol." Our images of God are other gods from which we make idols for ourselves. Aaron made a golden image of a bull from the peoples' jewelry which they then worshiped. Our great problem here is that our gods and idols we imagine look good in themselves. To imagine God as Father is not bad. The fact is that it is not real. It is just an image. But we must not make something that is good become the enemy of the best.

WHERE WAS GOD?

That question was asked by many after the Tsunami disaster in 2004. Where was God in the pain, loss and death that affected thirty-six countries and millions of people? It certainly got people thinking. As for Catholics, I have a sense that it was mainly non-practicing Catholics who were more honest and dared to confront God.

Practicing and respectable Catholics shied away for several reasons. One, we were brought up to believe that a good Catholic does not question God—nor the Church for that matter! Two, Catholics tend to focus more on the answer than the question. Three, it is too painful to articulate that kind of question.

I believe our answer to the question would go something like this: Who are we to question God? God knows what he is doing. We must accept God's will. Have faith. God has a purpose. God gives us free will. God is trying to get our attention.

The problem with this response is that it is presumptuous and arrogant. Because we Catholics are so conditioned to respond this way, we are unaware of our impudent behaviour. Imagine, we presume to know how God thinks! The truth is that we don't even know who God is much less how God thinks! Yet you I and spout off as if we had a hotline to God! How arrogant! I know my bishop quite well. But I cannot be so pretentious to read his mind and then tell the parishioners what he is thinking. Neither can a secretary presume to know what her boss is thinking at any given moment. But some do!

This attitude points to a canned God. Like canned music it is not the real thing. Our image of God is just that—an image. The problem is that we convince ourselves that the image is actually real. Then we pontificate and this is very dangerous. The smart insurance companies, too, cash in on this canned God. They will not cover you for a natural disaster because they label it "An act of God!" How do they know? More presumption and arrogance.

The pain of asking the question, "Where was God?" is two-pronged: first, in simply asking the question I drop my denial and admit that I don't have the answer. That's humiliating. Now I am plunged into ignorance, out of control and insecure. The rug has been pulled out from under my feet. God is no longer a tame God but wild and unmanageable. This is a death-of-God experience for us and very frightening.

The second point is that now responsibility for my brothers and sisters sits squarely on my shoulders. In other words, I now have to be God for them. And didn't the world witness this in the magnanimous response to the disaster? That outpouring of generosity, compassion and love is God in action. What would have happened if we all sat back and blamed God?

But the greatest pain is the thought of a change of lifestyle. The Tsunami disaster is a one-time all-out generous response. It affects our wallet a little but not our lives at all. The rubber hits the road when it does. For example, on December 9, 2004, UNICEF published statistics which are horrific and scandalous. Daily, yes every day, 29,158 children below the age of five die. That's about 1.4 million every year. All this because of human-made disasters caused by our injustice and greed. We in the developed world are responsible and must be held accountable. Our response to this appalling indictment cannot be short-term. No, we are in this for the long haul and we baulk at the thought of it. Now we have to ask, "Where are *we* in all this?" Leave God out of it.

During the Tsunami appeal the Prime Minister of England, Tony Blair, worried that the poor and dying would be over-looked, and called us to remember Africa in particular. The *New Evangelization* of Catholics calls us to a conversion of lifestyle that will move us to act justly, not only when we have disasters, but every day. Here we are doing no more than we ought. Every person on this planet has an equal right to a fair share of the earth's resources and to have a decent life. It is important to distinguish between charity and justice. The overwhelming response to the Tsunami was one of charity in that we all gave from our excess. But justice demands that we give from our substance to the poor, which is their right. We can, we must be God for them.

GOD: ELUSIVE AS A POT OF GOLD

Celtic culture oozes with folklore. This makes it very akin to the culture in which the Old Testament was written. We 'educated' Westerners tend to dismiss folklore as old wives' (husbands') tales fit only for the commoners! But folklore is replete with wisdom while many 'educated' don't have an ounce of commonsense, let alone wisdom! For those who have the wisdom to see, there is always a profound message in our mythology.

When I was growing up in Ireland, I believed there was a pot of gold at the end of the rainbow! The Irish do not believe this any more! Ireland has become 'educated' and now we search for drugs, alcohol and sex! To get that gold you first had to capture the leprechaun. And that was no easy feat. Then it got harder. You had to grip him good and tight with both hands. It was always 'him!' Then march him in the direction of the rainbow. But it got even more difficult! You dare not take your eye off him for a second till he handed you the pot of gold. If you did he slipped through your grasp like jelly.

Now all leprechauns are very wise! They will try every possible trick to distract you. St. Bernard one day was teaching about distractions in prayer, sitting on his horse. Someone boasted that they had mastered distractions. "If you can say the Our Father for me without any distractions, I will give you my horse," challenged Bernard. So the person began, "Our Father.........but deliver us from.... and will you give me the saddle too?" Bernard kept his horse! Murphy fought off all attempts by his little friend to distract him. They were within metres of the glittering pot when the leprechaun exclaimed, "Well look at all that gold!" And Murphy did! And the leprechaun vanished into thin air! And so did the gold!

God is like that. When you think you have him (it's always him!) pinned down, he slips through your fingers like the leprechaun. The great intellectual St. Augustine, says that "If you say it is God it is not God." It is only our *image* of God. When Moses asked for God's name so he could tell the folk in Egypt who sent him, God replied "I Am who Am." Not very helpful! There is a food product called *President's Choice* with a 'no name' brand. God is like that—a 'no name' brand!

One of the three great Eastern mystics is St. Gregory of Nyssa (c.335- c.394). For him and for us, the quest for God is endless. We just never arrive and when we think we do, we get distracted and God eludes us. He says, "The true vision and the true knowledge of what we seek consists precisely in not seeing, in an awareness that our goal transcends all knowledge and is everywhere cut off from us by the darkness of incomprehensibility."

However, he does stress that it is in this darkness that we truly experience the presence of God. You could say there is light at the end of the tunnel! In his *Life of Moses,* he speaks of Moses first experiencing God in the light of the burning bush. Then it was in a cloud on a mountain in darkness: "But when Moses rose higher he saw God in the darkness." For Gregory, every ending is a beginning, and every arrival is a new departure. But he is quite clear that this perpetual beginning is not repetition; it is something always new and fresh.

The great T.S. Eliot echoes Gregory's continuous quest:
> *"We shall not cease from exploration*
> *And the end of all our exploring*
> *Will be to arrive where we started*
> *And know the place for the first time."*

We are challenged by *The New Evangelization* to be explorers, pilgrims and pioneers in our pursuit of God. Our spiritual journey is unfinished business. While the pot of gold will always elude us, something energizes us to keep seeking. It can only be what Augustine experienced in his exploring: "Our hearts are made for God and will not rest till they rest in him." The good news is that the joy is in the journey, not the arrival!

GIVE UP YOUR PROJECTIONS OF GOD

"When you meet the Buddha, slay him!" This is what the Buddhists tell their disciples. It sounds awfully sadistic but it makes perfect sense. What they are talking about is one's image or projection of the Buddha which of course is not the Buddha at all. The Buddha is imageless so it's your own image of him you slay. The same teaching applies to Catholics: "When you meet *your* God, slay him!" What you are encountering is your projection or image of God because God too is imageless. We Catholics baulk at the mere mention of slaying *our* God! The truth is that it is a false god and conversion calls for its ejection.

It is incredible how much projection dominates our lives. Parents project their unmet needs on their children. If they did not have a good education or job they will drive their children to do better, all in the name of the child's benefit of course. Look at sports, junior hockey in particular. Witness the fights parents get into with referees and coaches. It's more about dad's projection of his unmet needs than his son's selection.

Projection is externalizing something going on inside us that we prefer not to deal with. It is like the old projector we used to show a movie. The special bulb would project the light on the screen away from the projector. I used to be scared stiff passing a cemetery in Ireland at night. So I would whistle or sing! I projected my inner fear in my whistle and singing and the latter was awful enough to waken even the dead! The proper thing to do was to admit to myself that I felt fear and deal with that instead. But it was too painful and scary so I found a scapegoat! Talking about cemeteries! I don't know why they put a fence around them. The people outside don't want to go in and the people inside cannot come out!

The most deceptive and debilitating thing about projections is that I hand myself over to them. This means that I live away from myself. I think it was James Joyce who said of one of his characters, "He lived at a distance from himself." When I cannot handle things as they are, as other than me, I impose my thinking on them. I then become more alienated from my true self. When I do this with God, naturally, I become more distanced from the reality of God. And the sad thing is that we are unaware we are living a lie. This is why conversion is a challenge because we don't see a problem.

Our concepts, images and symbols of God then, are projections that must be slain. It means that when I talk about 'my God' I have trimmed the uncontainable God down to my comfortable shape and size. All of us do this: in our prayers, writing, teaching and preaching. It's no wonder we have such a multitude of opinions about God! "There are as many opinions as there are people," says Augustine!

I believe it is primarily fear that keeps us in our projections—fear of the reality of God. I once attended a workshop by a psychologist titled, "Fear: The Demon Within." We know too well from our own experience that this is perfectly true. Fear of the unknown just paralyzes us. But it is in the unknown that we know God. Like the Israelites, don't ask us to leave slavery in Egypt and journey to the Promised Land! The devil we know is better than the one we don't know!

The psychologist Carl Jung gives a cryptic description of what is involved in giving up our projections: "Anyone who has lost the historical symbols [images and concepts] and cannot be satisfied with substitutes is certainly in a very difficult position today: before him [her] there yawns the void, and he [she] turns away from it in horror. This fear is far from unjustified, for where God is closest the danger seems greatest."[18]

---

18 **Kenneth L. Becker:** *Unlikely Companions: Footnote 1*

The writer of the letter to Hebrews reminds us that, "It is a fearful thing to fall into the hands of the living God" (Hb. 10:31). Our projections, our religious symbols, images and concepts are our substitutes for the reality of the living God. Of course, in our thinking, God is always a tame God! We fear risking the direct experience of the power, the length, the breadth, and depth of the reality we call God.

DROPPING YOUR PROJECTIONS OF GOD

Nature rebels and says enough is enough. Your projections are not fulfilling you so it is time to move on, to grow up and be real. The signs are common and you will recognize them.

For instance, you have little or no sense of God and feel that God has abandoned you. Guilt accompanies this because of your Catholic upbringing. Job's three phony advisers tried to convince him that he did something terrible to deserve his plight. Basically, they were laying a guilt trip on him, but he would have none of it. You can feel the same. The truth is that you are just plain tired of playing the projection game. Prayer is a burden, that's if you can pray at all like you used to. You are stuck, feel helpless and scared. "I must be losing my faith," is what I hear people say in this transition. Well of course you are losing your faith—in your false God! And that's the best thing that could happen to you! The young Simone Weil, never baptized, was ruthlessly blunt on this: "He who puts his life into his faith in God can lose his faith."[19]

You are being invited to drop your false faith and false God. But this is painful. It would be easy if you knew the next step and where all this is leading. For now you are in the dark. When I was struggling, a spiritual director friend of mine asked me this question: "Can you stay in the oven and be baked?" If you turn it down to low then I might! You too have to ask yourself the same question.

---

19 **Simone Weil:** *Gravity and Grace:* 162

Simone offers hope in this awful void, "Every separation is a link,"[20] she says. You are being linked to reality, the real God, but you have to be severed from the false one first.

This anxious transition can be over a long period of time; even years. It can also hit you suddenly in traumatic experiences like depression, burn-out, mid-life transition and awareness of your own death. The mystics call it the dark night of the soul. There is a shift of focus from you and *your* God; from outside to inside, from doing to being, and from saying prayers to praying. To put it simply, you are called to be real and all these different experiences are a taste of reality. You are now where you should have been all your life: on pilgrimage; on the journey to the God within for this is where the real God is found.

Now, perhaps for the first time, you are able to appreciate the truth that the only constant thing in life is change. The only stability you can now live is to be stable in change! This is reality and you are called to be grounded in it. Letting go of your false God is a major upheaval made all the more excruciating because you cannot first try it on for size! You either accept it or you don't. Maintaining your false image of God has been like swimming upstream which is crazy when you do not have to! You are not a salmon! So be real and swim downstream!

Although it doesn't feel like it, you are being called to a new freedom, a resurrection experience. It is a rebirth and a second baptism. Your first was with water. And you believed all your life that you were fully baptized! Now you see that too is a false image! Your new baptism is from above in the Spirit. You lived your first in control (you thought) worshiping images of God. Like your Master, baptized in the Spirit and blood, you are now called to be powerless. Once you were like Peter: you put on your own gown, tied it up with a rope and went where you liked. Not any more! Someone else wants to lead you and take you where you don't want to go, but where you must if you are to be real.

---

20 Ibid., 200

Keep in mind that Rome was not built in a day! Remember, you are in a process of conversion that will be completed only the other side of the grave. You will never be fully anything, including real, this side, so relax! Faithfulness is all God asks for, not success. The great Jesuit scientist, Teilhard de Chardin, offers you comforting advice: "Above all trust in the slow work of God.....give Our Lord the benefit of believing that his hand is leading you, and accept the anxiety of feeling yourself in suspense and incomplete." He speaks from his experience of the dark night of the soul. His writings disturbed the institutional Church and so he was forbidden to publish them. He died in 1955 on Easter Sunday in the home of friends with only a handful at his funeral.

THROW YOUR IMAGES INTO THE FIRE

"**I** will take the ring," he said, "though I do not know the way."²¹ Here we see Frodo's leap of faith in *The Lord of the Rings*. Like Abraham, he sets out on an unknown journey with the ring to the Mountain of Fire in Mordor—to throw it into the fire. Elrond left him in no doubt about this hazardous pilgrimage: "It is a heavy burden. So heavy that none could lay it on another. I do not lay it on you. But if you take it freely, I will say that your choice is right."²² And the ever wise Sam, Frodo's companion, muttered, "A nice pickle we have landed ourselves in, Mr. Frodo!"²³ Was he ever right!

The book and movie, *The Lord of the Rings,* strikes a chord in our hearts simply because it is the story of every human being. As Catholics, your ring and mine is our false image of God, our projection of God. Frodo had no peace of mind so long as he kept the ring and yet he hung on to it. Isn't that you and me? Deep down we sense the tension. We are restless. We might be happy but our false images are not fulfilling us. This is our struggle. We stand on the side of the pool dithering and shivering but will not take the plunge! To throw our images into the fire is indeed a heavy burden. We have to take personal responsibility because no one else can do it for us. It's like

---

21 **J. R. R. Tolkien:** *The Lord of the Rings:* Book 2, Chapter 2, 264
22 Ibid.,
23 Ibid.,

dying: I have to do my own dying. Even though it will land us in one hell of a pickle, it is the right choice. Since he had the ring, Frodo sensed that only he could burn it. He couldn't place this burden on anyone else. Neither can we. In this sense we stand naked before the real God.

Frodo felt under compulsion to destroy what he was clinging to: "I am commanded to go to the land of Mordor, and therefore I shall go. If there is only one way, then I must take it. What comes after must come."[24] 'His face was grim and set, but resolute. He was filthy, haggard, and pinched with weariness, but he cowered no longer, and his eyes were clear.' "I purpose to enter Mordor this way."[25]

I am afraid there is no compromise, no sitting on the fence, when the time comes for us to take our images to the Mountain of Fire in Mordor. Frodo had just done battle with old Gollum and while he came out victorious, he sure was beaten black and blue. Gollum represents our dark side, our shadow, and this is what sets up the tension in us: light and darkness war against each other. But we must do battle. I believe we create our false images of God precisely to circumvent the side of us we just do not want to look at. Until you face your darkness, forget about burning your false images and continue to live as best you can in your disharmony. Keep in mind, though, that the struggle will not go away. As Carl Jung suggests, make friends with your shadow, like Frodo did.

The first step in this is to be in touch with your emotions and feelings. Accept them by admitting to yourself that you feel scared and out of your wits. Remember, feelings are neither right nor wrong and have no morality. So embrace them. That's what Frodo did: "I know what I should do, but I am afraid of doing it, Boromir: afraid."[26] 'The wind murmured in the branches of the trees. Frodo shivered. Sam looked worried.' "Now where's he got to? He's been a bit queer

---

24 **J. R. R. Tolkien:** The Lord of the Rings: Book 4, Chapter 3, 624

25 Ibid.,

26 **J. R. R. Tolkien:** *The Lord of the Rings:* Book 2, Chapter 10, 388

lately, to my mind. He's *afraid.* He's just plain terrified. That's what his trouble is."[27] Sam's prophecy had sure come true! "I believe you speak more wisely than any of us, Sam,"[28] said Aragorn.

If you are wise, like Frodo, you will look for someone like Sam to journey with you to The Mountain of Fire. That person is a wise spiritual director or a soul friend. Be careful though, because they are hard to come by. You are better off without a pseudo director. So shop around!

---

27 Ibid., 394

28 Ibid., 394

FREE OF YOUR IMAGES OF GOD

What I possess possesses me. And anything I can't give up becomes *my* God. We have grown so accustomed to being possessed by our false images of God that exorcism may be required! Despite his good intentions, Frodo dug in his heels at the very last moment. He didn't realize how much the Ring possessed him: "I have come, but I do not choose to do now what I came to do. I will not do this deed. The Ring is mine [possession!]."[29] 'He slipped it on his finger and vanished from Sam's sight.'[30] That's what possession does. It consumes us.

He was plunged into his dark night of the soul, into the fire of purification. In the person of old Gollum, Frodo wrestled with his shadow side where he experienced exorcism! He emerged, wounded and battered, but set free of possession by the Ring. "Well, this is the end Sam Gamgee."[31] 'Frodo was pale and worn, and yet himself again. And in his eyes there was peace now, neither strain of will, nor madness, nor fear. His burden was taken way. He was himself again. He was free.'[32] But not without a fight! His pilgrimage to Mordor was a death and resurrection experience resulting in peace and harmony.

---

29 **J. R. R. Tolkien:** *The Lord of the Rings:* Book 6, Chapter 3, 924

30 Ibid.,

31 Ibid., 926

32 Ibid.,

"We only possess what we renounce,"[33] Simone Weil tells us. We have to lose our life to find it, Jesus warns us. The grain of wheat has to die in order to yield a rich harvest. We Catholics find this paradoxical language difficult to embrace. It's certainly not the language of the world that is ingrained in us and which possesses us. Becoming free of our false images of God involves learning a new language—the language of the contradiction of the cross. Jesus spoke and taught in this strange language using parables.

It is amazing that after two thousand years we have not learned to speak His language! We still speak off the top of our heads! We rationalize, intellectualize and speculate! Ours is the language of logic! To help our conversion process we could take as our patron saint the Wizard, Gandalf the Grey! He acted as spiritual director for the group commissioned to accompany Frodo. He was a wise director of few words! "In one thing you have not changed, dear friend," said Aragorn, "you still speak in riddles."[34] "A habit of the old," answered Gandalf. "The long explanations needed by the young are wearying."[35] 'He laughed.'[36] And so can we!

How true! All our long explanations and speculations about God are indeed wearying. And what's the fruit of it all? Maybe the time has come to be silent about God. Are not all our writings and speculation false images that keep us too busy to be quiet and listen? When the great St. Thomas Aquinas became free of his false images he told his secretary to put away his pen and paper, for he quit writing. He finally came to realize that, "Man's utmost knowledge of God is to know that we do not know him." Another intellectual, St. Anselm, arrived at the same conclusion. Speaking of the mystery of the triune God, he said that it, "Transcends all the vision of the hu-

---

33 **Simone Weil:** *Gravity and Grace:* 80

34 **J. R. R. Tolkien:** *The Lord of the Rings:* Book 3, Chapter 5, 485

35 Ibid.,

36 Ibid.,

man intellect. And for this reason I think it best to refrain from the attempt to explain how this thing is."

Sign language, not speculation, is our best response to the mystery of God. For example, you are asked a searching question. You are flummoxed! You indicate this by placing your index finger right on the cleft in the middle of your top lip just below you nose! That's all we can say about God! That cleft is there for a purpose so we need to use it more! About seventy-five percent of all communication is non-verbal. What do we do to quieten the children? Finger on cleft! Hush!

Even though you are freed of your false images, God will remain mystery to you. Perhaps even more so now. But you will be enlightened and on the road to conversion. You will now be discovering the mystery that *you* are. You will be *living* the mystery that God is. Now you are wise and you will speak a new language in riddles, paradoxes, parables and apparent contradictions! It's very exciting!

"LATE HAVE I LOVED YOU"

That is St. Augustine's prayer of lament. He put off his conversion because he was possessed by and addicted to his promiscuous lifestyle. During this time he broke his mother's heart because she observed the sinful life he was living. He had a mistress and a son! "O God, give me chastity, but not yet," he prayed. Now there's honesty for you! And I bet God loved him for that! It's not a sin being a sinner. But it is a sin not admitting it! We Catholics can make that prayer of regret and honesty our own. Look how long we Catholics have postponed a *New Evangelization*! In all fairness, it has been more out of ignorance than willfulness. Because of its emphasis on the institutional aspect, the leadership must take the blame. Institutionalized religion keeps us in our heads, on the outside looking in. Without the mystical element, Gerard W Hughes reminds us, the Church, "Will be intellectually alive but spiritually barren." We only have to look around!

Karl Rahner warns us: "Tomorrow's devout person will either be a mystic—someone who has "experienced" something—or else they will no longer be devout at all." He is not claiming that every Catholic must be a John of the Cross or a Teresa of Avila! But he is saying that mysticism is the vocation of *every* Catholic. We must reject once and for all the elitist notion of mysticism. That inner 'something' we experience is energy, grace and God's very self. Anyone living at this level is a mystic. By living I mean noticing and responding. It is unfortunate that we arrive at this late in our lives, if we do at all. Conversion demands that what was the exception must now be the norm. The remorseful Augustine gives us hope and encouragement!

In his *Confessions* he prays, "Late have I loved you, O Beauty so ancient and so new. For behold you were within me, and I outside; and I sought you outside. Being admonished to return to myself, I entered into my own depths, with you as guide; and I was able to do it because you were my helper. I entered, and with the eye of my soul I saw your unchangeable light shining over the eye of my soul. You touched me and I have burned for your peace."

As a brilliant intellectual he tried to find God outside himself in philosophy and theology. But all this knowledge was a distraction and an obstacle to experiencing God within. All the while, God from deep within was searching him out, but he was too preoccupied doing it his way. Enlightened, he lived in God as mystery within instead of speculating about God as object without.

One day he was thinking about the Trinity as he walked along the beaches of the Mediterranean. He looked up and saw a little boy on the beach in front of him. He went back and forth to the ocean with a little bucket and filled up a hole he had dug in the sand. Augustine approached and asked, "What are you doing?" The boy answered, "I am going to take that big ocean and put it in this little hole." He was touched by the boy's innocence. Smiling patiently he said, "You can't do that. That big ocean is too big to fit in that little hole." The boy looked up and said, "Easier for me to put that big ocean into this little hole than for you to take the big Trinity and put it into your little mind, Bishop Augustine."

Immediately the boy vanished into thin air. Augustine recognized that it was an angel sent by God with a message. He saw how small and limited his mind was when he attempted to grasp the things of God. While God cannot be known, God can be experienced. And one who experiences God is a mystic. A mystic is one who has come in out of the cold—one who is outside-in!

Augustine reminds us that our conversion from outside to inside is never too late. Remember the repentant thief on the cross and the workers in the Gospel who received a full day's pay for an hour's work! Like Augustine, God fast-tracks us too! He was baptized at 33, a priest at 37, and a bishop at 42! Having a mistress and a son was no obstacle either, for God writes best on crooked lines! He named his son, *A Deo Datus.* Translated, it means, "A gift from God." All is pure gift!

MYSTICISM IS 'catholic'

At the end of the Creed, which we rattle off every Sunday, we say we believe in the, "Holy catholic (with a small 'c') Church." The average Catholic takes this to mean the Roman Catholic Church, which of course it does not. Catholic with a small 'c' means universal. The Universal Church is more than 'Roman' Catholic. The Roman or Latin Church is only one of other groups of churches we call "rites" which are every bit as Catholic as we are. They are the Byzantine, Armenian, Chaldean, Coptic, Ethiopian, Malabar, Maronite and Syrian Churches. Mysticism too is catholic, universal and way larger than us. We Roman Catholics do not have the edge on mysticism.

The intellectual genius, Albert Einstein was a Jew. Yet, he didn't boast about his brilliant mind. But he did praise the mystical: "The most beautiful thing we can experience is the mysterious. It is the source of all true art and science. He to whom this emotion is a stranger, who can no longer pause to wonder and stand rapt in awe, is as good as dead: his eyes are closed." What an indictment! To think that we Catholics are almost dead and half-blind!

Notice where he puts the emphasis: we don't think our way into the mystical, we feel our way. It is experienced, not thought out. It's like pilots. They fly their planes more from the seat of their pants than the myriad of instruments in front of them! Being one with their machine they feel its pulse. That's how I rode fiery thoroughbreds! I felt every movement under me that signaled the next one. When I felt smug and thought I was in control, I ended up in a heap on the ground! Mysticism is all about noticing, being in touch with the within, the beyond, and being surprised.

Another Jew and philosopher, Ludwig Wittgenstein, has this famous proposition: "Of that of which we can say nothing, let us be silent." In saying this he was leaving room for the mystical. Before mystery he held that silence was the only possible response. He says that once we have reached the point at which language fails, stop talking. Don't go on nattering as though you know what you are talking about when, by the very definition of mystery, you don't. I wonder what theologians think about that!

We say that theology means 'talking about God.' But right here we have a huge problem on our hands! How do you talk about that which by definition you cannot talk about? How do you talk about absolute mystery? And yet we do! Look at all the wasted energy we put into this like volumes of books, endless lectures, useless debates while not to mention those darn meetings! I consider them an occasion of sin! A meeting is where minutes are kept and hours are wasted! Hopefully it is now plain and obvious how urgent is The *New Evangelization* and conversion. But we have a fight on our hands so prepare for stiff opposition!

Knowledge *about* God, albeit valueless, is control, and the theologians will fight tooth and nail to retain power. Just imagine how many bishops, priests, religious and laity this conversion would free up! The Vatican, seminaries and colleges could disperse most of their staff to work in parishes which would answer the shortage of clergy! The truth is that we need a new breed of teachers. Women and men living the mystery who can model to us how to be actively silent, how to listen with our hearts, how to get a feel for God, how to journey in wonder and awe before this mystery and be comfortable, how to be secure in our insecurity and to know that we don't know! In this sense they would be more mentors than teachers.

As the well-known Rabbi Abraham Joshua Heschel was dying, he turned to his friend and said, "Sam, never once in my life did I ask God for success, power or fame. I asked for wonder and he gave it to me."

The Irish comedian, Hal Roche, unintentionally, adds a spice of humour to mysticism! Asked directions by a visitor, Seamus replies: "Take the first left at the graveyard, right at O'Reilly's pub and continue for a mile to the chapel. Then you'll think you're there but you're not! Now cross the canal bridge, turn right at Murphy's farm and you'll think you are not there, but you are!" Surprise! Surprise! Intellectuals cannot be surprised because they already know the way—they think! The mystic, on the other hand, who is possessed by the mystery that is God, is forever being surprised! When you think you are not there, you are!

"WE NEED...A NEW SAINTLINESS"

Guess who called for this! Maybe a little more might help you but I really doubt it: "We are living in times that have no precedent...today it is not nearly enough merely to be a saint. We need the saintliness demanded by the present moment, a new saintliness, itself also without precedent. A new type of sanctity is indeed a fresh spring; an invention...it is almost the equivalent to a new revelation. The world needs saints who have genius."[37]

This person was about twenty years ahead of the Second Vatican Council which lasted from 1962-1965. The universal call of every Catholic to holiness (saintliness) permeated the gathering of over three thousand bishops. Faithful to the Council, Pope John Paul II continued to hammer home this priority: "I have no hesitation in saying that all pastoral initiatives must be set in relation to holiness."

When we look around we have to agree that we too are, "living in times that have no precedent." The sex-abuse scandals of priests, the failure of bishops to address these early on, and the immoral behaviour of some, have rocked the universal Church more than the worldwide catastrophe caused by the Tsunami in Asia. Disillusioned, feeling betrayed and severely hurt, hundreds of thousands of Catholics have walked away. Of those remaining, few have any confidence in the leadership of the Church in the West. European Catholics have reverted to paganism. Marriage, the very heart of society and Church,

---

37 **Simone Weil:** *Waiting for God: 51*

has almost disappeared. The average Catholic no longer lives by objective standards but by relativism, subjectivism, materialism and individualism. The Evangelicals are sweeping up the Catholics of Latin America at a phenomenal rate. It is estimated that 25% have been converted.

What would "A saintliness demanded by the present moment, itself without precedent," look like? That's a tough one to answer! But I am certain that it ties in well with the call of John Paul II for a *New Evangelization* of Catholics. If something is new then it is without precedent! The writer calls this type of sanctity a "Fresh spring.... the equivalent to a new revelation." Again, the optimistic John Paul II looked forward to a "New Springtime" for the Church.

We too must be hopeful. The risen Jesus is our primary source of hope. He, not the institution, is our 'New Springtime.' This means looking beyond the body to the head: Jesus. The body, the institutional Church in the West at least, is so anemic today that it has little hope to offer. For too long we have expected from the institution more than it can give. It is like spouses. Too often they expect from each other what he or she is incapable of sustaining: unconditional love. They marry believing all their needs will be met by their spouse, and of course they end up disillusioned. History shows that when the institutional Church no longer meets the deeper needs of its people they turn to Jesus. So there is hope. I believe that the institution has eclipsed Jesus, the head, to the point that it is now an obstacle to him. We must return to him. Meanwhile, we must not jump ship! We have to stay in this messy marriage with the body because we are all sinners. Reform comes from within, not from spectators in the stands!

The new saintliness and new type of sanctity the individual calls for is as old as Christianity! It is called *Mysticism!* But it is new for today simply because Catholics have neglected it. In this sense, we are like the prodigal son! His main sin was his denial of a relationship with his father to the point of disowning him. We too have walked out of a personal relationship with our brother, Jesus. We have squandered mysticism, our family heritage. Now we have to come to our senses and return home. Living a mystical life is as natural as breathing! We are born mystics! But, like a new language, if you don't keep speaking it, you lose it. Now is the time to start speaking a mystical language and living a mystical life!

Simone Weil is the most unlikely person to issue the challenge to saintliness so needed today! Born into a family of middle-class Jews in 1909 she died at the age of 34. Though she had close ties to the Catholic Church (she had a Dominican priest as her spiritual director) she was never baptized. Out of the mouths of babes....!

PEEL YOUR ONION

Ask anyone living in Northern Canada what you should wear for the winter and they will tell you to dress in layers! That's a very apt description of who we are. I am no biologist but I believe we are composed of layers from our skin to the very core of our anatomy. As part of my Clinical Pastoral Education training, I observed major surgery standing very close to the patient. To control her obesity, the surgeon stapled off part of her stomach. He had to cut through many layers to the point that his arm almost disappeared! As he inserted the staple gun he told us that the staples were made in Russia! That was before the collapse of Communism!

These are the outer layers that we can see. But at another level we are also made up of layers. This is the deeper level of our soul or spirit which we cannot see but definitely can feel. We cannot see the layers of our skull and brain, but feel that headache! Physically and spiritually we are like an onion. There will be no spiritual growth unless we peel our onion even though the cost is tears! Endless layers cover our inner life or spirit. We will never get to the core this side of the grave. But that makes it exciting for we continue to experience a new layer, new life, new insight, new awareness, and a new relationship with our God who *is* the very core.

"And then they feel rather than know."[38] This is how St. Bonaventure (he died in 1274) describes the relationship at what he

---

38 **Philip Endean:** *Karl Rahner and Ignatian Spirituality: 24*

calls the *"apex affectus."* Translated, it means: 'the soul's affective power' or the 'core of the soul.' He is speaking about a reality or a layer in us that is beyond the awareness of our intellect. God's presence at the very core of our soul cannot be known through our intellect. It is a *felt* presence which is deeper than feeling cold or warm.

In this regard, Bonaventure teaches that, "We must set aside discursive operations of the intellect and turn the very *apex of our soul* to God to be entirely transformed by him. This is most mystical and secret. No one knows it but he [she] who has received it. No one receives it but he [she] who has desired it. If you want to understand how this happens, ask it of grace, not of learning; ask it of desire, not of understanding; ask it of prayer, not of attentive reading; ask it of the betrothed, not the teacher; ask it of God, not of man; ask it of darkness, not of radiance. Ask it not of light, but of a fire that completely inflames you and transports you with extreme sweetness and burning affection. This fire is God himself."[39]

Notice how he says we are to peel the onion! It is all totally contrary to how we have been taught, which is to do it the Frank Sinatra way: "I did it *my* way." Bonaventure highlights the importance of the role of our senses in this journey within. We feel our way rather than think our way. We are not in touch with our senses because we have suppressed them. It will take time to befriend them and feel comfortable, so be patient. Sadly, too many Catholics leave their bodies behind in their spiritual quest. The body is still viewed as an obstacle so it is no wonder they are frustrated. If the Incarnation means anything, surely it says that God in the flesh meets us in the flesh. In stressing the place of our senses and affections, Bonaventure is simply affirming this truth.

Seven hundred years later, Karl Rahner confirmed Bonaventure's deep mystical insight. Praising it, he writes: "If God touches the deepest point of the soul from within, informing it as it were, the *apex affectus* (the core of the soul) will be able to have an awareness of this immediate union of love, without the intellect thereby

---

39 **Office of Readings:** Feastday, *July 15th*

becoming active." For at the core of our soul and deeper than our intellect, there is God.

The *New Evangelization* calls us to be like a sunflower and, ".....turn the very apex of our soul to God and be totally transformed by him." We keep turning towards our God within by peeling our onion, layer after layer, and tear after tear!

ATTENTION! ATTENTION! ATTENTION!

You go to your doctor. Has he or she ever asked you what you think about your particular illness? On the contrary, you are asked how you are *feeling*. You are in counseling or psychotherapy. If you cannot express how you feel you had better bow out before you are kicked out! That's how important it is for us to be aware of our emotions, our feelings and the affective side of ourselves. It's no big deal! But because we are trained from childhood not to be in touch with ourselves, it is a gigantic leap for the majority of us. The institutional Church, like society in general, is skeptical of anything below our shoulders! So it is top heavy, operating mainly from the neck up, and worships that lump between our ears! We really do need to lose our heads! But then we wouldn't be in control—so we fear!

Since we are mystics at heart (not our heads!) we become who we are by paying attention. It is comforting to know that we are not starting from scratch. There are still some embers glowing under the ash in the fireplace! Like Timothy, the fire had almost gone out, so Paul wrote, "I am reminding you now to fan into a flame the gift that God gave you when I laid my hands on you." Mysticism is indeed a gift that has lain dormant for too long and needs to be activated. We awaken the sleeping giant by paying attention, being aware, noticing and being in touch with the treasure within.

In one of her last letters to her parents, Simone Weil likens this treasure within her to a "Deposit of pure gold"[40] that she discovered. Unfortunately, this priceless treasure was disregarded by most and so she felt an urgency to hand it on. For her, and for us, a good place to start is to pay attention, not with our heads but at the affective level of our senses. "Attention," she writes, "consists of suspending our thought, leaving it detached and empty....above all, our thought should be empty, waiting, not seeking anything, but ready to receive. We do not obtain the most precious gifts by going in search of them but by waiting for them."[41]

This does not mean that we sit around and wait for lightning to strike! It is an active paying attention, like active listening. Simone calls it, "A kind of alert, receptive waiting."[42] Here we have to shed our Pelagian mentality that *we* search for God. This is heresy, but it is where most Catholics are at. Just look at our theology, homilies and prayers. It is we who take the initiative and demand God to bless it! All of which is in keeping with our Western superiority and arrogance.

The truth is that *we* don't find God. Anyway, we cannot and do not need to because God has already found us. The very desire to desire God, and to respond, is itself a pure gift. We just need to get off the roller coaster of thought, stop, and pay attention. "The problem" says Simone, "Is that we have wanted to be too active; we have wanted to carry out a search."[43] That makes us feel good because we are "doing" something. But all we are doing is spinning our wheels. It's all about control!

Attention is bound up with desire. "If we go down into ourselves," writes Simone, "we find that we possess exactly what we desire."[44]

---

40 **CBC Ideas:** *Enlightened by Love: The Thought of Simone Weil: 10*

41 Ibid., 30

42 Ibid., 30

43 Ibid., 30

44 **Simone Weil:** *Gravity and Grace: 67*

Paying attention then is noticing, being aware of the hunger in us, stirred up by God, which only God can satisfy. We don't figure this out in our heads. This has been the obstacle and problem all along. We attend with our antennae, our feelers. It is through our emotions, our feelings and at our affective level that we experience the God of our desire who first desires us.

When we are attentive to our feelings we will feel and notice only two experiences: We feel either consolation or desolation, either happy or sad. We talk to Jesus about the *feelings* we are experiencing, not the issue stirring them up: "Lord, I feel joyful, peaceful, a feeling of being one with nature as I watch winter become spring. I feel angry, frustrated and fed up with what is happening in our Church today." As you dialogue you will experience new feelings. Continue talking about *them* and you will be pleasantly surprised by God!

YOU CAN EXPERIENCE GOD

part one

※

While you cannot know God, you can definitely experience God. When looked at from everyday life-experience, this makes sense. Take a baby for example. Though not able to figure out a thing, he or she survives on experiences. While we cannot see the wind or pain, we definitely experience them. We in the West tend to associate experience with knowledge but it is at the sensing, affective and feeling level that we experience, not with our heads. I do not hesitate to say that the truth that we *can* experience God is basically commonsense—a 'sensing' that is common to all! These reflections are based on this fact along with Karl Rahner's categorical conviction that every Catholic *can* experience God.

"I encountered God; I experienced God's own self."[45] This was his insistent refrain in a 1978 writing. Shortly before his death in 1984 he referred to it as his "Spiritual testament." He speaks in the person of his founder, Saint Ignatius, writing from heaven to one of his present-day followers in the Society of Jesus. In this work, Rahner reads the life of Ignatius in terms of his own theology where he expresses his own deep convictions. Central in this is his utter conviction that we have the capacity to experience God. This is the best kept secret. Why has it been kept under lock and key for so long?

---

45 **Karl Rahner:** *Spiritual Writings:* 35

Reading and pondering on this stirs up some anger in me. Why did I have to wait forty-four years to stumble on it? It is a poor reflection on our leadership and a replay of the Garden of Eden story: That all can experience God is the tree of knowledge of which we were forbidden to eat—by our leadership. It is like one of the big pharmaceutical companies with a drug to cure cancer but will not release it. In effect, we are telling our Catholics that they cannot eat of the fruit because then their hearts will be opened and they will realize their dignity—that they are clothed in God. It is all about control. If the average Catholic can experience God directly then we in leadership lose power over them and this scares us. They don't need us! We in leadership must experience the *New Evangelization* at a more radical level than the rest if we are to facilitate their experience of God. We cannot give what we do not have.

With a passion, Rahner, as Ignatius' mouthpiece, did indeed proclaim from the housetops that the experience of God is our privilege and that leadership must recognize this: "But it remains true: human beings can experience God's own self. And your pastoral care must have this goal in sight always, at every step, remorselessly. If you fill up the storehouses of people's consciousness only with your theology, however learned and up-to-date it is, in a way train people only for devotion to the Church, as enthusiastic subjects of the ecclesiastical establishment; if you make the people in the Church no more than obedient subjects of a distant God represented by an ecclesiastical hierarchy; if you don't help people get beyond all this; if you don't help them finally to abandon all tangible assurances and isolated insights and go with confidence in that incomprehensibility where there are no more paths—if you don't help people *this* way, then, in what you call your pastoral care and missionary vocation, you'll have either forgotten or betrayed my 'spirituality.'"[46]

Our Catholic sisters and brothers are asking for bread and we give them a stone; for fish and we hand them a snake; for a relationship with their God and we teach them, give them books and send

---

46 **Philip Endean:** *Karl Rahner and Ignatian Spirituality:* 17

them on courses. We must cease playing mother hen and drop our messiah complex because they have the potential to have a direct relationship with God. They don't need teachers. They are crying out for mentors and leaders who can evoke, who can help surface the buried reality that they *can* experience God.

Rahner stakes this conviction on his founder's blunt warning to spiritual directors. In so many words Ignatius tells them to get out of the way. God is the director, not they. So they must not come between their directee and God but, "Let the Creator and the creature deal immediately with each other." We in leadership would do well to heed this. We make the introduction and then gracefully bow out! It's like matchmaking! We introduce couples to each other and then stand back! But only one who is in the process of conversion that brings freedom is capable of letting go.

part two

Up until recently, I would not have the knowledge and conviction to tell someone that they can experience God. A parishioner called me from her office feeling both excited and stumped. A co-worker (a young man in his thirties) for the second time asked her to tell him about Jesus. He is not a Christian and is interested in finding out who this Jesus is. On his own he started reading the book of Genesis! "I have a few books that might help," she said, "but I'm sure you have ones too." Previously I would have given him The New Catechism and a Handbook for Today's Catholic, among others! What a terrible blunder I would have made! In offering these I'd have totally ignored his question. The man wants to know about Jesus, not the Catholic Church.

"Give him nothing," I said, and the phone went silent for a while! I could hardly believe I said that. Surprise! I told her to just keep him talking and that she is the best book for now because he liked what she was living. How we sell ourselves short! I didn't say this, but I was telling her to evoke and not teach. Keeping him talking about his desire will help him to clarify, peel his onion and answer his own question. Good counselors don't answer your question. Because they believe *you* can, they challenge you to come up with your own answer. This young man *can* experience God and she must not get in the way of the, "Creator dealing immediately with the creature."

We leaders (popes, cardinals, bishops) commit the unforgivable sin of first teaching our people *about* God. So did Karl Rahner in his younger days till his conversion! Then he was quite clear that the experience *of* God is not the same as words *about* God. "I experienced God...," he says, "above all as beyond any pictorial imagining. God's own self I experienced, not human words about God—and the strength of conviction it brings renders not only theology but Scripture superfluous."[47] Although God, as Rahner insists, is imageless and nameless, God can be experienced.

In his early days, Rahner upset the Roman Curia with his then controversial ideas about the possibility of what he named, "anonymous Christians." He was saying that non-Christians can experience God without being full members of the Roman Catholic Church. The young man mentioned above is one such person. Hopefully, Rome and other leaders now agree on what to me seems to be utterly simple and blatantly evident. It is not denying in any way the importance of the institutional leadership. What it is saying, though, is that the institution remains secondary to the immediate experience of God. The institution is a means and not an end. It must know its place and keep behind, not in front of Jesus. When these roles get reversed we end up with a power struggle.

The Jesuit writer Philip Endean puts it this way: "Church authority may not be conceived simply as supplying the truth of God to an otherwise benighted, graceless humanity....Church authority offers us an indispensable rational context for working out our discipleship."[48] The Church does not supply the 'what' but dispenses the 'how.' The immediate experience of God is bigger than the Church whose servant it is. Rahner is emphatic that the "Immediate experience of God is not simply mediated by the ecclesiastical machinery."[49]

At the core of every person there is the well of living, refreshing water bubbling like a fountain! While the Church did not drill that

---

47 **Philip Endean:** *Karl Rahner and Ignatian Spirituality:* 15
48 **Philip Endean:** *Karl Rahner and Ignatian Spirituality:* 200
49 Ibid., 204

well it does help us draw from it and that's a fine balance that too often is not respected. God is that living well and Rahner reminds us that we should not be surprised that God would deal directly with us "In order to empower you, from your inmost centre in which he is present, to address this nameless one as person to person. This is a miracle beyond comprehension and which overshoots all your metaphysics."[50]

My parishioner's role is to lead the young man to the well within. There he will meet the God who thirsts for *him* and his God will empower him. Should we be surprised?

---

50 Ibid., 29

part three

❋

My philosophy professor Karl Kruger, like Karl Rahner, was German, and translated Rahner's major writings, his "Theological Investigations," into English. The Rahner that was presented to me was abstruse and his endless sentences did not help! It seemed there were no commas or periods in the German language! Needless to say I gave up trying even to read him, never mind understand him! But if the other side of Rahner, the one I know now, was proffered to me then, I would have lapped up his rich, spiritual, understandable and challenging writings.

The most revealing fact for me today is that his theology is profoundly simple! How come philosophers, spiritual directors, theologians and leadership never told me that? Another best kept secret, and, as the Jesuit Philip Endean says, "A message yet to be heard." He sums up Rahner's theology like this: "He is seeking to integrate the whole of Christian theology around one simple message: that God is a God of self-gift, a self-gift that can, however dimly and incompletely, be *experienced*. To refer all Christian doctrine, therefore, to the experience of God has the effect of concentrating and simplifying theology."[51] Simplicity! How we Westerners are scared of it, choosing instead complexity and sophistication! The *New*

---

51 **Karl Rahner:** *Spiritual Writings:* 26

Evangelization demands that we return to the simplicity of Jesus and the Gospels.

The glue that cements his theology and experience of God is prayer. Undoubtedly he was a man of prayer. How could he be an authentic and orthodox theologian otherwise? The fourth-century desert monk, Evagrius Ponticus, describes him well: "A theologian is one who prays and one who prays is a theologian." Once he concluded a philosophical argument with a former student of his with, "I believe because I pray."[52] Not the other way round! On the other hand, we are taught to believe first and then pray!

Needless to say that Rahner was a threat to leadership but he did have his admirers. His claim that 'spirituality' lies at the centre of theology was acknowledged and praised by many. Herbert Vorgrimler, a writer on Rahner, is one: "Rahner's theology has grown out of prayer, is accompanied by prayer, and leads to prayer."[53] How many leaders and theologians can lay claim to this and have it as their epitaph on their tomb? He was grounded in prayer because he says, "The spirituality of Ignatius himself, which we picked up through the regular practice of prayer and a religious formation, has probably been more significant for me than any learned philosophy or theology, whether inside or outside the Society (of Jesus)." What a humble admission from such a genius! Would that our seminaries could boast about forming their students in this manner!

We are born with the experience of God, as Jeremiah reminds us: "The word of Yahweh was addressed to me, saying, 'Before I formed you in the womb I knew you.'" Don't forget that 'to know' in scripture means intimacy. Speaking about his experience of God from infancy, Rahner likens his call to Jeremiah's: "There was nothing that I thought out or excogitated about you. Then my reason with its flip cleverness was still silent. Then you became, without asking

---

52   Ibid., 9

53   **Philip Endean:** *Karl Rahner and Ignatian Spirituality: 141*

me, the fate of my heart. You took hold of me—it wasn't that I 'comprehended' you."[54] All is gift!

Early in his life he expressed the above experience in a prayer: "Thanks be to your mercy, you infinite God, that I don't just know about you with concepts and words, but have experienced you, lived you, suffered you, because the first and last experience of life is you. Yes, really you yourself, not the concept of you, not your name which we give you.... [but] God of grace, my experience."[55]

"Six weeks before he died, he was at Heythrop College, London, for a celebration of his eightieth birthday. Many notable people were there to honour him and hear the guest lecturer, distinguished Oxford theologian John Macquarrie. Rahner sat centre-stage. Due to tiredness and little command of English he stopped trying to listen. Instead he took out his rosary, and began—quite visibly—to pray it!"[56] Here we have the beautiful, but rare combination of a brilliant theologian and devout and humble Catholic priest. No one has better articulated the simple truth: we *can* experience God. This is a new language that the average Catholic can learn and must be taught. But this will happen only if they first see it lived and hear it spoken by their leadership.

---

54 **Karl Rahner:** *Spiritual Writings:* 43

55 Ibid., 43

56 **Philip Endean:** *The Tablet*

part four

※

I am scared to take risks with the computer for fear of messing it all up and losing my document! Kids, on the other hand, are fearless and that's why they are so good on computers! Because the good news that *you* can experience God is foreign to Catholics, they are scared to risk it. We have such a poor self-image and false humility that it is going to take time to believe in ourselves. It is clearly implied that mysticism and the direct experience of God is only for the elite—whoever they might be!

The word "mystery" itself frightens us because we inevitably link it with the mysterious. When the Bible talks about "mystery" it means a definite plan that God has for God's people. The mysterious, on the other hand, is a dead-end street! The truth is that we all live mystery every day. Life, creation and people are mystery; not mysterious. We never fully understand this because the mystery is continually unfolding. God is not finished with us yet! Still, we talk as if we know all about ourselves but the truth is we know very little. In fact, what we call our 'self' is not self at all but our ego!

Living in mystery means living in experiences that are beyond our comprehension and totally transcend us. Why can't we simply admit that we are limited? We all can put after our name: "Ltd!" Whether we deny it or not, or are not even aware of it, we are in the "mystery." At the same time however, by the very fact that we are human, it means that we are capable of going beyond or transcending ourselves—with limitations of course. This is a tension that we do not like and will have to get used to.

Given this then, it is no big deal to include God as the ultimate mystery. The only difference is that God is infinite mystery. But that doesn't in the least pose a problem for us experiencing God, simply because our ability is pure gift from God. To put it crudely, we are wired for mystical experience!

It is in *awareness that we experience God as mystery.* But not head awareness! It is a sensed awareness of awe, wonder, of desiring what Ignatius calls the "more" even though we cannot name it; and what Sebastian Moore calls the longing for, "I know not what." This awareness is mystical and clearly a profound experience of transcending ourselves. We cannot find words to describe it but, as John Govan puts it, we are comfortable being, "Authentic in our inauthenticity!" This is because we experience a deep sense of harmony, oneness and peace. Accompanying all this is a profound sense of gratitude for life because we experience all as gift.

We find this beautifully described in Psalm 131: "I have not gone after things too great or marvels beyond me. Truly I have set my soul in silence and peace. As a child has rest in its mother's arms, even so my soul." We just rest in God. Most Catholics believe, wrongly, that you have to earn this by first enduring darkness. It's like purgatory first, then heaven! This portrays a mean kind of God who delights in making life difficult for us! John of the Cross offers this clear and comforting advice: "When the spiritual person cannot meditate, he [she] should learn to remain in God's presence with a loving attention even though he [she] seems to himself [herself] to be idle. Soon the divine calm and peace of God will be infused into his [her] soul. If scruples about inactivity arise, he [she] should remember that pacification of soul (making it calm and peaceful, inactive and desireless) is no small accomplishment."

Like me with the computer, we are frightened to take a risk and experience this mystical state. It's not our fault because no one has given us directions! When did you last hear a homily on this? Unfortunately, but it is the darkness that scares the pants off us! I was told that I had to first experience the darkness before encountering God. What that meant was that God was totally absent as if God had taken a holiday! Now I know that's just not true. So put this on your fridge: *THE DARKNESS IS NOT A PRELUDE TO EXPERIENCING GOD—IT IS GOD!* Yes, the darkness *is* God! God does not go on vacation!

The darkness that I experience is *me,* not God. It is the darkness of the inability of my intellect to experience God. So stop blaming God! Risk and stay with your darkness and you will experience it as light—as God. John of the Cross assures us that in this darkness all is well, "The soul feels the presence of someone and an interior strength; a certain touch of the divinity....experience and love of God."

part five

─✻─

Recent images of the distant Titan, Saturn's moon, were aired on television. Guy Consolmagno, a Jesuit, works at the Vatican Observatory. He pointed out the limitations of scientists to describe what their instruments had seen. Among other things, he had this to say about Titan: "We describe the unknown in terms of the things we know. That's the only way we can describe. All description is metaphor." What an apt description of God—the great unknown! All our descriptions of God are via the things we know and are therefore, not only limited, but naturally biased too. While we may not admit it or are not aware of it, God can be described only by way of metaphor. This means that whatever we say about God is severely limited.

Again, Karl Rahner points us in another and better direction: the experience of God which we *live* rather than describe. This experience is the result, not of intellectual analysis about God, but of surrender to the mystery that we are. Was that not also Mary's response? Realizing that her questioning and analyzing were going nowhere she surrendered, "Fiat." And then our good friend Job! After all his ranting and raving against God he too surrenders: "My words have been frivolous. I had better lay my finger on my lips....I will not speak again."

Rahner describes his own surrender: "My Christianity, when it understands itself aright, is the act of letting myself go into the mystery past all grasp. My Christianity therefore is anything but an 'explanation' of the world and my existence; it is rather the prohibition against regarding any experience, any understanding (however good and illuminating they may be) as finally and definitely valid, as completely intelligible in themselves."[57] Like Job, we have to quit banging our heads against the brick wall of intellect and surrender to the God beyond all that our mind can grasp.

This God of course is Immanuel, God-with-us, and more present to us than we are to ourselves. Jesus pointed to this in his teaching that the kingdom, the presence of God, is within us. Unfortunately, most Catholics are a rough block of marble waiting for a Michelangelo to come along and expose their potential to transcend themselves. There is a dire shortage of leaders who themselves are in touch with the kingdom within them, and so help bring it to the light of day in others. As an institution, we either forget or ignore the truth that every person is a God-bearer. So we teach and indoctrinate when we should be evoking. When I was in counseling and spiritual direction training, I was wrapped over the knuckles many times for teaching when I should have been calling forth and evoking.

We in leadership must get out of the mindset of teaching the 'experience of God' to our people. This is tantamount to indoctrination as if the person was devoid of an already existing relationship with God. As Rahner reminds us, what is at stake here is, "The coming more explicitly to the reality of the self, the free acceptance of the human constitution—a reality which is always there, mostly buried and repressed, but an inescapable fact."[58]

The presence of God in us he says is, "A reality of the human constitution." It is integral to who we are as children of God. It cannot be otherwise. So is the reality of the 'immediate experience of God.' It is not a question of importing God or imparting knowledge of God. But it is all about chiseling away at the block of marble to release that image buried and repressed in our people. The great Michelangelo's finished masterpieces always existed in the marble

---

57 **Philip Endean:** *Karl Rahner and Ignatian Spirituality:* 52

58 Ibid., 46

because they were first alive in his mind. Before we in leadership begin, the image we hope to release had better be alive in our minds too. If not, we will ruin an expensive block of marble!

Jesus, as always, is our model. He brought forth the best in people, less by teaching and more by evoking. He challenged them to reflect and come to a new awareness that ended in conversion. Take the woman at the well. Below her messed up life was a hidden energy that, when released by Jesus, launched her on a successful evangelization mission among her own people! Maybe we could take the woman of Samaria at the well as our patron saint for the *New Evangelization*!

WE TOO ARE LEPERS

For years, Fr. Damien was not accepted by the lepers on the Hawaiian island of Molokai. One night when he was washing his feet in hot water he sensed he had no feeling. He had contracted leprosy. That's when he began a homily one Sunday with the inclusive: "*We* lepers...." At last he spoke their language, was no longer an outsider and they welcomed him. We, the institutional Church, those of us in leadership, have to make a similar admission today. In general, we do not speak our people's language because we have set ourselves apart. When we teach and preach Evangelization we tend to stand aloof from our people. Like Damien the leper, we have to be inclusive.

Our people must experience us as much in need of Evangelization and conversion as they are—maybe even more so! Sadly there is no great evidence of this. The whole sex-abuse scandal is a blatant example of non-repentance on the part of bishops. Their fierce resistance to admit that they shuttled around abusing priests, and then step down, is a scandalous abuse of power.

A young priest from Ireland was appointed as assistant in a parish in Newmarket, England, the heart of British horse-racing! It soon became evident that he had a gambling problem. Not to mention that he spent his days visiting the stables and nights in the pub with the stable-lads! Instead of sending him to Gamblers Anonymous for treatment, his bishop assigned him to a parish in Slough at the other end of the diocese. The very first thing the priest noticed from his bedroom window was the dog-racing track! Talk about a coincidence! Conversion and Evangelization of the institutional Church cuts deep. Our Catholic people want to hear us begin our homilies like Damien: "*We* lepers...."

As long as we in leadership operate from the mindset of "them and us" we cannot be mentors of The *New Evangelization* and conversion. Spiritual pride is extremely subtle and very dangerous because it presents itself as something good. For example, we take it for granted that ordination automatically gives bishops and priests a leg up on the spiritual ladder!

I am shocked that even today seminaries are turning out priests who honestly believe they are 'spiritual directors,' like I did in my day. Ordination does not ipso facto make one a 'spiritual director.' But priests and bishops minister as if it did. This is a specialized field in itself requiring much study, emotional balance and lots of experience. The late James Gill, psychiatrist, priest and editor of the prestigious journal, *Human Development,* argued that Spiritual Directors should be licensed. This was mainly because of the damage that even trained Spiritual Directors can do. But also to affirm the professional status of trained Spiritual Directors.

Because we convey this erroneous belief to our people through our spiritual superiority, they come to believe it and in turn empower us in our sin! Now we have leadership and people living an illusion, a lie! It's the responsibility of us in leadership to shatter this and come off our 'spiritual' pedestal.

Health, while good in itself, got between Damien and his suffering people. Only when he became a leper like them did his ministry blossom. Titles, like good health for Damien, are obstacles to leadership in our ministry of Evangelization. They keep us perched on our spiritual roost and separated from our people. Furthermore, they are even blasphemous! In many countries, people call their bishop, "My Lord!" This is Feudalism and power at its worst. It's how the peasants had to address the gentry who literally lorded it over them like the slaves they were. Bishops are servants so the appropriate title would be, "My Servant!" Jesus called himself a servant and warned leadership to do likewise. If it was good enough for the boss then it is alright for the employee!

I cringe every time I hear people address the archbishop as, "Your Grace!" Because he is a step above a bishop, not in ordination but in power, this does not make him equal to God! Isn't Grace the gift of God's own self? For bishops and archbishops to continue this power-game betrays an addiction to control.

Perhaps our young people are seeing through all this hypocrisy. "John Paul 2, we love you," was their cry when they met with him. And he loved it! He didn't insist on titles like, "Your Holiness." He would have been the first to admit that he had no monopoly on holiness! Repeatedly he reminded us that holiness is the vocation of *every* Catholic. Accolades, honours, power and spiritual superiority are spots of leprosy and should be avoided like the plague! Damien the leper died on April 15, 1889 and was beatified in June 1995.

WE DON'T CREATE WE IRRIGATE

"Think of the heart as the soil. Is this soil to be condemned forever to barrenness? Is it a desert where the demons have their home? Or is it fertile land that brings forth eternity's fruits? The Church—so it can seem to us—sets up enormous and complicated irrigation systems in order to make the heart's soil fertile, through its Word, its sacraments, and its practices. Now all these "irrigation systems"—if one can put it this way—are certainly good and necessary...."

"Then what I am saying appears like this: besides these waters coming from outside, piped from outside that are meant to irrigate the soul's soil....there is a source, so to speak, drilled deep within the land itself. And so from this kind of source, drilled within, from the heart of the land itself, the waters of the living Spirit well up to eternal life—just in fact as it says in John."[59]

Karl Rahner's parable is a stern reminder that leadership is not creator but irrigator. It does not create the soil of God's presence in every person. Leadership's mission is to water a soil that is already fertile with the gift of God's self. It's fine for children to play God, but not for grown-up men in leadership roles!

The language leadership speaks suggests that they do actually create, and here is where we desperately need a new language. For instance, they talk about "The new life given in baptism." I think

---

59 **Karl Rahner:** *Spiritual Writings:* 68

most Catholics and leadership do believe that the institution pipes in this new life. Meaning, when a person is baptized, he or she experiences God and grace for the first time. This is not true. Neither is, "You will receive the Holy Spirit from the bishop in Confirmation."

This language smacks too much of the institution as spiritual creator. Through the celebration of the sacraments, leadership irrigates the fertile soil already created by God. Matrimony is one sacrament where we have it right. It is the couple who marry each other or celebrate the sacrament of Matrimony. The priest is simply a witness. Of course leadership's role is vital but it is always a secondary one. Why do we find it so difficult to know our place and keep it?

I headed for the missions in South America both as creator and irrigator! Well, I was not successful either way! I ministered alone in a large region that included a Leprosarium. In five years I didn't irrigate one wedding! But through operating out of this superior mindset, I did create lots of problems for myself. I felt frustrated, a failure and despaired at times. In my disillusionment I would often ask myself, "Is this all there is to being a priest?"

This idea of the institution being more a creator than irrigator is a throw-back to the Reformation. Among other things, the laity was excluded by heavy-handed clericalism. The main reformers like Luther, Calvin, and Zwingli, set about restoring the laity to their rightful place in the Church based on the priesthood of the laity. They tapped into the well of the fertile soil present in every person and irrigated it. This set the institution on the defensive, digging in its heels against reform. An enlightened laity was too much of a threat.

The reformers were four hundred and fifty years ahead of the institution, because only at the Second Vatican Council (1962—1965) did the bishops recognize the fertile soil. Up until then, any notion that the laity could personally experience God was anathema! What Pope Paul VI had to say in his introduction to a lengthy document titled, *Decree on the Apostolate of the Laity,* is very revealing: "The laity derive the right and duty with respect to the apostolate from their union with Christ their Head....they are assigned to the apostolate by the Lord himself." Notice that their rights, duties and assignment do not come from the institution!

Leadership's mission is to be a catalyst in helping people to become aware of their God-within and their dignity as a royal priesthood. This is less about piping in and more about extracting out! Since this style of leadership is more caught than taught, it has first to be lived. This will happen when leadership itself experiences radical Evangelization by drinking from the well. St. Francis of Assisi's advice to his Brothers is very relevant for leadership: They had been out all day evangelizing. During the evening meal one, disappointingly, said "but we didn't preach at all." "Your whole day was a sermon," replied Francis.

VATICAN STATE IS REAL ESTATE

The Vatican is the smallest sovereign State in the world: .44 sq km, with the Vatican City as its capital. In 2004 its population was 921, mainly staff, I presume. But how many actually work there? That was a question put to Pope John XXIII, and his answer: "About half!" Head of State is the Pope. Head of government is a Cardinal Secretary of State and the Cabinet is the Pontifical Commission, appointed by the Pope. So the Pope is not only a spiritual leader he is also the secular head of a country.

It came into existence with the Lateran Treaty between the Holy See and the Kingdom of Italy on February 11, 1929. This gave Roman Catholicism special secular status in Italy. Up to then, the Popes in their secular role ruled portions of the Italian Peninsula for more than a thousand years. In the middle of the nineteenth century, many of the Papal States [Real Estate!] were seized by the newly United Kingdom of Italy. Owning vast amounts of property and the abuse of wealth that went with it was a major cause of the Protestant Reformation in the sixteenth century. Popes took it for granted that it was a God-given right to be Real Estate agents and rule like kings. So much for the poverty that Jesus called for in the beatitudes: "Blessed are you who are poor....," and his warning to the wealthy: "Woe to you who are rich...."

Pope John Paul II rightly fought against the absolute power of world leaders whether communists or capitalists. Yet, ironically, he himself, like other Popes, retained it. The Vatican Website describes the Vatican State in these absolute terms: "The Vatican State is ruled in the form of an elected monarchy, for life. The Head of State is the Supreme Pontiff, who possesses full legislative, juridical and executive powers. These powers during the period of a vacant See, belong to the Sacred College of Cardinals." You cannot have more absolute power than that! As history proves, it is scary and dangerous.

While undoubtedly John Paul II achieved great things in his pontificate, he failed to reform his own house. In fact, he didn't even try. Instead, he chose to be a pastor and left the administration to the Curia and the folk had a heyday! A radical in-house *New Evangelization* is desperately needed. Pope Benedict XVI hinted that he would introduce reform but has backed off! Maybe he is not ready for martyrdom! Anyone who attempts to move round the furniture in the Curia had better be in a state of grace!

No doubt many, inside and outside the Curia, will argue for serving God and mammon, but the fact is that Jesus was absolutely clear that you cannot. The argument I heard growing up in Ireland for the wealthy Religious Orders educating the rich, was that they too had souls! That may be so, but the graduates of these elite institutions did not have much of a social conscience. You only have to look at Irish politicians to see the rogues, rascals and scoundrels that were turned out. The poor too had souls but they went to overcrowded and underfunded, government schools.

Jesus had no time for dabbling in Real Estate. For him; wealth, whether it be cattle, land, money or power, was an absolute obstacle to being his disciple. There was only one choice: get rid of it. He refused to be drawn into a problem two brothers had about sharing their inheritance: "Watch, be on your guard against avarice of any kind," he told them. Shakespeare echoed that with his, "Prosperity doth breed vice while adversity doth breed virtue."

Can you imagine what Jesus would say if asked about the Vatican State? "Get rid of it, right now!" Power and control are the root cause for holding on to Real Estate. This is nothing new in the history of the Church. Jesus had to contend with it and he didn't back down. The mother of two disciples, James and John, was on a power-hunt wanting a place of honour for them. Jesus knocked that one on the head right away: "You do not know what you are asking. Can you drink the cup [of suffering]?" Since his ministry was pure service he demanded the same of his followers—not positions of power.

THE COFFIN AND DIANA

Since I have lived most of my life without a television, I love listening to the radio. The Canadian Broadcasting Correspondent Laura Lynch, grabbed my attention when she reported on the funeral of John Paul II: "The power and the grandeur were on display but it was a plain cypress coffin that caught peoples' attention." Then a BBC correspondent in London was interviewed on the next day's wedding of Charles and Camilla. Well it was from the sublime to the ridiculous, the holy to the profane!

The correspondent left me in no doubt about what Camilla and Diana did *not* have in common. The British in particular and the world at large, blame Camilla for the break-up of Diana's marriage to Charles. They do not like her and the British public was not interested in her wedding. The correspondent went on to say that they were more taken up with the great British horse race, the Grand National, and were annoyed that it was delayed more than an hour to accommodate the wedding! The reason why the wedding was initially on Friday, he said, was so that the queen could watch the historical steeplechase on Saturday. But then the funeral of the Pope threw a spanner in the works, and she would be listening to Charles' and Camilla's repentance of adultery, instead of watching the race!

What does the Pope's plain cypress coffin and Diana have in common? *SIMPLICITY!* When Diana quit behaving as princess, acted like a human being, and reached out to the poor, the world sat up and took notice. While not a Mother Teresa, she opted for a relatively simple life, considering her position, and all the pressure that brought to bear on her. Yet, she was courageous enough to break free of most of the royal trappings and paraphernalia and be herself. The public loved her more as plain Diana than Princess Diana, and that is how they still remember her today.

It was not the grandeur and display of kings, queens, presidents, prime ministers, cardinals and bishops that touched the hearts of the millions who watched the Pope's funeral, but a simple, plain cypress coffin. That said it all. It stood out in total contrast to the ridiculous regalia and gaudy paraphernalia of cardinals and bishops. The simple coffin was a powerfully convincing homily, with not a word spoken! Francis of Assisi got it right: "Go and evangelize," he told his Brothers, "and use words only if you have to."

Like Diana, the Pope touched the world more by his humanness than his cleverness and need for power. He just had to be himself and, like Diana, break with ecclesial protocol—much to the annoyance of the Curia! His greatest gift was communication and that flowed because he was so comfortable with himself. He communicated what he believed and taught because, as one commentator put it, "He embodied the values he spoke." Like Diana, he did not have to lean on prestige, honour and power for support. As they say in the counseling world, he was totally transparent and congruent! The plain coffin was clear evidence of that.

Why does the simplicity of Diana and John Paul pull at the heartstrings of a world steeped in materialism, subjectivism, individualism and denial? It says they do not want to be there, that they feel trapped, helpless and unhappy. Most would not be able to articulate it as clear as this, but that is where they are at. Further, it speaks to the depths of who we are as human beings created in God's image and likeness. It tells us that the human soul has greater needs and aspirations which materialism, pomp and pageant cannot satisfy. And when people like Diana, Mother Teresa and John Paul II come on the scene, they stir into a flame that longing and restlessness for simplicity.

A plain coffin has spoken and reform for simplicity has to continue. First, the cardinals need to burn their regal attire because it reflects a monarchical bygone era. Second, the Curia must divest itself of power and control. Third, the Vatican State, as Real Estate, should go.

POPE TOO A DISCIPLE

When John Paul II was critically ill and the question of his resignation came up, many were absolutely scandalized at the mere mention of it. But the Pope himself scuttled that, as later we learned that he considered resigning in 2000! They not only had him on a high pedestal, but they refused to accept that the man was human and therefore limited. Peter, too, didn't want to let Jesus be human and go to his death when he tried to prevent him going up to Jerusalem. Failure to recognize a pope's limitations is tantamount to deifying him. They forget that popes were human enough to have mistresses and children!

It all goes back to detachment and trust. Jesus was only thirty-three, in the prime of his life, we would say, and yet he did not cling to power. And look at the ragtag that he left to continue his work! They were not only human but power-mongers, betrayers, cowards and had no theology degrees! But they did have confidence in the promise of Jesus: "I am with you always, to the end of time. Fear not." If it was alright for Jesus to let go then surely it is fine for a pope to resign because, after all, the boss is still around! John Paul was fond of repeating Jesus' assurance: "Do not be afraid." When we get upset about things like a pope resigning, the problem is less with him but points more to our insecurity. It means that we have put all our eggs in one basket! Dear old Peter is still alive and well in us!

I am fully confident that John Paul II would have been the first to admit that he too was a disciple of Jesus; that the student is not greater than the teacher; that no messenger is greater than the one who sent him; and the servant is not above the master. As one committed to the teachings of the Second Vatican Council, he would have been fully aware that his, "Teaching office is not above the word of God, but serves it...."

We give the pope a plethora of titles like, "Vicar of Christ," "Pontiff," "Holy Father," "Supreme Ruler," "Spiritual Head," and many more. How about throwing in a more appropriate one like, "Disciple," among these giants! A disciple is not only a companion of Jesus but is always a learner. The pope, like the rest of us, is never fully a disciple. There is still another title which we rarely use and I never heard it mentioned once by the media during John Paul's funeral: "*Servus Servorum Dei.*" It means, "Servant of the Servants of God." If you want the definition of a servant, don't look it up in a dictionary but go the Gospel of John, chapter thirteen, and observe Jesus washing the feet of his disciples. This is leadership in action and, don't forget, a picture is worth a thousand words!

A lot of attention was given by the media to Poland, the pope's home-country, stressing that he was the first non-Italian pope in four hundred years. Not a bad thing in itself! The story goes that John Paul had a vision of Jesus one night and put to him some pressing issues he had, like married clergy and women priests. Jesus assured him that none of these would happen, "In your lifetime, John Paul." Feeling relieved and confident, he asked Jesus if there would be another Polish Pope. Again, Jesus assured him: "Not in *my* lifetime, John Paul!"

On the lead up to the election of the next pope, people were speculating if it would be an African, Central American, Latin American or Asian pope. Europe and North America were not even in the running! But how about a Pope from Galilee? It's irrelevant where a pope comes from, for only if he is a companion and disciple of the Man from Galilee, does he have authority to shepherd and serve *His* Church.

A Pope from Galilee will, like his boss Jesus, be a sign of contradiction and just as upsetting as Him. Like Him, his strength to serve will not be in power, titles and prestige but in *weakness*. The macho Paul eventually came to this conclusion, to the extent that he was able to rejoice in his weakness and use it as his greatest vehicle to Evangelize. He pricks our balloon with this shocking claim: "In union with him [Jesus] we also are weak" (2 Cor. 13:4). We need popes who are weak enough to lead, not govern, and who are strong enough to resign!

EVANGELIZE THE CURIA

I t's often said that the Pope is a prisoner of the Vatican, meaning he is controlled by the Curia. Because of original sin this should not surprise us, but we must not make this an excuse against reforming it. Most new pastors are reminded in one way or another by parishioners: "This is how we do it here" meaning, don't rock the boat here! The great temptation for leadership is to settle for the status quo but then we hunker down to a comfortable existence and stagnate.

One could say that the Roman Curia is to the Pope what The Cabinet is to the Prime Minister. Some refer to it as "The Old Boys' Club!" The different groups which make up the Curia are called Congregations, Councils, Commissions, Committees and Services, numbering around thirty. They have a staff of about ninety. One very interesting fact stands out: Cardinals are in control of around twenty-five of them. If you were to pinpoint a specific group in the Curia to be *Newly Evangelized* it has to be the Cardinals because they wield the greatest power.

Listening to the radio on the first day of the election of Benedict XVI brought this home to me. The pomp, secrecy and mystery that surrounded what should have been an open and simple procedure, spoke of power-full men. For over a week they had been gathering informally in groups—with a bottle of vino!—to discuss the next successor of Peter. The Vatican vehemently denied that any politicizing went on but we all know differently!

Cardinal Ratzinger, the future pope, in his homily placed the responsibility mainly on the Holy Spirit and stressed the importance of prayer. However, if it is mainly up to God to decide then why gather to talk about it but instead, go to a monastery and spend the week alone in quiet prayer? I would love to know what the prayer of discernment was like! Was it prayer for enlightenment to guide their informal group discussions and then the formal ones? Or, I hope not, was it prayer bidding God to confirm whom they had already decided on in their small groups and vote as a block? All too often we take the latter route. I see it a lot with couples getting married. Little or no discernment goes on to know if God is calling them to the vocation of matrimony in the first place. Instead, the prayer of the matrimonial celebration is primarily about asking God to bless what *they* have already decided upon.

There are a lot of good principles on which to build reform but two stand out: the principle of Collegiality and the principle of Subsidiarity. Collegiality means a close working relationship of the bishops of the world with the Pope in shepherding God's people. The Second Vatican Council stressed the importance of this responsibility. But it has not yet got off the ground and the election of a new pope by a handful of Cardinals demonstrated this. Bishops will have to vigorously agitate to reclaim their rightful role and flatly refuse the 'privilege' of being 'raised' to a Cardinal. If they don't, then they have themselves to blame for being kept out in the cold. It's of interest to note that one does not have to be ordained to be a Cardinal and there have been laymen who were Cardinals. This is because being a Cardinal is about privilege and power. If Collegiality is working then *all* the Catholic bishops of the world, around four thousand, will be actively involved in the election of a pope.

The principle of Subsidiarity means that if someone else can do it I don't. When, as pastor I delegate, I empower my people. I am not granting them any privilege but giving them their rightful place in the parish community. Imagine if this principle were applied to the Curia! Look at how many cardinals, archbishops, bishops and priests would be freed up to work in parishes! They do not need to be in control of offices which could be well served by laymen and laywomen—maybe even better! But they would probably make money an issue! This is no excuse, for there are lots of semi-retired and retired Catholics who would gladly serve the church—salary free. And they are as capable, professional, and holy as the ordained—maybe even more! Then, instead of dishing out "Cardinal" titles, the pope would recognize that all Catholics have the grand titles of, "A chosen race, a royal priesthood, a holy nation and God's own people."

CARDINAL SINS

Every time, without fail, at forty-thousand feet they bank to the right exactly over the beacon. This has been their point of reference for up to fifteen hours non-stop flying from Asia to Vancouver and Western United States. I can see the flashing light of the beacon across the ocean on another island in the Pacific. It never ceases to amaze me the crucial role this little beacon plays in directing traffic from China, Korea, the Philippines and Russia to name a few.

As I reflect on the urgent need for reform in the Vatican, I ask myself what is the Pope's point of reference for appointing Cardinals?

The Vatican Internet, unashamedly, says of the College of Cardinals: "Among the College of Bishops, it has been a longstanding tradition of the Church, to raise certain bishops and archbishops to the College of Cardinals. The Cardinals have traditionally been seen as the "Princes of the Church." Because of their special devotion and holiness, they are called to assist the Holy Father in the governance of the Church. Most Cardinals are either Archbishops of the largest dioceses in their countries or regions, or the heads of the dicasteries of the Roman Curia (the Pope's Ministers of State, if you like)." I am not impressed! They are also given the honorary "governance" of one of the Parish Churches of Rome becoming the "parish priest" though living on another continent!

Hold up the beacon of the Gospel in one hand and the beacon of the world in the other, and the point of reference hits you between the eyes. The language alone, not to mention the mentality, speaks for itself. It is worldly, power-full, regal and monarchical. For example: they are *raised* to this position. They are seen as *Princes of the Church*. With the Pope, they *govern* the Church. They are the Pope's *Ministers of State*. Notice how it is not part of our Catholic Tradition, (large "T"), but a tradition, (small "t'), meaning a custom driven by the ways of the world.

Nowhere in the Gospels will you find anything that remotely points towards this. On the contrary, almost every page condemns such secularism and abuse. Poverty, Contempt for power and Humility characterize the beacon that is Jesus Christ. Power, Honour and Prestige describe the beacon of the world to which the College of Cardinals subscribe.

The mentality, language and behaviour parallel that of kings, queens, presidents and prime ministers. We see what corruption takes place in cabinets directly appointed by the prime minister. Favours are bestowed by the queen and powers of position given like we saw recently with Camilla as Duchess of Cornwall. The royal household, like the Pope, has absolute power to dish out rewards for loyalty. It's a case of you scratch my back and I'll scratch yours! The Pope's residence is called, "The Papal Household!" A priest, favoured with the title "Monsignor" is named to the Papal Household, a "Prelate of Honour." Proud of it, he puts PH after his name! I may be wrong, but I understand that the job of a Prelate of Honour was to empty the Pope's chamber pot in the days when there were no indoor toilets!

Attached to the Papal Household is the Diplomatic Corps where priests are trained as future diplomats to represent the Vatican State. They are given the grand title, "Apostolic Nuncio" and act like any ambassador does on behalf of the country he or she represents. What has all this got to do with the Gospel?

Up until 1978 the Pope was crowned, instead of consecrated, with a golden tiara similar to that of the pagan rulers of Persia. It was more a coronation rite resembling queens and kings. But John Paul I refused the crown choosing instead to be "installed" into his new "supreme pastoral ministry." John Paul II followed suit as did Benedict XVI.

Hopefully the next Pope will be a strong reformer who can break this unholy marriage with the secularism of the world and the purity of the Gospel. The College of Cardinals and the Curia will resist and fight it. So for a mitre he will need a helmet. For dress a bullet proof vest and for a crozier a pistol! Most important, he better always be in a state of grace!

RELATIONSHIP GRACE

part one

※

My oral exams for ordination were easier than preparation for First Communion! Both at school and at home I had pounded into me *the* definition of grace: "Grace is a supernatural gift bestowed on us by God for our salvation." There was no other definition! Only recently it dawned on me that what's missing here is *relationship*. Grace is defined as an item, a thing, an it, and doled out to us by a distant God. It is impersonal and concerned mainly about the next life. While it is a gift from God, there is nothing warm and intimate about this definition. We definitely do need a new language!

This definition is similar to how we defined matrimony prior to the Second Vatican Council: procreation was the main purpose. Again, no relationship. One priest I know put it crudely when he said that matrimony, in those days, was basically fornication legalized! Comments at baptisms by the parish priest in my home parish revealed the mentality that matrimony was primarily about parenting. After the baptism he would say to the parents, "I hope to see you all back here next year!"

The Council corrected this one-sided attitude by stressing that there is no primary and secondary end to matrimony. The couple's own relationship is equally as important as procreation, which makes perfect sense. After all, the couple came before the children and will remain after they have left the nest! Further, the greatest gift couples can offer their children is their love for each other. Matrimony is all about working on that relationship for their benefit as well as their children's. As in matrimony, we need to get a similar balance in our definition of grace.

I was taught that we ourselves could not earn this gift of grace which, of course, is true. However, in practice I was Pelagian, behaving as if I did earn grace, and the more the better! I think of all the plenary and partial indulgences I *earned,* particularly on the feast of All Souls. I was in and out of the church all day earning grace for the souls in Purgatory and sending them to heaven!

To speak of Jesus meriting grace for us is very abstract and non-relational. Along with this, it casts Jesus in the role of appeaser between God and us. It suggests that God was unwilling to give this gift freely and so someone had to earn it for us. That person is Jesus and he achieved this by dying for us. With this definition it is hard to see how grace is a *free* gift from God. Did it become a free gift after Jesus earned it? This, wrongly of course, depicts grace as independent of Jesus as if his part is pure mediator. In correcting this false image, Karl Rahner writes: "Grace is a concrete assimilation to Christ, a becoming part of *his* life. Thus it is the grace *of Christ,* not just in the sense that Christ has merited it for us...."[60] This means that we can only speak of grace *and* Christ as *one.* It moves from the image of grace *by him* for us, to grace *of him* in us. This puts it in a proper relational context.

Grace, as an intimate relationship of the gift of God's self, is clearly God's plan. We have only to read the scriptures to verify this. Grace as non-relationship is of our making and there is a reason for it. I believe it has to do precisely with the idea of relationship itself. The institution is all male and we know only too well how uncomfortable men in general are with relationships. Intimacy is very demanding because it calls for vulnerability. This in turn demands dropping our masks and giving up control, which we men find difficult.

---

60 **Karl Rahner:** *Spiritual Writings: 112*

Another reason why we shy away from grace as relationship is that we find it easier to give than to receive. At the centre of this is the control factor. When I give I am in control and when I receive I am vulnerable. God's grace is the gift of God's self and the response expected from me is the gift of my self. The couple is our best teacher here. It's not by chance that God and Jesus hold up sacramental couples as the prime example of how they love us. The two become one on their wedding day. The good news for us is that we experience grace and Jesus as one, like the couple, in a covenant relationship.

A COMMON LANGUAGE OF GRACE

part two

During the homily one Sunday I asked Joshua, a teenager, if he and his parents speak the same language. The whole family burst out laughing shaking their heads in disagreement! Initially at least, neither did Jesus and the woman at the well. When it comes to speaking a common language of grace, we in leadership, including teachers and catechists, fare poorly. Like Joshua and his parents, we are in two different worlds! We are outsiders looking into the heads of our victims (instead of their hearts) and stuffing them with knowledge. The conversion we need is to get inside and encounter the grace of God's presence that they already experience, and then talk the same language.

This should not be foreign to us if we are familiar with, and applying, the Rite of Christian Initiation of Adults in our parishes, schools and religious education. I am convinced that all religious formation, particularly sacramental preparation, should be based on the RCIA process (not program)! The final period of the journey, after reception into the Church, is called *Mystagogia*. It means deepening the celebration of the sacraments of Baptism, Confirmation and Eucharist primarily through reflecting, not teaching. Obviously something must be present to reflect on, so you will argue that we cannot have it at the beginning of the journey! Well, there is a lot present and much to reflect on right from the start! It all depends on whether your view is from a finite or infinite horizon!

Seeing the big picture, the infinite horizon, of God's relationship with us means this: every person, not just Catholics, is graced with the gift of God's-self from conception. The consequence of this is that we in leadership, teachers and catechists, do not lay the foundation. We build on God's foundation which is the person's immediate experience of God. This calls for a conversion in our thinking and approach, which must be primarily *Mystagogical*—right from the *start* of the journey and not only after initiation. This principle applies to all catechesis because we do not begin in a vacuum, as it were. Until we are convinced of this we will continue 'teaching' instead of facilitating reflection at *every* stage of the person's journey with God. Since we will not be speaking a common language we will frustrate a deeper encounter with God.

In 1960 Karl Rahner, utterly convinced of the *Mystagogical* approach, put it sharply, "When a person is summoned to the message of faith given by the visible Church, what this summons meets is not a person coming thereby (and hence through conceptual knowledge) into mental contact with the proclaimed truth for the first time. What the call does is to make reflectively available—in a way that is obviously necessary for a full and informed attitude about it—what was already there in the grace that was already encompassing them, inarticulately but really, as an element of their mental existence."[61]

This poses a tremendous challenge for leadership that, among other things, calls for great humility. However much we might like to believe it, we are not Jesus but we are John the Baptist pointing to him. To point a person in that direction means being more a facilitator instead of a teacher and this is something difficult for us in the West. Facilitating is an art that requires good listening skills, asks questions that help the person to reflect, is non-invasive, moves at the person's pace, has no hidden agenda, and is detached from any personal gain.

---

61 **Philip Endean:** *Karl Rahner and Ignatian Spirituality:* 48

But most important of all it means that we ourselves are in a responsive, living and growing relationship with our God-within. Only then are we on the same wavelength as our people, speaking the same language and being more their mentors than teachers. We must be like our computers: if we want them to speak to each other, they have to be compatible! And right to the point, Rahner declares: "These sorts of indoctrinations and commands from outside are only of any use if they meet the ultimate grace that comes from within."[62]

We have to move away from the prevailing mentality that grace is absent and somehow we make grace present through our teaching. That's not only seeing the glass as half-full, but as actually *empty!* As if God's glass could be less than full! As the psalmist says, "My cup overflows!"

---

62 **Karl Rahner:** *Spiritual Writings:* 69

GRACE IS ALWAYS ALREADY

part three

There is something about funerals that stir up in us a need to remember, not just the individual's life, but the immediate and extended families' as well. It's a time when they are vulnerable and feel the need to renew and strengthen family ties. I had this experience a few years ago at my mother's funeral. The persistent question I was asked by my relatives during the meal was, "Do you remember......?" Many of them I had not seen for years. Only when my cousin jogged my memory a bit did I recall particular happy times in the distant past. Soon I was caught up in this ritual and began asking the same question, "Do you remember....?"

Chatting with my ninety-year-old aunt flooded my mind with precious memories going back more than fifty years. She is a powerhouse of information and I could have listened to her all day. Recalling the past at a painful time like a funeral is good emotional and spiritual therapy. Of course there are other times when it can be embarrassing! Our neighbour, when I was still in nappies (no diapers then) never ceases to remind me about my tantrums! Apparently the cat kept a safe distance from me as I tried to grab it on my all fours! That's when I flew into a tantrum, but of course I don't believe it! Anyway, it keeps us bonded and gives us something to laugh about! The point is that we all have latent, lost, forgotten and even repressed memories and all it needs is a little prodding to surface them.

Grace, the presence of God's-self in us, is like that. For most Catholics, they have no memory of grace as God's presence in them, *always already*. At best, God is intellectually present, distant and recalled mainly in times of crisis. It's not their fault because no one has recalled for them the good news. But with a little jogging and prodding you would be amazed how quickly they connect with their hidden treasure: the God-within.

I experience this all the time in personal spiritual direction and guiding others. Coming to the overwhelming experience (not knowledge) of grace as God's self-gift, is like seeing the sun for the first time! What was always there, though smothered and unrecognized, stands out at the very forefront of one's consciousness. Now a relationship with God, that is as old as the individual, blossoms! Karl Rahner puts it better: "....the human person is always one who has already met God—and continues to meet God."[63] Why are we in leadership keeping such exciting news a secret from our people?

Maybe it's because we cannot get a handle on something that is constantly moving and changing. Grace as an object, a noun or a thing, we can control but grace as a verb, a living presence of God, is always surprising us and leaves us feeling redundant! As Rahner says, "A person is always a Christian in order to become one."[64] Relationships are dynamic, never complete, and so we cannot stand in the same river twice! This means that we are never fully anything; whether it is Christian, Catholic, married or ordained! We are always in a process of becoming!

Being in the process of a developing relationship with God means living with unfinished business: something which leadership in particular finds uncomfortable. How we love to tie up loose ends! To leave things hanging is totally alien to our Western culture because we look like we are not in control! While we may *take* control, we must not fool ourselves into thinking that we are *in* control.

---

63 **Philip Endean:** *Karl Rahner and Ignatian Spirituality: 155*

64 **Karl Rahner:** *Spiritual Writings: 133*

When we believe that we are, then we treat grace the same way that we in the Western world treat our planet. "The world about us," says Thomas Berry, "has become an 'it' rather than a 'thou.'" We look around us and see the irreparable damage we are doing because we view the planet as a mere object that has become the subject of our greed. To begin healing (because it is beyond repair) our planet these roles have be reversed: *we* must be the subject living in harmony with the planet that, like grace, is constantly emerging and in flux.

A practical start would be to change our language in speaking about grace. Since we experience grace as primarily a relationship, *always already,* we cannot talk about "actual" and "sanctifying" grace as we did. There are no categories, degrees or hierarchy of God's self-presence! Nor can we speak about being 'in' and 'out' of a "state of grace," and all the guilt with which we have burdened our people. This is a form of spiritual abuse. We are *always* in God's good grace!

THEOLOGIANS TOO ARE LEARNERS

On Sunday evenings I love to listen to "Sound Advice," an hour of classical music hosted by Rick Phillips. His detailed knowledge of composers and music is an invaluable source of education for an ignoramus like me! But his critique does have an air of arrogance when he rates a piece on a scale from one to five! Most of the theologians I have listened to and read would aptly fit into Rick's description! If so many believe that they are right and have a handle on God, how come they haven't got it right yet? They, too, need a *New Evangelization*!

As with grace and our planet, they treat theology as an object, as an 'it' instead of a 'thou.' It is heavily intellectual and lacking in relationship. But worse still, theologians teach theology without much evidence of it being personally integrated and transforming them into radical discipleship. As Karl Rahner rightly asserts, "*All theology must be theology of salvation [theologians' included]. It is impossible and illegitimate for there to be a theology that is merely "theoretical," fundamentally uncommitted.*"[65] I can count on one hand the times I heard theologians share their own personal experience of what they teach. They are as detached from it as the policeman is when he hands you a ticket for speeding along with, "Have a nice day."

"The gap," claims Avery Dulles, "that has developed since the sixteenth century between doctrinal theology (as something rigor-

---

65 **Philip Endean:** *Karl Rahner and Ignatian Spirituality:* 66

ously conceptual and scientific) and spiritual theology (as practical and hortatory discipline) has done harm to both theology and spirituality." Conversion for theologians will mean bridging this gap and, "Thus restore the idea of a Christian theology that takes proper account of worship, prayer, and the struggle to live according to the Gospel," says Dulles. In other words, says Dulles, practice what you preach!

The only definition of theology that I knew up until recently was that it is "The study of God." Like Paul, when I was a child I thought like a child and blindly accepted it! But now that I am grown up and think as an adult, I do not accept it because I see that something absolutely vital is missing: The 'thou' is absent! Moreover, how can we study that about which we can say nothing? The best that theologians can attempt (and with great limitations) is to describe God's *relationship* with us. This brings the *experience* of God to the forefront rather than dry intellectual theory about God. It shifts the focus to God continually communicating with us, and saving us, and away from theologians boxing God into a corner with all their clever arguments. It's the old control issue all over again!

Because the work of theology is to describe, not define, this experiential relationship with God, ".....it follows," says Philip Endean, "that it is always unfinished. We can never grasp it directly, but only move towards it. It is given us, not as something to be grasped, in a *Griff*, but as something calling us ever forward, a *Vorgriff*."[66] The latter is Rahnerian terminology and it means a "Pre-Conceptual Awareness" of that which transcends knowledge. It's somewhat like intuition or having a hunch about something. This points to the truth that I move and live in the realm of 'mystery.' I am driven forward with an insatiable desire for "I know not what" but nevertheless, I am aware of it though I cannot put it into words. This means that human knowledge is propelled by this 'Pre-Conceptual Awareness." With limitations, an analogy might help: My thoughts precede my

---

66 Ibid., 244

feelings so they cause my feelings. Likewise, "Pre-Conceptual Awareness" precedes knowledge.

I have worked for years with team-couples presenting Engaged Encounter, Marriage Encounter and Retrouvaille weekends. They speak with an authority because they speak from their relationship. When they present a talk on 'communication' for example, they first state the principles of good communication. That's the theory and not enough. They then go on to share how they live (and fail to live) these principles in their marriages. It is said that what is most personal is most universal. Only when theologians share from their own relationships with God, will they speak with authority. Jesus taught with authority because he spoke from his lived experience with God whom he called his "Abba."

THEOLOGIANS MUST KISS!

The mark of a great teacher is that he or she can break down what is complicated and make it intelligible and simple for the students. Recently I listened to a panel of high-powered intellectuals debating Einstein and how important his theory of "Relativity" is for the ordinary person like me! Thanks to their 'fairly simple' explanation and directions I went to the library and read a few books on Einstein! Something I always believed that was way beyond me. But it was one of the panelists who really got me going when she said that she teaches "Relativity" to twelve-year olds! Isn't she simply a great teacher!

If anyone told me that Rahner fits into this picture and that I would be studying him late in life, I would have mocked them! I am grateful to the Jesuit Philip Endean for this miracle today! As a great teacher himself, he has the gift of dispelling the lie about Rahner being untouchable! He makes him intelligible and enjoyable too!

Speaking about Rahner the theologian, Philip Endean says, "In one way, therefore, Rahner's theology—for all its verbal difficulty and intellectual subtlety—is profoundly simple. He is seeking to integrate the whole of Christian theology around one simple message: that God is a God of self-gift, a self-gift that can, however dimly and incompletely, be experienced. To refer all Christian doctrine, therefore, to the experience of God has the effect of concentrating and simplifying theology."[67]

---

67 **Karl Rahner:** *Spiritual Writings:* 26

Who would have ever thought that the giant Rahner could be described in such clear language that the layperson can understand! "One simple message!" It reminds me of John the Evangelist. In his last days, we are told, his constant and simple message was: "Love one another." Jesus, too, kept it simple and yet profound. The conclusion for today's theologians is obvious: They must "KISS:" Keep It Simple Somehow!

We see something of Rahner's humility and simplicity in his work where he is Ignatius speaking to a modern Jesuit: "People have often accused your theology of being cheaply eclectic [selective]. There is of course something right about that charge. But if God is the 'ever greater God,' who outstrips every system within which humanity seeks to bring reality under its control, then your 'eclecticism' can also perfectly well be an expression of how God can be too much for humanity and of how humanity willingly accepts that divine being-too-much. After all, in the end there is no system within which a person, from the one point at which they stand, could take in the whole. Your theology should not operate lazily, in cheap compromises. But a thoroughly elaborated, transparent system in theology would be a false system. In theology too you are pilgrims seeking the eternal homeland of truth, in an Exodus ever new."[68]

Clearly, Rahner is talking to himself here but his message is universal, particularly for theologians. If people put him on an intellectual pedestal, he had no illusions about his limitations. And, as Philip Endean tells us, he was not ashamed to admit them: "In his last years, Karl Rahner would often speak of the permanent tension in his theology arising from its two different starting-points: the historical and the transcendental. He did not know how they fitted together. He could only retreat into piety: maybe God would show him the answer in heaven."[69]

Mistakenly, theologians start from the 'divide and conquer' approach breaking up theology into tracts like Grace, Sacraments, God

---

68 **Philip Endean:** *Karl Rahner and Ignatian Spirituality: 259*

69 **Karl Rahner:** *Spiritual Writings: 149*

and the Trinity. I prefer to call this 'the control' method! One of our seminary theologians used to demonstrate this when he would come out with sayings like, "I want to finish off Grace (Sacraments, even God and Trinity!) today!" He felt he had conquered something by tying up some looses ends! It's like the difference between men and women shopping: men are conquerors while women are hunters!

Theologians have to start with the big picture: God's loving relationship with us, and let things hang loose! It's so simple! Rahner warns them that they can only come to his non-neatly parceled expression of theology....."with an indulgent benevolence, to see its approaches, basic tendencies, ways of putting questions, as more important than its 'results'—results which, in the end, cannot after all be definitely valid."[70] It goes totally against the grain for the institution and theologians to ask questions.

> *He who gives the asker answers*
> *ties the asker.*
> *But he who makes the asker answer*
> *makes the asker answer-master!*

---

70 **Philip Endean:** *Karl Rahner and Ignatian Spirituality: 149*

BENEDICT BENEDICT BENEDICT

There was a lot of speculation as to why the Pope chose the name Benedict XVI. A glance at two other Benedicts might give some indication.

Pope Benedict XV was an Italian Archbishop who became Pope in 1914 and is remembered best for his attempts at peacemaking. He proposed a peace plan to end World War I in 1917, but was basically ignored. The French called him the German Pope while the Germans called him the French Pope! You are damned if you do and damned if you don't! But he persisted in his efforts. It is said that he was so dedicated to war relief that when he died in 1922, the Vatican was almost bankrupt and they had to borrow money for his funeral!

The present Pope has come on the scene when the world is split at just about every level: marriages; parishes; dioceses; rich and poor; West and East; subjectivism and objectivism; First world and Third World. But the big one is the split between the conservative and liberal, the right and the left-wing Catholics. As a peacemaker, he sure has his work cut out for him, and he will be damned if he does and damned if he doesn't!

Then there is Saint Benedict, the founder of Benedictine Spirituality. The Benedictines' motto is "Pax," meaning, "Peace." Do you know the reason why there is just one Benedictine monastery in Ireland? You would never get the Irish to live in peace and subscribe to the Benedictine motto, "Peace!" As a young man, Benedict went to Rome to study but he soon became disillusioned and threatened by the vice and sophistication that he encountered there. So he left, embraced the ascetical life and became a hermit on Mount Subiaco. That was fifteen-hundred years ago and things haven't change since! They say that if you want to lose your faith, live in Rome!

His life of prayer, penance and solitude attracted the monks of a neighbouring monastery and they invited Benedict to be their superior. But his serious way of life was too much for them, so they rebelled and they tried to poison him! Because of the hostility of a parish priest, Benedict left Mount Subiaco for Monte Cassino where he spent the rest of his life.

If the present Benedict, like his Benedict predecessors, sees himself as a peacemaker and reformer he had better be under no illusion. His greatest opposition will come from within his own household: the Curia. The folk will be hostile like the parish priest and rebel like the monks! So Benedict XVI would be smart to make his own cappuccino and never leave it out of sight! We don't want a repeat of 1978 when the Cardinals had to go back to Rome after a month to elect another pope!

The English writer, Lavinia Byrne painted a delightful picture of where Benedict needs to begin his reform: "The late John Paul was the captain of the ship who left the steering to his first officer. He spent his days chatting with the passengers, playing with the children, singing with the teenagers and waving to the passing ships. Meanwhile the engineer neglected to service the engine, so Benedict needs to don his overalls, go down into the engine-room and get his hands dirty. A mere oil change will not do because the engine is in immediate need of a major overhaul." She is of course referring to the Curia! While many ask if Benedict is up to the challenge, she pointed out that the problem lies less with him and more with the structure.

Clearly the Benedictine "Pax" is not peace at any price as is evidenced in the life of Saint Benedict. It is the peace of Jesus which disturbs people and leads them to conversion. To initiate this, the present Benedict will need to be as free as Jesus. This will come from, as John Paul repeatedly encouraged, a fresh and personal encounter with Jesus. In this sense, Benedict, like the rest of us, is in need of daily conversion.

Hospitality and care of the poor are very special Benedictine virtues. The greatest legacy to our Benedict's reform would be, like Benedict XV, to leave the Vatican broke and we had to pass around the hat to bury him!

SACRAMENTS ARE SECONDARY

I 'made my First Communion' in 1948. The Second Vatican Council lasted from 1962-1965 and the Catechism of the Catholic Church was published in 1992. All three dates have one thing in common: They give the same definition of sacraments: "A sacrament is an outward sign instituted by Christ to give grace!" Vatican II said: "....they do indeed impart grace, but, in addition, the very act of celebrating them disposes the faithful most effectively to receive this grace in a fruitful manner...." The Catechism teaches: "The sacraments are efficacious signs of grace, instituted by Christ and entrusted to the Church, by which divine life is dispensed to us."

This definition forces me to ask: Did Jesus institute sacraments as we define them today? Is the institution putting words in his mouth? What do we mean when we say Jesus entrusted them to the Church? Or did the institution stage a coup d'etat? It would appear it did because it fits in with our Constantine model of a monarchical Church which Jesus definitely did not entrust to us! In this respect, as in so many other examples, the institution has lost touch with its roots. In the celebration of the sacraments, at least in practice, the institution sees itself as primary while God's relationship is secondary.

The writer of the fourth Gospel, John, reminds us how we must reverse that order and not rush and take our seats at the head of the wedding table! Being human, the institution loves to take the best seats! "This is the love I mean," he says, "not our love for God, but *God's love for us*...." And like all good teachers, he repeats it later on: "We are to love then, because *"he loved us first."* Sacraments are celebrations of our response to God's life and love already in us, in which case, the institution is enabler, and not initiator or dispenser of grace.

It follows that sacraments, like the institution, are secondary because without God loving us *first* there is nothing to celebrate. The institution does not lay the foundation but builds on that laid by God. Therefore the institution's teachings and involvement in the sacraments are of no value unless, as Karl Rahner reminds us, "They meet up with the ultimate grace from within."[71] In other words, the institution is always John the Baptist, pointing to and helping people to appropriate the grace *already* present.

What Rahner says about the process of assisting a non-Christian to come to this appropriation, will help to clarify: "Fundamentally, the Christian can only do the following: presuppose that there is already present within the person who hears, in the root of their being, an understanding offered to the freedom of faith, and tell this person, through an objectifying articulation, the understanding they have already been given. If the hearer also accepts the Christological statement explicitly, the speaker in this case has not in any proper sense brought forth this understanding of faith, in its primordial unity, but only brought it to itself in objectifying concepts."[72] The institution is like a midwife who helps to bring a baby, which it did not create, to the light of day. It clarifies and articulates for the non-Christian God's presence already residing in him or her.

Going through different immigration stages in coming to Canada reminds me of similar juridical stages that the institution calls for in the celebration of the sacraments. First, I came on a student visa, then a visitor's, followed by a work visa and now I am a Landed Immigrant, but not a Canadian Citizen. However, my fundamental status as an Irish Citizen has not changed at all; nor would it if I became a Canadian Citizen. Baptism, Confirmation and Orders stand

---

71 **Karl Rahner:** *Spiritual Writings: 69*

72 **Philip Endean:** *Karl Rahner and Ignatian Spirituality: 231*

out as examples of this secular pattern of the institution which only reinforces its power.

As things stand today, Baptism is incomplete because you do not get all the Spirit! In most dioceses, you have to wait as long as twelve years for that in Confirmation! But Orders is even more disorderly! The priesthood of Jesus is divided up into priesthood of the people, deacon, priest and bishop. How presumptuous! The institution is like Immigration Canada dishing out various sacramental visas along the way! It presumes the right to divvy out categories of relationships with God, forgetting that sacraments, like me with Immigration Canada, do not alter our fundamental status with God. God shares God's life one-hundred percent with us *before* and *after* the sacraments.

"Rahner's account," says Philip Endean, "acknowledges the real presence of God's grace outside official sacramental channels, and thereby represents a liberation which Catholic awareness still needs to appropriate."[73] The institution too needs to be *Newly Evangelized*!

---

73 Ibid., 247

POWER OF SACRAMENTORS

After we were ordained, we carried around with us the Oil of the Sick (the 'holy oils' in those days!) in case of an accident and we gave the "last rites" there on the spot. I can smile now but we were serious and meant well because that was our Catholic tradition then.

I am writing this reflection during the 'holy week' of Cheltenham races where the Irish clergy gather in droves! Give them their due, they teach their housekeepers not to lie, so they have this to say when parishioners phone to see Father: "Sorry, but he is on a 'course' for the next four days and will be back Saturday evening." Most Irish clergy consider it their right to be chaplains to the racecourse and golf course! Two stories highlight what I mean about the "Power of Sacramentors:" Last night I checked the Internet for the winners at Cheltehham and came across the following headline: "Fr. Seán Breen is an avid [compulsive!] race-goer."

Before flying out from Ireland to England, the article said, he made a pastoral visit to an Irish stable to bless the horses due to race in Cheltenham! In fairness, it didn't say he anointed them, but it wouldn't surprise me if he did! One fancied horse in particular, became a doubtful runner due to 'sudden' illness and was even scratched a week prior but then 'miraculously' recovered, after the blessing, to win the Cheltenham Gold Cup—at a good price! Knowing what I do about the crooked racing world, it ain't no miracle! Then on St. Patrick's Day he "held mass" at one of the hotels for the Irish (for their good intentions of course) attended by two hundred, supporting "race cards!" And on it went!

The serious side of this is that it portrays the clergy (and institutional Church) as powerful dispensers of grace—including the grace to back winners! It's a case of going from the sublime to the ridiculous! We in leadership have an inflated view of ourselves when it comes to celebrating the sacraments.

My other horsey story points in the same direction. One racing correspondent spiced his report on the English Grand National with a bit of humour and cynicism! Monday's headlines of the Daily Express read: "Paddy Farrell was seriously injured when Overshadow fell at Becher's Brook and as he lay on the turf, half the grandstand stood up to give him absolution!"

It is inevitable that priests and bishops are addicted to power which we are not always conscious of, and this makes it more dangerous. Our ecclesiastical language speaks for itself. We talk about the 'power' of ordination, the 'power' of the sacraments, the 'power' of the Mass, grace as a 'powerhouse' and so on. We need to watch our language! Coupled with this is the fact that we are male, and men are macho, powerful and take control. So we operate out of this illusion that we are 'spiritual' powerhouses!

Contrast all this with our boss, Jesus, and one questions if we are working *with* him (not *for*) at all! When we work *for* him we call the shots. Not only did he speak the language of weakness, he lived it to the hilt. This is the primary quality he looked for in his disciples and he blasted the powerful. The writer of an article on seminary formation put the following question to seminarians: "Are you *weak* enough to be a priest?"

For this to be effective and taught, the seminary staff need to ask themselves the same question. If not, priests will continue to be turned out under power-full illusions. Because they read a few books, attend a few lectures, write an essay and get a Masters in Theology, they believe they are fully equipped. Imagine, mastering the study of God! If they want more power, then they read a few more books, attend a few more lectures, write a longer essay and they are Doctors of Theology! Or better still, Doctors of Divinity! Now they believe that they can actually diagnose God! It is from this power base that they, and the rest of us, operate as sacramental dispensers of grace.

"Sacraments," says Karl Rahner, "are celebrations of what is already there [a "thou" relationship with God] in human experience." Our role then is secondary and simple. It's like the rider of the horse who lies when he takes the credit for jumping the fences. The horse deserves all the praise while the rider's role is secondary in assisting the horse to clear the big obstacles.

FIDDLING WHILE ROME BURNS

The Roman Emperor Nero was an absolute tyrant and incapable of feeling. From what we know about the human psyche today, we can conclude that he was a psychopath. He had his mother and wife killed while he kicked his mistress to death when pregnant. In the year 67 he had Peter and Paul put to death.

The city of Rome burned down in the year 64 and Nero, a pagan, blamed the Christians, though it's likely that he set fire to it. Meanwhile, as it continued to burn he played on his violin. Hence the saying: "Fiddling while Rome burns." The Roman historian Tacitus tells us how he treated the Christians: "He covered some with skins of wild animals and left them to be eaten by the dogs. Others he nailed to a cross. Many he burned alive and set on fire as torches at night."

When we personally dither, don't take responsibility and pass the buck instead, we too fiddle while Rome burns and we know others who do the same. It means that we continue to work as normal and not pay any attention to something important and unpleasant that needs to be addressed. Among others, the international priest sex-abuse scandal stands out. Bishops around the world and Rome itself fiddled, and continue to fiddle, while Rome is burning. It's a weird twist of irony that, two thousand years later, Rome still fiddles!

One of the most blatant and recent examples is that of Bishop Krenn of Austria. News of the horrific scandal of homosexuality and pornography in a seminary in his diocese eventually broke. Pictures were published of the rector and vice-rector kissing and fondling seminarians at a Christmas party. One seminarian was charged for downloading 17,000 images of child pornography. Of course the usual response was denial. The rector and vice-rector protested their innocence although they admitted the pictures were genuine. Krenn described the pictures as "boyish pranks" and compared the goings-on at the seminary to English people kissing under the mistletoe at Christmas—and refused to step down.

A courageous Cardinal Christoph Schoenborn, Archbishop of Vienna, stepped in and lashed out at the Vatican for fiddling while Rome burns: "I cannot hide my distress and anger and don't see why the Austrian Catholics should have to put up with this," he wrote. "The seminary scandal had "once again" discredited the entire priesthood," he said.

It was not as if the Vatican was ignorant of what was going on. The Austrian bishops, two years earlier, had warned Bishop Krenn against opting out of the nationwide formation programme for seminarians. They also protested against his policy of accepting candidates who had been rejected by other dioceses but Krenn ignored them. The Austrian Bishops and papal nuncio to Austria warned the Vatican saying the scandal over homosexuality and pornography could have been avoided had Rome listened. Two year's fiddling makes you ask "when is enough, enough?"

The then Cardinal Ratzinger, now Pope Benedict XVI, eventually became involved and attempted to calm the storm. Asked by the media why the Vatican fiddled, he replied: "Church management does not always function the way people want it to. Rome needed to proceed slowly and be quite sure before acting, but of course a fire can break out before we have collected all the evidence. In general, we should all face crises more calmly." Meaning, we should all fiddle while Rome burns. And so the denial and power-game continue to be played out.

This kind of insensitivity and irresponsibility clearly points to a leadership that is focused more on its own reputation than the truth. How do we hold bishops like Krenn accountable for his abusive behaviour, and the Vatican for its silence? During the height of the clergy-abuse scandal, the President of the United States Conference of Catholic Bishops was in no doubt about where accountability lay. Asked why bishops did not resign because of the role they played, he made it clear that they are accountable to nobody but the Pope. That's like claiming diplomatic immunity for a crime! While the call for The *New Evangelization* by John Paul II came *from* the Vatican, we have yet to see signs of it taking root *in* the Vatican!

Nero and the Vatican have three things in common: absolute power, accountable to nobody, and fiddling while Rome burns.

PEOPLE STRENGTH

Tens of thousands of mothers, fathers, brothers and sisters of the soldiers met them head on in the streets of Manila and dared to look down the barrel of their guns. Not a shot was fired and peacefully, the Philippine dictator Marcos was toppled. For weeks, the people of Ukraine took to the streets and eventually ousted their pro-Russian dictator without violence. The Lebanese people ended their oppression by Syria through peaceful protest.

In so-called democracies the people are meant to exercise their right through the ballot box. The problem is that when they kick out one corrupt Party they replace it with another because honest politicians are a rare specimen. Such is politics worldwide and our Western capitalist system is no different. No wonder they call politics a dirty game. In Canada, the theft and squandering of hundreds of millions of tax-payers' hard-earned money through the Sponsorship Programme scandal, is just the tip of the iceberg. Here we have institutional sanctioned theft which is fair game, till you are caught. But if I cheat on my tax-returns for as little as a hundred dollars I am hauled before the courts.

While governments steal our money, among other things, we have the Vatican stealing our rights, among other things! And the root cause of both is abuse of power which translates into disrespect for the people and no accountability to them. The politicians soon forget that it is the people who put them to govern in the first place. The Vatican has long forgotten that the people, a royal priesthood, are the Church and have a God-given right to be heard and have input into decision-making.

It is time we spoke a new language when we refer to the "Church." Let's be quite clear that the Church is the *whole* people of God. Leadership is included but is *not* the Church. Ask the average Catholic who the Church is and he or she will tell you it is the pope and bishops. Catholics just do not know who they are and leadership will not tell them! The pope and bishops will have to clean up their language because when they speak about Church they mean themselves. When they make statements on certain topics and use language like, "The Church teaches....," it is not true. The people had no input and most of them probably disagree anyway with the particular teaching. What they should make explicit is that leadership, the pope and bishops are the magesterium and teach, which is their job. But they must not equate leadership with Church and be clear that the Church is more than them.

The laity have no say in choosing a bishop, for example, and the secrecy surrounding the election of the Pope is almost like that of the Freemasons. It was not until 1059 that popes were elected by the College of Cardinals. During most of the first Christian thousand years, they were elected by the laity and clergy of Rome because the pope is the bishop of Rome. This raises an interesting question: Is the bishop of Rome the pope or is the pope the bishop of Rome? Right now it clearly appears that the pope is the bishop of Rome which seems like the cart is before the horse.

If the pope is first the bishop of Rome, then that really simplifies matters and it makes more sense too. Let the Vatican return ownership to the people as before and they and the clergy elect their bishop who automatically becomes pope. This would eliminate a grand performance of pageantry by the Cardinals which has no precedence whatsoever in the Gospels.

Without the Church (the people, and in particular, parents) there would be no pope or bishop! It's they who have the final say because they are the suppliers of leadership and today they are voting with their feet. In North America, 60-percent discourage their children from being a priest, 20-percent are indifferent, so only 20-percent are supportive.

Leadership in the early Church recognized and respected the priesthood of the people. Cyprian was elected bishop of Carthage by the clergy and people around 250. Later he wrote: "I decided to do nothing of my own opinion privately without your advice and the consent of the people." Pope Celestine I in the fifth-century was more explicit: "No bishop is to be imposed on unwilling subjects, but the consent and wishes of clergy and people are to be consulted." Later in the same century Pope Leo I was even more emphatic: "On no account is anyone to be a bishop who has not been chosen by the clergy, desired by the people, and consecrated by the bishops of the province with the authority of the metropolitan."

Politicians cry out: "Give us your vote," and that's the last we hear of them till the next election. The Vatican and bishops plead with parents: "Give us your sons." Maybe they need to demand: "Give us back our rights!"

THE SALMON AND THE TRIDUUM

Many Catholics do not know what "The Triduum" means and few experience it. Holy Thursday, Good Friday and Easter Vigil make up the three days we call "The Triduum." They are three actual days but are celebrated as one event. One rolls into the other. At the end of the Eucharist on Holy Thursday there is no blessing, dismissal or final hymn like on Sunday, because we have not finished, but will pick it up again on Good Friday. The same happens again here; there is no blessing, dismissal or hymn because we will continue with the blessing of the fire at the Easter Vigil. Without this rudimentary understanding, you will not make the connection between the salmon and The Triduum and my own personal Triduum experience.

I live on an island in the Pacific, about one hundred miles off the Northwest coast of British Columbia where salmon abound. My first catch weighed over twenty pounds, more than ten kilograms! Recently, I visited a fish hatchery where salmon are reared and then let loose in the Pacific. After three to five years of swimming around the world, they return either to the hatchery or natural habitat where they were spawned. This is a miracle. The effort they make to swim upstream to this point leaves them in poor shape; battered, exhausted, and near death.

So many crowded the river at the mouth of the hatchery that I could literally stoop down and pluck a twenty to thirty-pounder out of the water. They were so tightly packed that I could risk walking across them! Watching these giants leaping, desperate to get into the very hatchery where they were reared, made me feel very sad, because they were denied entry! They had to move on quickly and find a natural spot to spawn in the river and die. That's exactly what happens: after she lays her eggs the salmon dies. And all this to provide the likes of me with new delicious salmon steaks years later! They literally give their lives for me! Like Jesus at the Last Supper, they say to me: "This is my body given for you."

That's the story of the salmon and The Triduum! It's similar to the celebration of the Easter Vigil where I celebrate the new life Jesus gives me in his resurrection. Each time I eat salmon, I am celebrating the new life that this salmon's parents gave me! And so the dying and rising cycle continues!

That is all nice in theory, academic and even nostalgic. The great challenge is to apply it and live the salmon and The Triduum experience on a daily basis. If discipleship and The Triduum are not practical, they are useless. They were dead practical for Jesus and they are for the salmon too! My personal Triduum experience could not be more earthy!

My fourteen-year old pick-up truck and I have gone through turbulent times lately, almost ending up in divorce! Erratic starting, letting me down and not being able to diagnose the problem brought out the worst in me. In preparation for my Sunday tour of the island I started it at nine and again at ten. But at eleven when I was leaving it failed like it did the previous Sunday! Frustrated and angry and running behind time for the one hundred kilometre trip, I went begging for the second time! I hate begging because I don't like being vulnerable and dependent.

The previous Sunday, a neighbour heard me trying to start and gave me a ride to the nearest mission station. Several times a parishioner has brought me home. This Sunday I asked a lapsed Catholic for a loan of her car and, to my surprise, got it! When I returned it in the evening I was shocked: she had a delicious meal prepared for me! Resurrection experience!

I experienced death in my anger, frustration and begging. The important point here is that I was *aware* of those negative feelings at the time. I was *aware* that I was called to die to being in control. While the feelings did not disappear, awareness cushioned the blows! My resurrection *awareness* was how this death called me to reach out for help, involve others in my helplessness and come home to a fine meal. This is living The Triduum, death and resurrection in the raw of daily life! It is the daily cycle of desolation and consolation, and *awareness* is the key to new life.

WE HAVE COLONIZED GOD

Bursting with excitement and enthusiasm I headed for the missions in South America as a spiritual colonist! The colonizers had conquered the people and their land for themselves but I would conquer them for God! While the ends were different the means were the same—the imposition of a superior, western religious culture. I never heard about 'indigenization' which means respecting the local culture, and believing that God had already arrived there long before me! Instead of exposing their inherent experience of God, and building on it, I imposed my Irish version of Catholicism!

I didn't go as far as my brother missionaries in Africa, baptizing the local boys, "Patrick" (and of course St. Patrick's Day was celebrated with the same gusto as back home!) We didn't know better, we did our best and God continues to write straight on crooked lines! The proof is that today we have what we call 'mission in reverse' with African priests ministering in Ireland and former colonizing countries. Hindsight is twenty-twenty and today we focus on indigenization which involves receiving as well as giving.

It's amazing how the original sin of 'control' has so much power over us because that's what colonization was all about. We were so good at it that we even attempted to colonize God too, in obvious and subtle ways. But this is not our big sin! Our greatest sin is that we actually believe we have domesticated God, got a handle on God as it were! We are confident that we have achieved this through our power of reasoning, logic, theology and philosophy.

We started colonizing the God of the Bible through imposing our rational approach on the scriptures. We largely ignored the fact that the Old Testament people and writers were not the least interested in our philosophical speculation. Their view of God's relationship was more concrete, earthy and intimate, more to do with the heart than the head. The distinction between essence and existence, for example, was totally foreign to the Hebrew mind. Like me on the missions, we imposed rather than exposed.

The approach to theology, up to the twelfth-century, was primarily mystical and spiritual. With the coming of universities at this time, the emphasis became mainly intellectual. This was the age of what we call Scholasticism, meaning 'Schoolmen.' The great thinkers like Bernard of Clairvaux, Anselm of Canterbury, Albert the Great, and Thomas Aquinas, introduced the place of reason in their attempt to understand God. They opened up the need for a critical reflection on the faith.

Scholastic theology was correct to teach that reason does have a role to play. But Scholasticism had its weakness too in that it did not always recognize the limitations of reason. The Scholastics tended to rely too heavily on reason and logic. Unfortunately some took the new emphasis on reason to its extreme which reduced theology to mere terms and concepts. The Bible and the writings of the Fathers, which influenced theology up to this era, often took second place.

"Read the text," was the constant refrain of my scripture professor! He stressed the importance of studying scripture in its original setting and literary meaning. This meant going right back to the culture in which the writer spoke and wrote and what it meant for *them.* For example: What were the *actual* words of Jesus? Who was he addressing and where? What did the apostles *speak* before they wrote? For whom did they write? The Scholastics tended to ignore this and treated scripture as a collection of independent sayings which they used to support their particular theological or philosophical arguments. In other words, they were colonizers! As an aside, it is vital to know that scripture was taught and lived before it was written. In other words, the people came before the book!

We see the extreme their distinctions and sub-distinctions in theology went to in absurd questions like: "How many angels can dance on the head of a pin?" This points to the useless arguments that emerged at that time. Sadly, this attitude still lingers in the minds of theologians and philosophers today.

"The Protestant Reformers," says Richard McBrien, "accused theologians of trying to domesticate God by making God a topic among topics in our theological and philosophical systems." The pendulum towards rationality has swung to the extreme and needs to be balanced with a more mystical approach. The greatest thinker of that period, Thomas Aquinas, came to that conclusion when he wrote: "Man's utmost knowing of God is to know that we do not know him." This was when he underwent a profound conversion experience and quit working on his famous *Summa Theologiae:* "The whole of Catholic theology." Asked why he stopped writing, he replied: "I cannot go on....all that I have written seems to me like so much straw compared to what I have seen and has been revealed to me." He died three months later in 1274.

SLOW LEARNERS!

Many bishops around the world just don't seem to get it. The magnitude and pain of the horrendous sex-abuse scandals seem to run off them like water off a duck's back. It appears that they are impervious to the appalling damage this is doing to the *whole* Church. Among other things, they lack *feeling* for the wounded victims, and the embarrassment priests and people are enduring. They rationalize it all, go on the defensive and utter a shallow *mea culpa* when the honourable response in many cases would be to resign.

For the umpteenth time this attitude was played out in a recent report on the sex-abuse scandals in Ireland. The Irish have a very close relationship with the United States to the point that they ape whatever the Americans do. The large cities like Dublin and Cork are just as American as New York and Chicago. So it's not as though the Irish bishops do not know what has been happening in the American Church. Yet, some bishops choose not to learn from its mess because they themselves are repeating it all over again.

At their gathering in March 2005, the Irish bishops once again dealt with the whole sex-abuse scandals that have rocked the Irish Church. Their focus was on payments to the victims coming from a Stewardship Fund they had set up. This is noble and the victims probably feel reasonably satisfied. But not the parishioners! The question on their minds is: "Where is the money coming from to pay for all this?" Land and property have been sold but clearly this is not enough to compensate the victims. Since 1996 they have paid out US$8.8 million in compensation and that leaves the kitty empty. Meanwhile, the number of victim-claims keeps growing.

The fact that the Irish people are asking questions is a very healthy sign because it means they no longer will pay up and shut up. For all too long that's how they were treated by bishops and priests, but now they are coming of age and are assertive. So where is the money coming from? Two bishops admitted that they had imposed a levy on the parishes without telling their people. Unbelieveable! You think that by now they would be learning something from the way other bishops have been behaving. Hats off to one bishop who apologized to his people and this should have been the first step towards his resignation. But, like the American bishops, he did not. It was a struggle to get Cardinal Law to step down and this was due mainly to the constant pressure put on him by the people.

Most Irish bishops either said nothing, or that the money was raised by other 'means'—whatever that means! Maybe some of the clergy winnings at Cheltenham and Aintree races! The fact that they could not be up front makes people feel very suspicious. No wonder they are very angry and asking for accountability, which is entirely their right. The truth is that in no way should the people be expected to pay for others' sins; the sins of omission of their bishops moving clergy around, and the sins of commission of the sex-abusers. The bishops and the priests must come up with the money through digging into their own savings and selling off their property. I am willing to bet that some have a racehorse or two that could be auctioned off!

The editor of the Irish Catholic newspaper hit the nail on the head when he wrote: "Only a full and transparent approach to finance, in a spirit of openness and genuine consultation with the laity, will deal with this issue. Unless this happens, it will be hard to believe that any lessons have been learned and even harder to believe that Catholics will want to pay for the [bishops'] mistakes."

Maybe the time has come when Irish Catholics have to hit where it hurts most: the collection plate! Refuse to put a euro in it till they are satisfied that bishops are capable of learning from their mistakes.

Bishop Patrick went to Ireland in 432 to evangelize the pagan Irish. Now it is the Irish bishops, along with the rest of us, who need a *New Evangelization*!

WATCH YOUR LANGUAGE

Language is a tool, a vehicle, a means to an end. Because I speak Gaelic doesn't mean I can deliver my homily next Sunday in Irish in North-western Canada! In the West of Ireland, yes! Just before he was elected, the then Cardinal Ratzinger (and later on as Benedict XVI) gave his homily in Latin. I bet most of the Cardinals had a quiet nap because few would have understood him!

The point is that language matters, simply because it is the second best form of communication. Non-verbal is the best and is how we communicate around seventy-percent of the time. The argument the Vatican puts forward for keeping Latin is that it is the official language of the Church. But since only a few understand it, the rest of us are kept in the dark—guessing. If we must have an official language, why not Italian?

Confucius was a great Chinese philosopher who lived five hundred years before Jesus. He made a relevant point when he said, "The reform of society begins in the reform of its language." We desperately need to apply this principle to the institution, not only in respect to Latin, but at every level.

We even use a profane language when we refer to the celebration of the Eucharist. How often have you read the following: "A *special* mass (notice lower case) was *said....*" "They *held* mass for....." And, "Father offered a mass of *thanksgiving.*"? The Eucharist *is* 'thanksgiving' and can be nothing else, and *every* Eucharist is special. Further, you cannot 'say' or 'hold' a Mass. Is not our language blasphemous when we say the Pope is 'the *representative* of Jesus Christ.' Impossible! Jesus is both human and *divine* so nobody can possibly re-present him. In thanking the Cardinals (in Latin!) for electing him, Benedict called them his *Lord* Cardinals. They had to grab hold of their mitres! This kind of royal language is fine for Queens and Kings but surely not appropriate for the *"Servant of the Servants of God."*

Dolly is a retired x-ray technician, and recently with her retired husband, came to fill in for a few months in our local hospital. At coffee-break one of the staff asked her if her *partner* was with her, to which she immediately fired back, "Yes, my *husband* is with me." Now we have to be careful and clearly qualify what we mean by 'partner.' Not too long ago you could boast about having had a *gay* time but not any more. Until recently we all knew the definition of *marriage*. Now we have to spell it out. The point is that language matters in every aspect of life.

Leadership in particular will have to tidy up its language which has it roots in the secular, stretching back to the Roman Empire. Where else did the language like Hierarchy, Office, Apostolic Palace, His Holiness, Govern, My Lord, His Eminence, Your Grace, Most and Very Reverend, Archbishop, Monsignor and Canon come from? You will not find them in the Gospel, that's for sure. These are all titles and terms belonging to a Feudalistic era and are more about power than service.

The editor of *The Tablet* argues that words do matter because, "In them we find fundamental beliefs and thoughts, and a predominantly male vocabulary in relation to God can be damaging to faith, understanding and action." The dominance of men and absence of women in the liturgy of the Pope's funeral was evident to the world. The row upon row of cardinals, bishops and priests spoke a clear and solid non-verbal language: the institution speaks only one language.

Jesus is our model and it is from him, not the secular, that the institution must take its cue and watch the language scripture uses to describe him. It is simple, clear, concise, unequivocal, challenging, dangerous, demanding and summed up in one word: *Servant*. "The Son of Man came to serve and not be served....if anyone wants to be first, he must make himself last of all and servant of all....his state was divine, yet he did not cling to his equality with God but emptied himself to assume the condition of a slave....it is the God of Abraham, Isaac and Jacob who has glorified his servant Jesus....God raised up his servant....Herod and Pontius Pilate made an alliance against your holy servant Jesus...."

THE DARK SIDE OF JESUS

Each of us has our dark side which Jung calls our "shadow." The vast majority of us go through life avoiding it because we don't like what we see. The result is that we do not grow into mature, holistic and individuated people. Like the leaning tower of Pisa, we remain lopsided!

What I mean by Jesus' dark side is that side of him that we don't like, that doesn't fit into our picture of him. Even as adults, he is still gentle Jesus meek and mild and we want to keep it that way. Like couples, we want a relationship with him that is better, richer and healthier. Forget about the worse, poorer and sickness part of the marriage! Can you hear him blast us like the Pharisees: "You hypocrites!" Marriage is a package-deal where you don't pick and choose and a relationship with Jesus is exactly the same. But we settle for being cafeteria Catholics: picking and choosing what we like about Jesus.

The death of John Paul and the election of Benedict got me reflecting on this dark side of Jesus. Although John Paul may be on his way to canonization, he too had his dark side as does Benedict. The side that rubs people the wrong way; what they do not like or accept. It is said that saints are difficult people to live with! Be careful though! It doesn't follow that because you are difficult to live with you are a saint! The last thing we would dream of doing, although it should be the first, is to tell Jesus what his dark side stirs up in us, not what we think about it.

I am learning that when I am struggling, it is best not to pray *to* Jesus, as I was taught from childhood. Instead, I invite him to come into my mess and then tell him how I am *feeling,* not what I am thinking. That's what the two despairing and disillusioned disciples did after Jesus died. When they met up with him as they were on their way out of Jerusalem, they invited Jesus to stay with them and told him their painful story.

Jesus is as much with his Church today as he was with the two disciples, so extend an invitation to him because you cannot handle his dark side alone. On a practical note then, what does this dark side of Jesus look like, and how does it affect your thinking and attitude towards him? Among other things, Jesus excluded women from his ministry. He enforced God's law with absolute rigour. He demanded celibacy of at least his twelve apostles and that they leave their wives, children, parents and work. He was an extremist in the eyes of most. Divorce was just not up for discussion. How does this dark side of him make you feel?

Like divorce, he was not beaten down on the Eucharist either. In his long teaching in John 6, he refused to tone down his language and was willing to lose the twelve rather than compromise. He tolerated no gray area in discipleship. To those who wanted to go home and say farewell or bury their father, he let them go—for good! One religious Order, when vocations were plenty, had the following sign on the front door of the novitiate: "These doors open from the inside!" Only the totally committed were welcome.

His language is shocking and outrageous! Just looking at a woman lustfully was equal to committing adultery with her. Those who gave scandal were to be dumped into the sea with a millstone around their neck. The rich were doomed to hell! A camel could pass through the eye of a needle easier than for them to get to heaven. He broke up families with his version of peace.

"He had a habit of refusing to fit into anyone's paradigms," says Fr. Andrew Greely. "Half the time he reassured people and the other half the time he scared them. He was patently a troublemaker. Jesus is as troubling to us as he was to the men and women in his own time. We find him attractive and want him as a friend. However, we don't like his elusiveness, his challenges, his paradoxes, his weird parables," continues Greely. We don't like his dark side! We need to be *Newly Evangelized*!

INSTITUTION AS AN OBSTACLE

The Church as institution is meant to be like a sign on the highway: it points you in the right direction. The personal experience of God within the individual Catholic is the end to which the institution is meant to lead each one. When these roles become reversed then the institution becomes an obstacle to God. Drawing more attention to itself, it diverts people away from a direct encounter with God. We see this all the time with politicians. In their campaign to be elected they promise their people the sun, moon and stars! Their party will have the people's and country's best interest at heart—always! Clearly, they will be the means to that end. But when elected, there's a sharp reversal: the party and the individual politicians, become ends in themselves. The first thing they do is give themselves a fat pay-hike! Being human, and in whom original sin is alive and well, we shouldn't be surprised that the institution should behave in a similar fashion.

The institution is still suffering from the edict of the Roman Emperor Constantine in 313. In it he declared Christianity as the official religion of the State. This was a 'blessing' in that it ended State persecution. But it was, and still is, a 'curse' in that the institution took on the mores of civil governing with social status being a major one. As part of ordination, bishops and priests were then invested with civil authority. The Vatican, as a recognized State, the smallest in the world, personifies the Constantine model today. This hardly fits in with Jesus' model who had no where to call home, not even a place to lay his head.

Clinging to this secular image, the institution exhibits models that describe it in secular terms. There is the "business" model: What drives the diocese and parish is efficiency and success. Hence all the committees and meetings! The bishops and pastors are CEOs who are expected to be good organizers and produce results. These are judged by how many baptisms, confirmations, converts and marriages a diocese had last year. Then the "White House" model: The bishop of the diocese is president and has his cabinet officials to head up the diocesan programs! Just look at our Chancery offices! How many work there? Maybe half!

During his public ministry, Jesus was the leader, not Peter. That got turned around after his resurrection and ascension. Now the focus was more on Peter as the head of the institution as if Jesus had totally disappeared off the scene. From then on, the institution placed more emphasis on itself, forgetting that Jesus promised to be with the Church always—not as an absent landlord—but in the very heart of each member. The *New Evangelization* of the institution calls for a reversal of roles.

Using the image of the barque of Peter, the institution describes itself as a 'safe haven' for its passengers. This is good up to a point so long as it resists being protective, paternalistic and restrictive. In which case it becomes a kind of ghetto institution into which people escape from the demands of the radical discipleship of Jesus. Karl Rahner was very much in tune with this danger: ".....the Church of today and tomorrow, a Church in which, almost, people can no longer bear the silent solitude of God and instead seek to flee into an ecclesiastical collectivity—even though in fact a Church community can only be built up from spiritually aware people who have really met God, not from those who use the Church in order ultimately to have nothing to do with God and God's free past-all-graspness."[74]

The God of 'past-all-graspness' is encountered at one's deepest core and this requires an inner journey of quiet and solitude. The truth is that many of us, including leadership, cannot tolerate very

---

74 **Karl Rahner:** *Spiritual Writings:* 40

well external, never mind, inner solitude. This kind is not loneliness, isolation or aloneness. It is just word-less and thought-less communication with God. It sounds incredible that the institution would become a form of escapism for Catholics, but it is true. It's like a daughter or son running home to mom and dad when her or his marriage calls for renewed commitment. Providing there is no abuse, wise parents will send them right back to their spouses.

SHUT OUT BY THE INSTITUTION

Institutions like the government and police are notorious for keeping the public locked out of information they have a right to know. They operate under a cloud of secrecy and feel accountable to nobody. We have to thank the media for its relentless pursuit and exposure of scandals in these institutions. What they reveal is often alarming and shocking, like innocent citizens sent to Syria to be tortured; all in the name of cracking down on terrorism.

The institutional arm of the Church also shuts people out, and in this reflection I will focus only on one specific way it behaves. It's nothing new because Jesus had to deal with it and he let the folks have it: "But woe to you, scribes and Pharisees, hypocrites! For you lock people out of the kingdom of heaven. For you do not go in yourselves, and when others are going in, you stop them." Jesus constantly did battle with these so-called religious leaders and had no time for them whatsoever. They preached a purely external religion by which they controlled people, while Jesus led them within to freedom, through a relationship with himself and God. The kingdom of God, Jesus preached, is right inside you and not a place or an institution outside, not even a religion.

The institution shuts us out of the kingdom within by its preoccupation with maintaining an outward religion that can be measured and controlled. Good things like doctrine, knowledge, creeds and even the sacraments, point us more to a relationship with the institution than with Jesus. Because they are a series of hoops to jump through, they lack the intimacy of a relationship and keep us on the outside looking in. Jesus, on the other hand, invites us to come in out of the cold and to look out from inside! It's much more important to know the teacher than to know what He taught! The institution places more emphasis on the teaching than on the person of Jesus. Here we can learn from the success of our evangelical brothers and sisters who preach Jesus Christ first just like Paul did.

We have to depend on a handful of good spiritual writers who speak the language of the inner journey, when in fact this should be the primary work of the institution. Is it that the institution cannot handle very well the *freedom* that results from experiencing the kingdom within? Free people tend to be a pain in the neck for the institution and as unpredictable as the weather! I do not mean freedom to do as we like, but the freedom Jesus brings—the freedom that results from *experiencing* oneself as a child of God and a loved sinner.

No human being was more free than Jesus (and he was a nuisance) so the religious leaders had to get rid of him. He certainly did not do his own thing. On the contrary, he was so free that he was totally obedient to the Father. And here is the paradox that the institution seems unable, or unwilling, to handle: freedom and obedience go hand in hand, and in that order too. You cannot be obedient till you are free. What the institution often calls obedience is in fact subservience, and Jesus wants to free us from this. The most obedient Catholic is a free, not independent (nor dependent) Catholic!

If the institution were to place more emphasis on the kingdom within, it would make the transition in mid-life more meaningful and a lot smoother for us. We call this natural progression 'mid-life crisis' because we are not prepared for it and so do not know how to handle it. It is more correct to call it 'mid-life transition' because human nature is now moving us from outside to inside. What worked for us in the first half will not in the second half of life—hence the crisis and confusion it stirs up in us. We are now compelled to find meaning, purpose, and fulfillment inside, and this is a whole new ball-game for us. It's made all the more difficult because there are no colleges, universities or novitiates to prepare us for the journey within—the longest journey!

However, if the institution is doing its job, we will come to mid-life *already* living from within, living a relationship with our God and drinking from the well within. It is in this sense that the institution must repent, be converted, be *Newly Evangelized* and blaze the trail for us by personal witness. Remember, a picture is worth a thousand words! It's easy to see the damage the institution does when it keeps us bound in the first half of life *all* our lives!

PATRON SAINT FOR THE INSTITUTION

Our man is Job! The book of Job is less about an individual but more about you and me. The writer of the book represents us and is grappling with the question every human being asks at some stage: Why suffering?

The book is divided into two parts: before, when Job had everything going for him and after, when he lost all and found much more. With the knowledge we have today about ourselves, we can apply Job to the suffering stirred up by mid-life crisis or mid-life transition. Like Job, in the first half of life, we sail along feeling that we are in total control of our destiny. Life is good to us and we even thank God for "blessing" us with riches, prestige, honour and power. At this stage we have all the answers to the meaning and purpose of life, or so we think.

Then, from around age thirty-five when we enter the second half of life, we begin falling apart and are plunged into desolation, depression and despair. We lived on the surface of the ego in the first half but now we are sucked into our unconscious to confront our shadow. The truth is that we did not actually live at all in the first half; we just existed. It is now that we are called to really live and the first step is to lose everything, including God. The God we created in our own image and likeness, in the first half, must go because it is a pagan god, an idol. With Job, we are called to wrestle with this god and if we do, like Job, we will come out battered but enlightened.

Seen in this light, Job's experience, and ours, is not a disaster but a pattern of life that's natural and necessary for holistic growth.

While we, the individuals who are the Church, make this transition, so must the Church as institution undergo the process and wrestle with its god. I have yet to read or hear about institutional mid-life crisis! Job is a good patron saint for the institution! All that has been said about the experience of individuals in the first and second half apply equally to the institution too. A cursory glance at the institution suggests that it needs to be *Newly Evangelized* in order to spark off the crisis and move it into the second half.

There is a great similarity between the institution and Job's three advisers: they represent the institution in the first half of life with all the answers! Scripture scholar, Roland E. Murphy, sums them up well: "All the workings of divine providence must be clear to them, explicit, mathematical. They have fallen victims to the occupational hazard of theologians [the institution too]: they forget they are dealing with mystery. They have 'studied' God as a subject to be analyzed, predicted and understood. And in forcing facts to agree with their understanding, they become willfully dishonest." The Vulgate version of 13:7 has Job seeing through their dishonesty with the question: "Does God need your lies?" Then, enlightened, Job reminds them, and the institution, that, "God does not fit man's measure" (33:12). Try as we may, we cannot tame God!

Another interesting point is that they talk in the abstract *about* God but never *to* God! Job, on the other hand has a fiery dialogue going with God, is totally honest and God likes this. Satan's question to God, "But Job is not God-fearing for nothing, is he?" skeptically interprets Job's virtue as mere self-interest because of how he is "blessed" by God. Satan puts the same question to all of us, particularly the institution: "Are you serving God for your own profit or strictly for God's sake?" Are you in it for the consolation of God or the God of consolation? Is disinterested service possible? Spiritual writers call this, "Purity of Intention." Ongoing conversion and evangelization demand that the institution daily examine its intentions for, as the Greek philosopher Socrates reminds us, "The unexamined life is not worth living."

Like Job's three pseudo advisers, the institution wants to look good, secure and in control as we all do in the first half of life. To be authentic, like Job, it must lose everything, wrestle with the whole question of God, look weak instead of powerful and have more questions than answers. It must constantly remind itself that it is dealing with mystery, acknowledge its limitations and, as Murphy says of the advisers, "....to write after each of their theses, 'If God so wills.'" With the enlightened Job of the second half of life, it must humbly confess: "I have been holding forth on matters I cannot understand" (42:3).

PATRON SAINT FOR BISHOPS

Before he was elected Pope Benedict XVI, the then Cardinal Ratzinger spoke about the need to reform the Curia. We are hoping that he will soon tackle this head on but I have a feeling he might have changed his mind! It's one thing to play hockey or soccer in front of the television but a horse of a different colour on the ice or pitch! The people who can best support him are the bishops worldwide—around four thousand. But they have to be more assertive, band together and confront Curia abuses. As with politics, people get the government they deserve, so do bishops get the Curia they deserve! In this regard, they could do well to adopt the late Basil Hume, Archbishop of Westminster, England, as their patron saint.

One of his flock, Sister Lavinia Byrne, got into trouble with the Congregation for the Doctrine of the Faith over her book, *Woman at the Altar.* The Cardinal rallied to her assistance and fired off the following letter to Archbishop Bertone on September 15, 1998:

Your Excellency:
On Monday, 14 September, I met with Sr. Lavinia Byrne IBVM and her provincial, Sister Cecilia Goodman.
The purpose of our meeting was to discuss the aftermath of the publication of Sr. Lavinia's book, "Woman at the Altar." I explained to the two sisters that I had no mandate to interfere in the affairs of their religious institute. I also said, that whereas I had to make certain that the teaching of the Church was known and accepted by the Catholics of England and Wales, at the same time I had to ensure

that no harm would come to the Church. I, too, had to be concerned that every individual be treated with justice and charity.

Having considered the present matter carefully, having spoken with Sr. Lavinia and her superior, taking also into account the sensitivities of the people in our country at a delicate moment in the Church in this country and abroad, I concluded that I must advise, and strongly, that no further action be taken by the Congregation in the matter of Sr. Lavinia's book.

You will recall how Sr. Lavinia had explained that her book, "Woman at the Altar," was completed and with the publisher when the Holy Father issued his document entitled "Ordinatio Sacerdotalis." It was Sr. Lavinia who insisted that "Ordinatio Sacerdotalis" should be printed at the end of her book, even though this caused the publishers considerable inconvenience.

I have read Sr. Lavinia's press release of 1 August, 1998 and this confirmed my view that no further action should be taken. She wrote: "Woman at the Altar was a book of that moment. There is no way in which I or any other theologian could write it nowadays. I have not spoken in public or lectured about the question of priestly ordination since I was asked not to do so by my legitimate superiors in the Institute of the Blessed Virgin Mary in July 1, 1995. I should add that I believe and profess all that the holy Catholic Church teaches and proclaims to be revealed by God."

This statement was given publicity in the press. Sr. Lavinia is a much-respected person in this country, and not only in the Catholic Church. She has done much good and will continue to do so.

I am sure the Congregation will act wisely and with prudence, and now leave the matter to rest. Any other policy will be harmful for the Church in this country. Please accept my advice.

Yours respectfully,
Basil Hume
Archbishop of Westminster

That was the end of the matter for the Congregation kept silent after receiving it. Like Basil Hume, instead of complaining, more bishops need to be as courageous and forceful. If they cannot be assertive it's because they do not want to rock the boat but settle for peace at any price. Either they want to appear nice and not get on the bad side of the Curia or, they are hungering for positions of power. Because Basil Hume was free of these attachments he was able to confront.

He was renowned for his humility, simplicity and holiness, a sign that he had a personal relationship with Jesus. Here was one bishop who took The *New Evangelization* seriously: the call to a fresh encounter with Jesus.

PATRON SAINT FOR EXCLUDED WOMEN

A laywoman and member of the Third Order of the Dominicans, with no formal education and who died at the age of thirty-three, might be considered an unlikely advocate for women's active participation in the running of the Church. Catherine of Siena (1347-1380) was an extraordinary young woman who confronted popes and princes in a very messy period of church and political history. Her more than three-hundred dictated letters were addressed to people from all walks of life: popes, cardinals, bishops, monks, politicians, princes and queens, among others.

She was canonized in 1461. In 1970 Paul VI declared her a "Doctor of the Church" and referred to her unique call to be peacemaker, as her "Charism of Exhortation." She not only exhorted but she also confronted and challenged leadership. Not bad for someone who could not read or write! She lived in an embarrassing and turbulent time for the Church known as the "Western Schism" (1378-1417), which the Papacy brought on itself. When the Emperor Constantine granted secular power to the Popes in 313, they surrendered the purity and simplicity of the Gospel and aligned themselves with kings, emperors, princes and princesses. They constantly vied with the latter for control, believing that the Pope was granted the divine right to be both spiritual and secular leader.

This was the unhealthy background that lead up to the "Western Schism." As the saying goes, love of money is the root of all evil but we can also add power, control and pride to the cause of such scandalous papal leadership. Because of the infighting in Rome, the pope at the time, Clement V, moved the papacy to Avignon in France in 1309 where it remained till 1378. He considered Avignon a safe place enjoying more independence as an imperial territory under the rule of the French King. Catherine was to play a major role in sorting out this upheaval and moving the papacy back to Rome.

Catherine was fearless and, not intimidated by authority, told the popes and others to behave themselves! She rebuked the cardinals who supported the anti-pope with, "You are flowers who shed no perfume, but stench that makes the whole world reek." She had harsh words too for Giovanna, Queen of Naples, who also supported the anti-pope as well as murdering her husband: "You know what you do is ill, but like a sick and passionate woman, you let yourself be guided by your passions." The Popes respected her and in 1378, on her advice, Pope Gregory XI left Avignon and returned to Rome; ending 69 years of popes in Avignon. Right away he sent her to Florence to make a fresh start for peace and reconciliation.

Gregory lived only one more year, and then his successor, Urban VI, summoned Catherine to Rome to work for the reformation of the Church. He too got an earful from her since he was well known as a very irascible character. Catherine knew that reform had to begin with self, so she ordered him to control his harsh and arrogant temper. Amazingly, he appreciated her honesty and forthright advice! So much did he confide in her that, by dictating to others, she wrote in the same vein to both high and a low alike. Like Jesus, she was no respecter of persons!

So enormous was the papal chaos during this time, into which Catherine was drawn, that in a period of forty years there were five popes! For a whole thirty-eight years there were two popes: Urban VI in Rome and Clement VII in Avignon, each with his own College of Cardinals and Curia. This sparked off the "Western Schism." A General Council in Pisa in 1409 attempted to solve this by electing a third pope, Alexander V, but he died quickly and was followed by the infamous anti-Pope, John XXIII! It's very interesting that the pope, whom people loved and who called the Second Vatican

Council, took that name! This scandalous situation continued until 1417, when the Council of Constance elected Martin IV and brought an end to the schism.

Like Jesus, reconciling the thief in his last moments on the cross, Catherine directed her final work of political reconciliation from her deathbed in 1380, between Urban VI and the Roman Republic. The mess and scandals that men created were finally fixed by a woman! We need Catherines today to straighten out the men at every level of the Church: parish, diocese, papacy, Vatican and Curia!

PATRON SAINT FOR EXCLUDED LAITY

He will not be canonized because he didn't keep his nose clean! Cardinal John Henry Newman (1801-1890) was ahead of his day as an advocate for lay involvement in the Church. Much of what was written about the role of the laity in the Second Vatican Council was already promoted by him. But he blotted his copybook with his article, *On Consulting the Faithful in Matters of Doctrine,* in 1859. One writer commenting on this said, "His publication was an act of political suicide from which his career within the Church was never fully to recover; at one stroke......he gained the Pope's personal displeasure." While Benedict XVI is fast-tracking John Paul II for canonization, Newman hasn't even gotten to the starting stalls! So if you hope to be canonized do not upset the folks in Rome!

When his bishop asked Newman, "Who are the laity?" he replied: "The Church would look foolish without them." After founding the university in Dublin, he came down hard on the Irish Hierarchy's discrimination against lay involvement. He lamented, "One of the chief evils which I deplored in the management of the affairs of the University twenty years ago, was the resolute refusal with which my urgent representations ever met that the Catholic laity should be allowed to cooperate with the archbishops in the work. As far as I can see there are ecclesiastics all over Europe whose policy is to keep the laity at arm's length, and hence the laity have been disgusted and become infidel, and only two parties exist, both ultras in opposite directions. I came away from Ireland with the distressing fear that in that Catholic country, in like manner, there was to be an antagonism, as time went on, between the hierarchy and the educated classes." Add the sex-abuse scandals in Ireland and you have mass anti-clericalism and distrust of leadership.

Newman was a prophet because what he wrote in 1873 is now a reality, not just in Ireland but all over the Western world. The laity are indeed kept at arm's length and divided into two camps: the ultra liberals and ultra conservatives. In his essay, *On Consulting the Faithful in Matters of Doctrine,* he warned that to cut the laity off from participation in the life of the Church, "In the educated classes will terminate in indifference, and in the poorer in superstition." How right he is! A vociferous and critical laity is much healthier than an indifferent sidelined people.

Because Newman firmly believed that the laity *is* the Church and that the Tradition of the Apostles was committed to the *whole* Church, he wanted more for them than mere participation as Lectors and Extraordinary Ministers of the Eucharist. They should be involved in every aspect of the life of the Church like in decision-making and matters of doctrine. He draws on two major Church events to support this vision for the laity.

The first was his book called, *The Arians of the Fourth Century,* which dealt with the heresy of Arius that Jesus was merely a creature. The Council of Nicea in 325 condemned him, teaching that Jesus is also God. Newman's point was that this very same belief was already "proclaimed, enforced, maintained and preserved, far more by the *Ecclesia docta* (the people) than by the *Ecclesia docens* (the teachers) that the body of the episcopate was unfaithful to its commission, while the body of the laity was faithful to its baptism..." The Nicene dogma was maintained during the greater part of the fourth century, "not by the unswerving firmness of the Holy See, Councils or bishops, but by the *consensus fidelium* (the agreement of the people)," wrote Newman.

The other event that he cites is the lead up to the doctrine of the Immaculate Conception defined by Pius 1X in 1854. The pope required bishops to get the feeling of the clergy and the laity towards this doctrine and its definition. When he issued the definition, he explained that although he had already known the sentiments of the bishops, he had wished to know the sentiments of the people also. Here was a pope who respected the dignity and royal priesthood of the laity and treated them accordingly!

Newman's theology of the laity does not pit bishop and people against each other. Rather, they complement each other and promote the full life and mission of the whole Church. Whatever collaboration there is so far is one way: the laity collaborating with leadership. It has to be mutual, with leadership collaborating with the laity. During the Second Vatican Council (1962-1965) Cardinal Suenens of Belgium asked his fellow bishops, "Why are we even discussing the reality of the church when half the church is not even represented here?"

PATRON SAINT OF SEX-SCANDALS

John Profumo died on March 9, 2006 at the age of 91. One London paper put it bluntly: "Profumo the sex-scandal minister is dead." Yet I hold him up as a patron saint for my brother priests, bishops and religious whose sex-scandals have devastated the Church.

Profumo had a high profile political career in the British Conservative government. He was Secretary of War during the reign of Prime Minister Harold Macmillan in the 1960's. So popular was he that many said he would become prime minister one day.

In 1963 rumours began to circulate of sexual impropriety in the life of one of the nation's most elite and well-liked men. The woman named was the infamous Christine Keeler, a prostitute he met at a party at Lord Astor's country home in Berkshire. He was introduced to her by one Stephen Ward, an osteopath accused of running what the newspapers called a, "Top people's vice ring." The story went that Profumo first caught sight of her climbing naked out of a swimming pool. She was 19. He was 48. Most dramatically, among Keeler's other clients was Commander Eugene Ivanov, the assistant naval attaché in the Soviet Embassy in London.

In March 1963, Profumo went before Parliament and he denied any misbehaviour with Keeler. But details of the relationship began to emerge and three months later he resigned admitting that he lied to lawmakers. He wife stood by him throughout the scandal until her death in 1998.

But here is the other side of the story: redemption. Profumo's first job after the scandal was cleaning toilets. It was his self-imposed lifetime of atonement which lasted for 43 years at Tonybee Hall in London. This was a large centre for poor families—children, parents, the elderly and alcoholic—with a large percentage from Bangladesh. He was closely involved with Tonybee Hall right up to a few months before his death.

The chief executive officer of Tonybee took him off cleaning toilets because he recognized Profumo to be a good fund-raiser. And he used well his contacts in high society to rescue the charity from its poor financial state. Luke Geoghegan, CEO, said of him: "John Profumo was an inspiration to us all. His passion was people who were at the bottom of the heap of society. I think through his 43 years of tireless volunteering the message was that you can actually change society for the better. You become a better person by giving yourself away."

Profumo believed he had to make reparation and atonement for his sins and he did it bravely in public. He was a man who took scandal seriously and was ready to make amends to the scandalized. I have yet to hear of any of the hierarchy and priests make public reparation for their sexual scandals. When I was growing up in Ireland and a priest stepped out of line in a serious matter he was banished to a monastery to do penance for the rest of his life.

One bishop I know personally fathered a son while he was a bishop. Instead of heading for the Trappists he worked in a parish in a nearby country. Recently he retired to a large rectory given to him in the very diocese he was bishop when carrying on! Times have changed! Another bishop I know well fathered a daughter as a priest and then became a bishop! Whatever happened to public penance, reparation and atonement? As a layman, John Profumo had not only a private but a well developed social conscience. He also knew that sin always has social consequences.

What a shot in the arm it would be for the *New Evangelization* of Catholics if we had more Profumos among our sex-scandal bishops, priests and religious! Like him, their scandals too could be redemptive. A start would be to admit publicly with the adulterer, King David, "Peccavi," I have sinned. That would be a powerful challenge to the rest of us to admit our sinfulness which is the first step of conversion called for by the *New Evangelization*. Our sin also would be redemptive; we would be wounded healers and sinners evangelizing sinners.

BUT WHAT DO *YOU* THINK?

Jesus respected people's intelligence and he expected them to use it as well. He rarely answered a question, but got people to think for themselves—the mark of a great teacher! On one occasion, he put his disciples on the spot with the question, "But who do *you* say that I am?"

It's too easy for leadership to take refuge in scripture and Tradition when it comes to discussing hot issues like the role of women in leadership and married priests. Of course we must ask what scripture and Tradition tell us, but we must also ask ourselves: "What do *I* personally think about women in leadership and married priests, and what feelings are stirred up in me?" What we think and how we feel definitely colour our interpretation of scripture and Tradition, so we need to stand back and be objective with ourselves. It is common knowledge that we men are programmed from childhood to see ourselves as superior to women and treat them as second-class citizens.

Along with a swimming pool, John Paul II made it known when he was elected that he liked his Polish meals so he imported Polish nuns to cook! Why not men? And why not a woman secretary? Women in the kitchen are no threat but women in the Vatican in leadership roles?

Because of our high-powered technology we are instantly aware of women abused, unjustly treated and discriminated against worldwide. Has it ever dawned on the institution that it might be guilty of one or more of the above? To argue that our alienation of women in leadership is based solely on scripture and Tradition is too simplistic. It doesn't take into account our long historical cultural bias against women, and male superiority.

While we accept that Revelation is complete in Jesus, we must also acknowledge what the Catechism of the Catholic Church teaches: "Yet even if Revelation is already complete, it has not been made completely explicit: it remains for Christian faith to grasp its full significance over the course of centuries" (#66). This echoes what the Second Vatican Council taught in the Constitution on Divine Revelation: "For there is a growth in the understanding of the realities and the words which have been handed down....For, as the centuries succeed one another, the Church constantly moves forward in the fullness of divine truth until the words of God reach their complete fulfillment in her" (#8).

What this says to all of us, but to leadership in particular, is that we have not yet arrived at the full knowledge of and articulation of God's Revelation. There is always what we call *the more,* for Revelation is not a bookish event but a personal God who continues to unfold the depth and breadth of God's mysterious relationship with us. For leadership to close the door on issues like married priests and women in leadership is to manipulate God.

I believe most Catholics would be less critical if leadership took a more humble approach, instead of what they experience as fundamentalism, authoritarianism and absolutism. When we look at the big picture of God's revelation, we see how slow God works! The Universe began around 15 billion years ago; the Earth 4.5 billion; and the first humans 2.6 million. Abraham was 4 thousand years ago and Jesus only 2 thousand! We Catholics are merely the young kids on the block! If this is any indication, God has a lot more to say, so leadership must keep on listening and be open to be surprised by God!

Leadership would do well to make Thomas Merton's prayer of trust, openness, certainty in uncertainty and security in insecurity, its own:

*My Lord God, I have no idea where I am going.
I do not see the road ahead of me
Nor do I really know myself.
And the fact that I think I am following your will
Does not mean that I am actually doing so.
But I believe that the desire to please you
Does in fact please you.
And I hope that I will never do anything apart from that desire.
And I know that if I do this,
You will lead me by the right road
Though I may know nothing about it.
Therefore I will trust you always
Though I may seem to be lost and in the shadow of death
I will not fear, for you are with me,
And you will never leave me to face my struggles alone.*

DUC IN ALTUM

There must be something catchy about the title, even if it is Latin, because I hear the clergy speak it a lot these days! You could call it John Paul's theme for the New Millennium when he called on Catholics to "Duc in altum" meaning, "Put out into the deep." He is challenging the laity to move out of the security of the sanctuary and be effective witnesses in a pagan society! In other words, go and evangelize. His words are those of Jesus to his disciples who had been fishing all night and caught nothing. He commanded them to "Launch out into the deep water" where they immediately filled their nets.

We in leadership must be careful and not see this as an invitation, yet again, to a flurry of activity, a trap we continually fall into. It should be no surprise to us that our attempt to implement the *New Evangelization* is bearing very little fruit because we place our emphasis on 'doing.' John Paul followed the same plan and sequence of events that Jesus did with his disciples. He first of all called them to be his *companions*. Only after being formed in a relationship with him did he send them out to evangelize. Relationship preceded activity. In 1997 John Paul, in his call to *The New Evangelization,* stressed repeatedly the primacy of a personal encounter with Jesus. In other words, Catholics must first be evangelized before they can dream of evangelizing, which was his command in 2000 with "Duc in altum."

To be evangelized and then to evangelize, calls for depth experiences. A companion of Jesus, as opposed to being a follower, or bearing the title 'Christian,' is about an intimate relationship with him. For the vast majority of Catholics this is unknown territory and quite scary, so they back off.

When it comes to evangelizing, Catholics find themselves in unchartered waters and completely out of their depth. They need lots of support and affirmation to believe that Jesus believes in them, that they are capable of launching out and making a deep impact on society. This requires deep conviction, deep confidence, deep commitment and deep concern for a world that's quickly destroying, not only the planet, but itself as well.

I live on an island in the Pacific Ocean where fishing is the backbone of the economy. After some fierce stormy experiences on the ocean, once for twenty-three hours, I have come to have the utmost respect for the water! I now fish from the shore and leave it to the seasoned and wise fishers to launch out into the deep! They tell me that the delicious halibut, that can weigh up to two hundred pounds, are found only in deep waters where they feed on the bottom of the ocean. I will starve to death sooner than sail miles out into the wild ocean and launch out into the deep!

There's an array of modern navigational gadgets fitted on just about every fishing boat in this area and they have their limitations. One experienced captain I know uses them but does not rely on them while the younger fishers depend totally on the latest technology. He has his back-up: the stars! And they have been working since creation! With a big smile across his face, he boasted that when the young guys' equipment fails, they call out to him like Peter did to Jesus when he was sinking! The lesson for the institution here is that a relationship-theology has always worked and is far superior to a conceptual and academic theology. We have to return to what works and help our people to experience a relationship *with* Jesus instead of knowledge *about* him, because the latter is not working.

Many claim that the cardinals did not launch out into the deep in electing Benedict XVI. Instead, they kept the status quo, fished from the shore and settled for a caretaker pope! At 78 they figured he would not be around too long! They were not prepared to take risks with a pope from Africa, Latin and Central America or Asia. So they played it safe! Catholics cannot use the cardinals' fear of risk as their excuse for not being evangelized and consequently, not evangelizing.

NO SHORTAGE OF PRIESTS

Strictly speaking there is no shortage of priests because every fully initiated Catholic is a priest. Peter, the first pope, was very clear on that: "You are a chosen race, a royal priesthood...." (2 Pt 9). In praise of Jesus, John the Apostle says the same: "....and made us to be a kingdom, priests serving his God and Father...." (Rev. 1:6). And like a good teacher, he repeats it later: "....you have made them to be a kingdom and priests serving God...." (Rev. 5:10).

The bishops at the Second Vatican Council, in the *Dogmatic Constitution on the Church*, confirmed this: "The baptized, by regeneration and the anointing of the Holy Spirit, are consecrated into a spiritual house and a holy priesthood" (# 10). Of course there were priests long before Jesus. Back in the days of Moses the whole tribe of Levi was priestly. But Jesus extended this to the *whole* people so that the *whole* Church shares his priesthood and not just some elite. We need to speak this inclusive language of priesthood more and restore to every Catholic his and her dignity. What the Church in the west is experiencing today is a shortage of *ordained* priests.

While just about every Catholic would be shocked and even embarrassed to be called a priest, leadership would disagree with it because it restricts priest to the ordained. If Jesus calls all of us priests why should leadership have a problem with it? It's because leadership does not speak the same language as Jesus. He was no philosopher or theologian so he did not speak an academic, theoretical and impersonal language. Rather, he spoke a relationship language and everyone could understand him. Basically, then, it is a language problem.

For centuries, the institution defined matrimony mainly as a contract even though scripture always defined it as a covenant. It was only recently that the Second Vatican Council finally came round to speaking the language of scripture, using covenant terminology for matrimony. Covenant in scripture is always relational. The priesthood of the *whole* Church is simply an extension of a relationship with Jesus and not a concept or an idea to be defined.

Not for one moment do I believe that Jesus is mean and niggardly and divvies out his priesthood in layers and tiers. Meaning, some get a bit more than others! Unfortunately, that is how leadership portrays priesthood because it divides it up into categories and structures. For example, we have the bishop, priest, deacon and laity—four categories of priesthood in all! The bishop, it says, shares in the fulness of the priesthood of Jesus while the priest, deacon and people get the left-overs! There is only *one* priesthood and it is the priesthood of Jesus in which the *whole* Church shares. Jesus is no scrooge! In defining priesthood, leadership says that there is a difference in *essence* and degree between the ministerial (ordained) priesthood and the *common* priesthood of the laity.

Since essence is more to do with metaphysics and philosophy, Jesus would not have known what it meant and further, would not have been the least interested! He just did not speak that kind of abstruse language. What does leadership mean when it refers to the priesthood of the laity as 'common?' It can be an insult or a compliment. When we speak about something or someone being common we mean ordinary, standard, nothing special, kind of drab, coarse, and so on. And when we speak about what we all have in common, we mean equality, on the same footing, no distinction, sameness and so on.

Certainly there must be order in how we all exercise our priesthood and so we call ordination the sacrament of *Holy Orders*. To ordain is to appoint, to install or to commission an individual to order, not order about, a portion of the Church like a parish, in living out our priesthood in everyday life. This is a ministry of service and should not convey in any way the image of a two-tier priesthood with the ordained a step above the priesthood of the laity. Sad to say, but our behaviour and the language we use as ordained say that we are superior. When we speak about a 'vocation to the priesthood' we imply that the individual is now called to be a priest. The truth is that, like every fully initiated Catholic, he is already a priest so his vocation is a call to serve, to minister and to help the laity live the priesthood in an orderly fashion.

During his visit to Germany in 2006, Pope Benedict XVI hinted that it is time for the institution to speak a new language. He said: "We have heard so much about what is not allowed; now it is time to say we have a positive idea to offer....all this is clearer if you first say it in a positive way." Apply this to priesthood and it means that we must stress what the ordained and laity have in common: they share equally in the priesthood of Jesus.

INVOLVE THE CHILDREN

To keep Johnny quiet during a Sunday Eucharist, his parents had him write in his scribbler the number of times Father repeated "so" in his homily. After ten minutes, and noticing Johnny looking bored, his dad asked if he would like another word. "Sure," said Johnny, "the word *Amen*."

That funny story has a sad side to it. All too often children at the Sunday liturgy are there to be seen but not heard. Parishioners view them as distractions to their prayers and make parents feel guilty to the point they often leave the celebration. Imagine the hassle it is for mom and dad to organize themselves and three small children for a Sunday Eucharist. By the time they get to their pew they are already exhausted from their heroic effort.

Parents like these should be congratulated at the beginning for such generosity and commitment! Instead, they get dirty looks when their child does what is natural. It's even worse if the presider should in the slightest way hint at their "disruptive" presence. In my young days the clergy ordered parents to take their children out. Jesus' condemnation for those who scandalize children is a warning to presiders: "It is better that a millstone be hung around their necks and then drowned in the depths of the sea." You have to agree with parents who have experienced anything like that for not returning the next Sunday, or ever again.

The reality is that the Sunday liturgy is mostly unwelcoming for children, though this is not intentional. We just don't appreciate their presence and are not aware that children too have a God-given right to fully participate in the Eucharist. I recently heard a dad relate a joyful story about his little three-year old daughter's happy experience of being made to feel welcome. For the readings and homily the small children were taken downstairs for theirs which proved to be a delightful experience for her. One weekday as they were driving past the church little Sarah began pointing and clapping because of the fond memories she had the previous Sunday!

Needless to say that little Sarah will have very happy memories of Sunday Eucharist as she grows up and will likely continue to celebrate as a teenager. Unfortunately, she is in a minority. What about all the children and parents who have negative and even hurtful experiences? And they are a majority. We can conclude that the Sunday liturgy, among other things, is a time and place to create happy memories for children and parents. But we need not and must not use gimmicks to achieve this. Over and over again parents tell me that they do not show up on Sunday because they have small children. What is that saying to presiders and parishioners?

Those of us who know a little bit about the liturgy are fully aware that liturgy, among other things, means *the work of the people.* But we tend to focus more on the adults and not involve the children in the work. If we don't, then we are the problem, not the children. A classroom teacher knows too well that if she or he does not involve all the students all the time they can expect trouble!

Where a parish has a school, it is easy to involve the children in celebrating the Eucharist and for the most part we do this well. The challenge comes on a Sunday where the children are scattered over several celebrations and the majority by far are adults. I honestly believe that the solution here is not to have a children's Sunday Eucharist. While the intention is good the message we send is bad. We are saying that children and adults cannot celebrate well together which I don't accept for one moment.

Again, with the best of intentions, we build children's crying rooms, but look at the negative message it sends. We would never dream of doing that for blacks and whites or rich and poor. But it's alright to discriminate against children. I am not suggesting that children be allowed to act unruly and run wild during the Eucharist. They are part of our worshipping family and must not just be tolerated, but lovingly accepted and involved. While respecting the integrity and flow of the liturgy, there is room for creativity that will include them.

WAYS TO INVOLVE CHILDREN

The Sunday Eucharist is a family celebration and not a time for private devotion. Since children are an integral part, parishioners must welcome them as they are and not expect them to behave as adults. Jesus was often "interrupted" by the people when he took time out for quiet but he didn't complain. On the contrary, he welcomed children while the apostles wanted to chase them away.

A welcoming and hospitable atmosphere is the first step to involving children and their parents. This points to the importance of the ministry of hospitality, where certain parishioners are in the foyer to welcome everyone. It's like when you visit someone and they meet you at the front door with a warm smile and big handshake, or even better, a hug! But the responsibility falls on the presider more than anyone else to make children feel at home and wanted in the Sunday Eucharist.

While we presiders are not a John Paul II, we can learn from him some good communication skills. People need to experience us alive, happy and excited while we don't have to kiss every baby! After all, each Sunday is a little Easter when we celebrate the joy of the resurrection of Jesus. A step in this direction might be to reduce the number of Eucharistic celebrations because it is very difficult to celebrate well more than two.

Involve the children at every Eucharist in taking up the collection, which might go up because it's hard to refuse a child! Have them bring up the gifts and hand out the bulletin. Younger children have their own Liturgy of the Word. Invite them up for a prayer by the presider before the first reading and send them out quietly with their teachers. Once a month the children could be the focus of the homily at all the celebrations. I invite them up to the front pews, which are always empty, because Catholics are so humble! Then I simply chat and dialogue with them while also including the congregation. Children get a great kick out of seeing adults put on the spot!

For immediate preparation for the sacraments of Confirmation and First Eucharist, our diocese has a series of six sessions for the parents and children. For years I battled away at 'teaching' the parents on a Tuesday night till eventually I saw the light. They were in no way ready for a series of lectures. Some did not want to be there; all showed up tired and most were themselves children in the faith. And there I was waxing eloquently on the Holy Spirit about whom I could say little! I should have listened to St. Paul much earlier and learned from him. Because the Corinthian adults were infants in the faith he told them: "I fed you with milk, not solid food, for you were not ready for solid food." Not me! I stuffed them with potatoes and meat! Our Catholic parents today are unevangelized and, like the Catholics of Corinth, infants in the faith.

I adapted the sessions to a more hands-on-experiential approach and inserted them where they rightly belong: in the celebration of the Eucharist. How this didn't dawn on me earlier I don't know, because the very titles make this the obvious setting: *"Called By Name" focuses on baptism; "Sealed With the Spirit" on Confirmation; "Come" deals with the Gathering Rite; "Listen" with the Liturgy of Word; "Do" focuses on the Liturgy of Eucharist; and "Go" on the Rite of Dismissal.*

Parishioners knew well in advance that the eleven o'clock liturgy for the next six weeks would be focused on the parents and children. They had an option of two other liturgies but in fact the numbers stayed the same for the eleven. I use the Eucharistic Prayer for Children which has short and simple responses throughout. When I invite the children up, they bring their homework which I expect them to do. I collect it, pass it on to one of the catechists to correct it and return it the next Sunday. I find the people come alive and get as much, if not more, from it as the children. Since the session, *Called By Name,* is about their baptism, I have a live baptism and invite them around the font.

Here is a very brief overview of the other sessions: For, *Sealed With the Spirit,* I show them the oils and get them to watch for when I stretch my hands over the offerings at the consecration, invoking the Spirit. For the session, *Come,* we gather in the foyer and, after explaining, we process in. For, *Listen,* we pause before the first reading and I try to create a library atmosphere. Before the Gospel I give them a brief introduction and warn them that I will be asking questions on what they heard! The session *Do* centres on Jesus' command: "Do this in memory of me." They bring up the bread and wine and watch for when I extend my hands over them. And for the session, *Go,* I talk about it before the final blessing and dismissal.

The result? Six fewer meetings! The Eucharist is both the goal and the means to the goal. Teaching is done through doing. It is experiential, practical, tangible and a celebration with the parish community instead of dry pedagogy on Tuesday night! It is holistic instead of cognitive and abstract. And it creates happy memories! It's another step in implementing the *New Evangelization* with children, that's new in *ardour, method and expression.*

DUALISM SHUTS US OUT

A Sufi is a Muslim mystic who, like Jesus and other mystics, speaks in parables: "One day a Lover approached the home of his Beloved. He knocked at the door. A Voice within responded to the knocking: 'Who is there?' The Lover answered: 'It is I.' The Voice within spoke, almost sadly: 'There is no room here for me and thee.'

The Lover went away and spent much time trying to learn the meaning of the words of his Beloved. Then one day, some time later, he once again approached the home of his Beloved and, as before, he knocked on the door. Once again, as had happened earlier, the Voice within asked: 'Who is there?' This time the Lover answered: 'It is Thou.' And the door opened and he entered the home of his Beloved." The point here is that the Beloved and Lover are *one*.

This is a simple and powerful truth that clarifies what I mean by dualism. We Catholics; pope, bishops, clergy, religious and laity, are steeped in it and we don't recognize how much it keeps us shut out from our Beloved. We behave as if God is out there somewhere, so we are separated and spend our lives trying to make contact. Standing before God, we always say: "It is I." The great divide by Michelangelo with God reaching across the chasm to Adam, but doesn't make contact, sums up the dualism embedded in us. The opening prayers of the Eucharist, contained in The Sacramentary, are riddled with this notion of God and us in our separate worlds.

Dualism presents itself in the form of contrasts, opposites and polarization like light and darkness; above and below; flesh and spirit; life and death; good and evil; truth and falsehood; heaven and earth; God and Satan. These are opposing forces locked in conflict and do not coexist. For most of our lives we live this dualistic illusion that we exist independently of God.

The Celts and mystics on the other hand, experienced the presence of God in creation itself and not apart from it; they felt the divine mystery present all around them. The Indian mystic, Krishnamurti, puts it like this: "There is no separation between the observer and the observed, between the subject and the object; they are a seamless continuum." The truth is that we cannot even exist apart from God, not to mention be in a relationship with God. While I am clearly not God, and therefore distinct from God, I am not separate either.

The great Saint Augustine leaves us in no doubt about our oneness with God when he prays: "Since nothing that is could exist without you, you must in some way be in all that is. And if you are already in me, since otherwise I should not be, why do I cry to you to enter into me? O God, I should be nothing, utterly nothing, unless you were in me—or rather unless I were in you, of whom and by whom and in whom are all things. So it is Lord; so it is. Where do I call to you to come to, since I am in you? Or where else are you that you can come to me?" He speaks from experience for he regrets that he wasted most of his life looking for God outside himself while God was all the time within him.

The greatest villain and the one mainly responsible for this dualistic spirituality is our ego. It places us at the centre of reality and objectifies God as somewhere 'out there.' The result of this ego-centred focus is isolation and separateness from God. The truth is that God is the centre and we orbit around God like our planet around the sun. Paul reminds us that, "It is in him that we live and move and have our being" (Acts 17:28). And the Jesuit poet, Gerard Manley Hopkins, confirms that there is no dualism when he writes: "The world is charged with the grandeur of God." When we truly believe this, we can confidently say like the Lover, "It is Thou." We will no longer use a dualistic language like "getting in touch with God," and "let's put ourselves in the presence of God." We do not need to make contact with God. We just need to become aware that we are the fish in the ocean and stop looking for it!

Due to dualism our prayer is primarily a talking-*to* God outside ourselves. The Benedictine, John Main, calls this ego-centered prayer: "An *I* to surrender and a *Thou* to be surrendered to." Drop the dualism and prayer simply is being-*with* God in whom we live. Main stresses that, "We cannot surrender to the one with whom we are already united." But we can speak about a surrender *of* ourselves.

The second villain of dualism is the philosopher Rene Descartes (1596-1650) who had a great influence on Western culture. His separational philosophy led him to make, what many would consider famous, this proclamation: "Cogito Ergo Sum," (I Think, Therefore I am). Considered from a spiritual point of view, it is blasphemous because he gives the illusion that I exist independently of the Other. Notice too how it's all about *me, I, control, independence.* Cartesian philosophy is essentially subject-object dualism that has prevailed in the West leading to a 'God and me' dualism. Descartes puts the cart before the horse!

Hindu mystics are much closer to the truth when they say, *"So Hum"*—"You Are, *Therefore* I am," (*Estis, Ergo Sum*). It's like the baby in its mother's womb saying, "You are mom; therefore I am!" This transcends dualism; erases the I; inserts the Thou; and admits us into the home of the Beloved.

We would do well to pay less attention to Descartes and ponder on Jesus' own awareness of his oneness with the Father and the oneness he desires for us. John 17 is his passionate prayer for not any kind of oneness for us, but the same oneness he has with the Father.

NO EXPECTATIONS NO DISAPPOINTMENTS

We are all unbalanced to some extent and it's more than being a few sandwiches short of a picnic! I am not speaking primarily about psychic unbalance, though it is of course related. Take a few examples: We live unbalanced lifestyles, eat unbalanced diets and we are totally out of sync with our ecosystem. It all begins with our distorted thinking which in turn is rooted in power and control.

The Province of British Columbia is presently experiencing two natural phenomena: forest fires and the pine-beetle epidemic. The latter is destroying thousands of hectares of healthy pine trees and it will continue to spread. Because of our unbalanced reasoning we label them disasters, which they are not, so we battle to control them. They are disasters only for the rich who want to make a quick buck regardless of damage they do to the environment.

The truth is that this is nature's way of replenishing itself but we blatantly refuse to accept reality and work with it. Instead, we spend millions of dollars fighting fires. I am told that Russia allows nature do its cleansing by letting the fires burn. When I listen to reports I hear things like, "We are hoping that Mother Nature will cooperate with us so we can bring this under control." Notice the arrogance and unbalanced thinking! Imagine! Nature must cooperate with *us*! No, it's time we cooperated with nature, respected its cycles, lived in harmony with it and stop raping our forests. In this regard, the First Nations people have a lot to teach us.

We set ourselves up to be disappointed because we expect things to submit themselves to our control. Then we go on to blame nature and others whereas in fact we ourselves are the ones who bring disappointments on ourselves. Of course we would never admit this because we live in denial—a more subtle and dangerous form of unbalance! Look how we blame the weather for our disappointments when nature is behaving as it should. We moan and complain with sayings like, "What a miserable day it is." It is we, not nature, who are miserable simply because we are unbalanced!

If we drop our expectations we will not be disappointed, but this is easier said than done. It's become our first language to the point that we proudly boast over and over again, "I expect to...." Meaning, "I am in charge and I will!" Illusion! The best and most you can say, and should is, "I *hope* to...." Now you are being real! We had a lovely saying when I was growing up: "I will see you tomorrow, le cunabh Dé," meaning, with the help of God or God willing. If we want to live a balanced and happy life we will need to speak a new language, and this calls for conversion.

When we substitute *hope* for expectations the picture changes, our thinking is balanced and we are not disappointed because we accept the uncertainty of reality. When you hope you are open. When you expect you are closed. It all goes back to a spirituality rooted in the Gospel and what Jesus promised that if we lose our life (give up control) we will find it. We leave room to be influenced by all kinds of events, positive and negative, and most of all, to be surprised! You will never be surprised living with expectations but you will be constantly disappointed and frustrated! Only the salmon can swim upstream, but it costs them their lives because they die after spawning. When we behave like salmon and attempt to swim against the flow of life, we kill ourselves in the process! So, go with the flow!

We get all worked up about four-letter swear-words but they do us little or no harm. But there are other swear-words and we use them hundreds of times a day! Even though they do us irreparable damage, we don't bat an eyelid! Words like *expectation, always, never, have to, must* and *should* are swear-words because they keep us unbalanced and retarded. So quit swearing! Stop controlling!

Our best teacher here is right on our own doorstep: our breathing! Just become aware and notice all you experience. For example, you cannot hold on to it! Try and you will die in less than three minutes! Neither can you hold the incoming air because you haven't got it till you let go of what you have in your lungs! And what you have you cannot keep there! This is a simple yet powerful exercise in non-control and therefore, non-expectations! Further, give up the illusion that *you* do the breathing because you don't! It's that little muscle you call your heart that's doing all the work and you simply cooperate with it. Try controlling it and not cooperating with it and see what happens!

Breathing is about detachment and balance. Expectations are about attachment and unbalance. Breathing is about the present moment. You can't breathe in advance! Expectations are about an illusionary future. The *New Evangelization*, like breathing, is essentially an exercise in detachment from everything, including expectations. Life unfolds literally with every breath. To notice this is to be wise and real and grounded in the present.

SAME-SEX MARRIAGE AND OUR RESPONSE

A day after Canada legalized same-sex marriage, Spain followed suit and so the domino-effect continues. Rather than curse the dark, we Catholics, leadership in particular, must strike a match and carry out a postmortem on ourselves. It would be hypocritical to bemoan the past, complain and criticize the government without looking into our contribution to this sad affair. Catholics, including leadership, are partly responsible for governments taking us down this dead-end road. In Canada at least, there is a great similarity here to the apathy and indifference of Catholics in the closure of Catholic schools in Newfoundland and Quebec.

Many Catholic couples are no different to other married couples in how they live their commitment. They do not portray the Sacrament of Matrimony as special and so they fail to be light and salt of the world. Cohabitation, infidelity and divorce rates are just as high among Catholics as the rest of society. We are not doing a good job presenting matrimony as permanent, attractive and fulfilling. However, there is a small minority of couples who, at great odds, are living their vocation to the fullest and these are our hope. Sad to say, but we in leadership are not giving matrimony the priority it deserves. We say the family is the domestic church, the first cell and leaven of society but for the most part this is just rhetoric.

When the new code of Canon Law was promulgated in 1983, canon lawyers advised the Canadian bishops to break with the government and cease witnessing civil marriages. But, true to form, the bishops chose to remain wedded. Since the days of the Emperor Constantine bishops have been hand-in-glove with the State wanting dual power. But today the tide has turned, and the marriage has gone sour. The government of Canada, under a Catholic Prime Minister, has jilted the bishops!

Bishops owe it to their priests not to throw them to the lions by continuing to witness civil marriages. There just is no advantage but there are lots of disadvantages! The consequences for a priest refusing to witness a same-sex marriage are grave and he should not be exposed to this. The bishops did not do a good job protecting their people from priest sex-abusers. Let's hope they will do better this time around, be proactive and look after their priests.

Good can come out of this evil and so we must be hopeful. The great challenge now for leadership is to be creative and courageous and hold out hope for our people. First we must work with the remnant; the few solid couples who are are serious about, not just being married, but living the vocation of matrimony. Then those great couples who give generously to marriage preparation, enrichment and troubled marriages, need our encouragement and involvement. There's something radically wrong with our priorities when we pay staff to annul marriages but do little to prepare couples and prevent break-up. How high on the priority list is matrimony and family ministry in our dioceses and parishes?

Further, since the title "marriage" is now a misnomer, let's drop it from our language altogether and instead use the language of *matrimony*. This would send a clear message to society and governments that we do distinguish between marriage and matrimony, the secular and the religious. It would also form the basis of good catechesis for matrimonial preparation. Couples would be matrimonied into the Church and then married by the State as happens in most countries around the world.

The title *matrimony* is rich in meaning. The root word *mater* is Latin for mother. An offshoot of mater is *matrix,* which contains the mother and womb image. Matrix literally means, "That which encloses anything or gives origin to anything, like a womb." Another definition of Matrix is, "The form or mold in which something is shaped." So matrimony conjures up images like mother, womb, birth, mold and shape.

We refer to the Church in the feminine as, "Holy Mother Church." On their wedding day, the couple is matrimonied into us. They enter the womb of their Mother as it were. This is the beginning of a birthing or molding process in which a couple's relationship will continue to be shaped as long as they live. Marriage can't trump that!

MORE DREAMS—FEWER MEETINGS

There is no record in the Gospels that Jesus called a meeting! But there are umpteen dreamers in scripture! He lived at home for thirty years and spent only around three preaching and teaching. He accomplished a lot in a short time because he didn't attend any meeting! If he did, it would have taken him thirty years! Meetings don't cost us anything because we pass the buck by forming sub-committees and so on it goes and nothing gets done! Dreams, on the other hand, can be nightmares and even cost us our lives!

The Old Testament Joseph, as a kid, dreamed that he would rule his family and clan. Look what it cost him! His brothers hated him, threw him into a well and then sold him off as a slave in Egypt. Although Jacob his father rebuked him for his dreams, nevertheless, scripture tells us that "...he kept the matter in mind." He pondered on it. Joseph of the New Testament was told to marry Mary and was shuttled back and forth to Egypt via dreams. They didn't call a family meeting but pondered and reflected instead.

On another level, Martin Luther King had a dream for the black people of America and look at what it cost him! The *"Live 8"* concert has a dream to "Make Poverty History" in Africa. Nelson Mandela, at age 86, attended the concert in Johannesburg and shared his dream: "I retired and shouldn't be here but as long as poverty and injustice last in Africa, no one can rest." Dreams will hurry the process of the *New Evangelization* of Catholics, but meetings will scuttle it.

Biblical dreaming, like prophecy, is less about the future and more about the present. Both are primarily about change, discipleship and conversion resulting in a greater commitment to God's plan. This is exactly what the *New Evangelization* is calling Catholics to.

Meetings have no depth because we are in touch only with the conscious, surface side of ourselves and talk off the top of our heads! Dreams, on the other hand, are very deep because they deal with the unconscious part of us and so are more real. Jesuit writer Kenneth L. Becker says: "In fact, the unconscious psychic processes constitute more of one's life than one's consciousness does. For they go on day and night, an important part of psychic life, processing experiences, working over problems, elaborating responses, directing life and development, as they did before one was conscious of oneself at all."[75] It makes sense then to pay more attention to our dreams and less to meetings. A priest I know avoids meetings because he says they are an occasion of sin for him!

I am noticing that my dreams have a pattern and are connected to things that happened the previous day. I had a dream last night but I will begin first with the previous day's connections. It was Sunday and the Gospel was about Jesus' *yoke*. A parishioner brought the beautiful *wooden* church sign she made for our new building. My next door neighbour's name is *Mike* to whom I delivered the chickenfeed which I collect on my way home from one of the mission stations. We prayed with Emma's *family* at the Eucharist for her son-in-law recuperating from *brain* surgery to remove a malignant growth. In the evening, I spent ages in the *bush* looking for eight lost hens!

Now to my dream. Like many others, it was a nightmare. Not consulted, I was assigned to "special" a patient called *Michael* in a huge old asylum institution. He was shackled to the large bed by *a wooden frame* around his neck. He looked wild and tried to attack me and I was scared but remained at the end of the bed. I then found myself leading him on a rope attached to the *wooden frame* for what felt like a day and we got on alright. Then he escaped and ran into

---

75 **Kenneth L. Becker:** *Unlikely Companions:* 78

the *bush* with me pursuing him. I felt sorry for him and sad that, after a long search, I couldn't find him. I returned to the institution but couldn't find anyone to whom I could report.

Then about four members of his *family* showed up, were angry with me and said they found him. I went with them to a very muddy pond where several were trying to raise his body supported by a blanket. My rubber boots filled with the mud as I helped to lift his *head* but it broke in pieces in my hands like an *eggshell*. The feel and noise made me feel sick to my stomach. Unlike other nightmares, I woke up feeling different.

After previous nightmares of this kind I would wake up feeling exhausted and this would last most of the morning. But this morning I woke up feeling fresh and alive! I am pondering it! Maybe Michael is my shadow, my dark side, my unconscious and I spiraled down to a deeper layer of awareness making friends with it. This connection at the very core of our being is evangelization in the raw, is holistic and genuine which no meeting can achieve.

A MATTER OF JUSTICE?

I am workshopping Fr. Phil's talks for his first Retrouvaille weekend as a team priest. The Retrouvaille program is for couples experiencing problems and presented by three couples and a priest. Phil was married for forty years, and then after his wife died 4 years ago, he was ordained.

This exercise got me reflecting on the question of married priests. I recall the exodus of Anglican priests in Britain in 1999—two hundred and ninety-four—from the Church of England to the Roman Catholic Church because of the ordination of women. Since then more than one hundred and thirty-five, who were married, went on to be ordained in the Roman Catholic Church and are now working in ministry as married Roman Catholic priests. There are also Catholic married men who had a civil divorce and then had their marriages annulled. They were later ordained priests and are now working in parishes.

On further reflection I concluded that the Roman Catholic Church does have many married priests in ministry worldwide. Since the Roman Catholic Church does not recognize Anglican Orders as valid, the men had to be validly ordained. So here were married men who were ordained! What's the problem, then, ordaining Catholic married men? Anglican married men and Catholic married men are on the same footing. Because one has studied theology does not make him superior to the other. The conclusion I arrived at is that this is an injustice, discrimination and a violation of a right.

Our Catholic laity have a *right* to the Sunday celebration of the Eucharist. This is implied in the Code of Canon Law: "Christ's faithful have the right to be assisted by their Pastors from the spiritual riches of the Church, especially by the word of God and the sacraments" (#213). We say, and quite rightly, that the Eucharist is the source and summit of the life of the Church. It is the high-point of a Catholic's life. In not having their right met they are being discriminated against and unjustly treated.

I am not advocating an either-or situation: celibacy or married priests. Rather, I am arguing for a *both-and* solution: celibacy and married priests. The reality is that we do have a *both-and* situation: Anglican married men are ordained while we still maintain celibacy. All I am asking is that we include Catholic married men who surely have a greater right to be ordained. It's so simple that I cannot understand what the problem is! It is neither a biblical, moral or theological one, but strictly a discipline. In this case, surely a right supersedes a tradition and a discipline. Here we have something that is good (celibacy) being the enemy of what is best: the rights of the people.

The first Pope was a married man! If I had the opportunity to ask the Pope and the Roman Curia why they continue this practice of excluding Catholic married men, I suspect they would take refuge in a long theological treatise! But I would press for their own personal thoughts and feelings on this issue. I would act like Jesus did with the apostles when he asked a question and they waffled on in generalities. He was not interested and pinned them down with, "But who do *you* say that I am?" I would ask, "How do you *feel* when the question of ordaining married men comes up? Insecure, uncomfortable, threatened and out of control?" Ultimately, I believe it is more about power and control than theology.

Since I do not have a snowball's chance in hell of asking that question, what hope does the Catholic laity have of representing themselves? They are at the very bottom of the hierarchical ladder more than forty years after the Second Vatican Council. I reflected on their plight during workshopping Fr. Phil, when the local government agency called me and asked if I would act as an advocate for people seeking social assistance. They are the poor and at the mercy of government bureaucrats who withhold information they have a right to. I gladly accepted.

Bishops are our advocates to speak on behalf of the ordination of Catholic married men. I know some who have raised this question on their ad limina visits to Rome without success. But the vast majority of bishops are timid and will not ruffle any feathers in Rome. They have to be more assertive and speak up for their Catholic married men. Don't go to Rome with cap in hand as beggars and inferiors. Go with a plan as equals and present it with conviction. Be clearly seen to be part of the solution and to not continue contributing to the problem. Go as advocates on behalf of a disenfranchised laity and in particular, our Catholic married men. Argue with passion and fire for their rights and needs to be met. They say the squeaky wheel gets the most oil! They must confront Rome on why it has one law for Anglican married men and another for Catholic men. After all, what's good for the goose is good for the gander! A fresh encounter with Jesus will inspire them to risk and to dream.

They could take as their patron saint Cardinal Danneels of Malines-Brussels, Belgium. For some time now he has been a squeaky wheel as an advocate for innocent AIDS victims. He is showing some backbone in arguing for the use of condoms to protect an innocent spouse from contracting AIDS where his or her spouse is HIV positive. The moral issue here is not about contraception but protecting someone from a deadly disease. It appears that Rome is listening!

THE RABBI AND EVANGELIZATION

A very wise spiritual director and good friend of mine says you can pray with the telephone directory! Rabbi Shmuley Boteach is a husband and father of eight children. I have learned from his book, *Ten Conversations You Need To Have With Your Children,* that good parenting can teach us a lot about the *New Evangelization*.

Most parents raise their children on the premise or principle of what they will *do* when they grow up. So they form them accordingly. But Rabbi Boteach strongly disagrees with, "What do you want to *do* with your life?" It's the wrong question. The correct question is, "*Who* do you want to be when you grow up?" The shift is from *doing* to *being*. The first question is work, career and success-oriented while the second is *value*-focused. The kind of person I am is much more important than what I do. It is from my values that I develop a healthy self-image and good self-esteem. Sadly, but most adults look to their profession and bank account for these essential qualities.

When parents are preoccupied with what they want their children *do,* they operate out of the mindset of what the Rabbi calls "External will." It's a do, command and military style of parenting. Children will respond, not because they want to, but because they fear the consequences. They soon form the habit of responding to social pressure and this wanting to please others becomes a negative and even destructive pattern of behaviour.

The secret of good parenting, he says, is to have children respond from their "Internal will." This means helping them to listen to their inner voice: conscience, soul, spirit and deepest self. When they are living at this level this will want to respond regardless of any external influence. Good parenting is about putting children in touch with their innermost self and reconnecting them with their essence.

Since we live in the fast lane, we want instant results. This is the external will syndrome, the short but the longer way. Orders and commands will get immediate results but because they are primarily out of fear, they will not last. The child is simply conforming and more like a robot than a human being. Internal will behaviour on the other hand, is the long but shorter way. Dialogue with their children takes longer for parents but the results are lasting. Parents take time and help them to listen to their inner voice and this helps them to a process of internalization.

Two days ago a little three-year old was crying as she and her mom left the church. When I asked what the problem was her mom explained that she had been misbehaving during Mass and now she would be spending time in the corner at home. Quite oblivious to it but the mom was taking the short but longer road, the external will approach. I felt sad and wanted to help her to see a better way: the long but shorter route of the internal will way but I didn't.

The Church as institution parents like this mother using the external will style which is very impersonal. Through commanding and exhorting it imposes a response. In leading primarily from the outside it takes the short but longer way. It's like the seed that fell on rocky soil and because it did not develop any roots, it soon withered away. I look at the Catholic church in Ireland and see this being lived out today. How could such a Catholic country turn pagan over night? It's because of how we were parented by the institution. We were not taught to integrate our faith and so we buckled under the pressure of the fastest growing economy in the European Union known in Ireland as the "Celtic tiger."

Jesus, on the other hand, the source and summit of the *New Evangelization*, applied the internal will method. He gave very few directions but asked a lot of questions. In this way he led people into a self-discovery process to listen their own inner voice; their conscience, soul, spirit and deepest self. These people were like the seed that fell on fertile soil and produced a bumper harvest. The classical example of taking the long but shorter way, is his patient dialogue and non-judgmental approach with the woman at the well. Having led her to listen to her inner voice she went on to be a powerful evangelizer of her own people, the very ones who initially rejected her.

The institution needs to be *Newly Evangelized* by Jesus and must look to him as her model and mentor. Another Jew, Rabbi Shmuley Boteach offers her the model of good parenting, one that will teach her the lasting benefits of the internal will approach.

A MIRACULOUS MARRIAGE!

"*Tuesday 8 May 2007 represents an important moment in our history—the day that marks a new beginning for everyone. After many difficult and dark days we believe this is an unprecedented opportunity to deliver a better future for everyone.*"

This is an excerpt from the joint statement of the Northern Ireland Executive: Ian Paisley, First Minister and Martin McGuinness, Deputy First Minister. It is nothing short of a miracle that a Protestant and a Catholic are now working together to restore peace and economic stability to a war-torn Northern Ireland. What's important is to know how they arrived at this point.

Ever since the battle of the Boyne in 1690 when the Protestants defeated the Catholics, they have been at each others throats. Since the late sixties more than three thousand innocent people were killed, hundreds maimed and the economy in a shambles. Each side dug in their heels refusing to dialogue. Each believed they were right and refused to budge an inch. Each hated each other. Each was convinced that success could be brought about only at the point of a gun and the mayhem of indiscriminate bombing.

Decades of attempts and failures to bring the two sides together and talk eventually won out. Violence was renounced in favour of dialogue and now Protestants and Catholics can feel hopeful that commonsense will prevail. For me this is a vivid picture of the *New Evangelization* in progress. Here we see personal conversion, repentance and a fresh beginning marked by a newness in *ardour, method* and *expression*. The advice of the spiritual writer Thomas á Kempis (d. 1471) was heeded by both sides: "It is better to feel compunction than be able to define it."

Had the Vatican listened to his words less than fifty years later, the Church would be in a far healthier state today. Like the Protestants and Catholics in Northern Ireland, there was fierce mud-slinging meted out to each other by the Vatican and the Reformers. Instead of dialogue and personal reform, a self-righteous arrogance prevailed. When in October 1517 Martin Luther attacked the scandalous sale of indulgences, Rome rebutted by ordering him to be silent and make his submission. Cardinal Cajetan was dispatched to procure his submission or his arrest and transportation to Rome. From then on the latter went on the defence in all its dealings with the Reformers and that negative mindset still prevails today to a great extent.

Both sides became so entrenched in theological controversy and polemics (refute, attack, argue) that they lost sight of each other. Just like when a couple in a marital fight focuses only on the problems instead of one another. A little known mystic and preacher of the time, Peter Faber, a Jesuit, tried to turn this around. His preaching dealt not with theological controversy but personal reform. Had the Reformers and Rome listened to him there could have been an Ian Paisley and Martin McGuninness-style reconciliation. The Church would have spared itself nearly five hundred years of wasted energy defending itself. When a soccer or a hockey team goes on the defence it doesn't score goals! A Church on the defence is not open to fresh thinking, new insight, personal reform, a fresh encounter with Jesus and taking risks.

Much closer to our own day, a great theologian tried to inject some positive thinking into the Church and move it from its defensive position. Hans Urs von Balthasar was born in Switzerland on August 12, 1905. He sought to reinvigorate theology and recover essential aspects of Christianity that he believed had been lost in the polemics of the Protestant Reformation. Along with others, he turned his attention to spiritual theology so evident in the early church fathers.

Balthasar argued, and quite rightly, that we must first come to know Jesus. This is where reform and the *New Evangelization* begin. He taught that Christian truth is like a symphony: it is harmonious rather than isolated definitions and statements. It is "Less a collection of positions and doctrines than an organic, dynamic and narratival display of divine love. Theology fails in its task if it presents us simply with something that is true," he taught. He called the institution to be humble, come off its pedestal and recognize its sinfulness. Balthasar remarked that a Church that is "sinless" and "all-knowing" would have nothing in common with the Church of Jesus Christ. And reflecting on the state of the Irish Church today, Bishop Willie Walsh added: "If our Church today appears weaker and more broken, then perhaps it is more Christ-like."

The 'marriage' of Tuesday 8 May 2007 marked a new beginning for the people of Northern Ireland. If taken seriously, the *New Evangelization* will usher in a new era for Catholics.

LITTLE SHOCKERS!

Sometimes it takes a good shock to wake us up! A brush with death in a car accident, diagnosed with cancer or suffering a heart-attack really shake us out of our illusory world. For the first time in our lives we now begin to really live. We take one day at a time, smell the roses, live each moment to the fullest, take nothing for granted and finally admit that we are not in control. Above all, we become grateful people. We have experienced a conversion!

To help us embrace the call to the *New Evangelization*, a call to conversion, we need other kinds of shocks. These are the wise sayings and wisdom of those who see beyond the surface of life and who are in touch with reality. Hopefully, the following little shockers might make us sit up and take stock of life:

"There are more things in heaven and on earth than are dreamed by your philosophies," warns Shakespeare, (d. 1616). I would include 'theologies' so that theologians might come to accept that they are merely scratching the surface. A clear awakening would be to admit that for every answer they come up with they have ten more questions!

"Clap your hands. Don't beat your breast!" Just after I was ordained I remember the pastor describing the Sunday nine o'clock Mass as the hypocrites' Mass! These were what he called the 'craw-thumpers' with heads bowed and beating hell out of their breasts!

Things haven't changed very much. Look at how self-centered and sin-focused we are at the beginning of our Sunday Eucharist.

You would think that Jesus never came! Surely our focus should be on not how bad we are, but how loving, forgiving and great Jesus is. It's time to clap our hands in praise and gratitude instead of beating our breasts!

"We can make our mind
so like still water
That beings gather about us
that they may see,
It may be, their own images,
and so live for a moment
With a clearer, perhaps even with
a fiercer life because of
Our quiet." W.B. Yeats (d.1922).

We keep ourselves busy precisely to avoid encountering the quiet. While we desperately long for inner quiet we fear it and run from it. The good news is that it is primarily in the poverty of the void and the vacuum that Jesus is encountered. He reminded us that the kingdom of God is within and we experience it in silence.

"Life without a lonely place, without a quiet centre, becomes destructive." Henri Nouwen (d. 1996). The most common form of self-destruction is workaholism. And we end up workaholics when we lose our soul, our quiet centre. Sad to say that as individual Catholics and at the institutional level, we are ridden with this sickness.

"Many of our major problems derive from our inability to sit still in a room." Blaise Pascal (d. 1662). Due to advanced child psychology, hyperactive children are now diagnosed with what is called "Attention Deficit Disorder." It's an illness that places a great challenge on teachers and parents. The psalmist tells us, "Be still and know that I am God." Once when the priest was sitting still with his eyes closed after Communion, an anxious and restless parishioner went and shook him thinking he had fallen asleep! We are not comfortable with stillness!

"Two roads diverged in a wood and I
I took the one less travelled by
And that has made all the difference." Robert Frost (d. 1963).

The inner journey, where life in abundance lies, is indeed a road less travelled by us because we fear the unknown. Once we dare to risk, however, we will for sure find it makes all the difference in the world.

"I want to unfold
I don't want to stay folded anywhere
Because where I am folded
There I am a lie." Rainer Maria Rilke (d.1926)

We remain unfolded when we resist change. The *New Evangelization* challenges us to a profound conversion experience that will cause us to unfold and blossom. This happens when we unfold ourselves to Jesus in the form of a fresh encounter with him. Since Jesus calls us his friends, relationship is of the very essence of being a Catholic. To remain folded, and therefore isolated, and attempt to be Catholic is to be a lie.

ACKNOWLEDGEMENTS

I wish to thank Lori McGinlay, R.N., for taking time out of her busy nursing schedule to proofread the material and offer valuable suggestions.

The use of selections from copyright material has been granted by the following publishers and copyright proprietors:

Unlikely Companions: C.G. Jung on the **Spiritual Exercises** *of Ignatius of Loyola,* **Kenneth L. Becker (Leominster 2001) copyright Gracewing Publishing and Inigo Enterprises**

Gravity and Grace: **Simone Weil copyright Putnam Publishers, New York 1952. Translatedby Arthur Wills**

*Enlightened by Love: "***The Thought of Simone Weil,***"* David Cayley, CBC Radio One, broadcast April 8-12, 2002

Waiting for God: **copyright 1951 by G. P. Putnam's S, New York**

Rembrandt: **His Life and Paintings, copyright Gary Schwartz, 1985**

The Lord of the Rings: **J. R. R. Tolkien copyright HarperCollins Publishers London, 1995**

KARL RAHNER and Ignatian Spirituality: **Philip Endean copyright Oxford University Press, New York 2004**

Karl Rahner: Spiritual Writings **edited by Philip Endean copyright Orbis Books Maryknoll, New York 2004**

The Church in America: **Post-Synodal Apostolic Exhortation of**

Pope John Paul II, 1999

At The Beginning of the New Millennium: **Apostolic Letter of Pope John Paul II, 2001**

The Eucharist as the Source and Summit of the Church's Life and Mission: **Pope Benedict XVI copyright CCCB Publications, Ottawa**